AROUND THE WORLD

Beverly Caruso

YWAM Publishing
A Ministry of Youth With A Mission
Seattle, Washington 98155

Dedication

To those fathers and mothers like mine who have released their daughters and sons to follow the Master's call to whatever land He leads them.

Acknowledgments

The gathering of devotions from workers in over 100 countries involved scores of individuals. Without a foundation of prayer, this collection of stories would never have made it to print. Thanks for your prayers to Ted and Edith Adams, Dr. Richard Austin, Libby Bordewich, Lucy Caruso, John and Alice Donar, Dorothy Hall, Frank and Joan Hartman, Paul and Linda Linzey, Juan and Edna Medrano, Hope Nelli, Gail Nicholson, Donna Peterson, the Dean Peterson family, Pat Wickham, Frank and Gloria Wilson, and the women of New Life Community Church.

My editing team included Teri Anderson, Frances Bradley, Joy Cooley, Myrtlemay Pittman Crane, Regina Dagen, Joanne Holden, Nancy Kington, Marianne Miller, Shirley Sells, Dianne Shober, and Shirley Walston. A special thanks to Penny Henry and Carolyn Case. Pam Warren's invaluable patience, diligence, and long hours gave the book coherence and flow.

I am especially appreciative of Randy and Pam Piepenburg, Art Henry, and John Lindskoog for their computer expertise.

My husband, Pete, and my son Dave gave frequent and appreciated suggestions and encouragement, and they kept the household going.

I'm grateful to my publishers—Tom Bragg, Warren Walsh, and Jim Rogers—for believing in this project and providing me opportunity and oversight.

I'm grateful to my Lord and heavenly Father, who shared with me the privilege of passing on these stories to you, our readers.

Foreword

In October 1991, I watched the birth of an idea. Youth With A Mission (YWAM) evangelists of a dozen nationalities had gathered in Switzerland for a writers' workshop. As so often happens, however, it was not during the scheduled class times that the liveliest conversations took place, but at meals, in hallways, on paths overlooking a mountain lake.

What did they talk about, these YWAMers meeting one another for the first time? They talked about the personal discoveries they were making as they sought to follow God.

A counselor from Argentina told what he was learning about ministering to marriages in trouble. A teacher from India said she was finding Christ to be stronger than ancient prejudice. A sculptor from Albania described the vacuum of faith in his country, and the adventure of filling the emptiness with Jesus.

As they shared an insight here, a breakthrough there, the excitement in the group was palpable, the level of our faith rising like the water level in Lake Thun when the snow melts and the spring runoff begins.

That's when I saw the idea take shape. If this sampling of YWAM workers had such inspiration and encouragement to offer one another, why shouldn't YWAMers everywhere be invited to set down their own discoveries in faith?

Male and female, young and not-so-young people go into YWAM ministries at personal cost. For many it means giving up a career and an income, leaving home and friends, accepting difficult living conditions. For all, it means exchanging security for the privilege of bearing another's burdens.

And since we can never out-give God, He showers on them...wisdom, understanding, peace, and joy.

In this book, YWAMers pass on some of what they've received as they heed His call to "go into all the world." To keep the treasures of God, we must give them away. That's what the contributors to this book have done—offered their experience of Him to you and me in the hope that each of us, in turn, will pass our own faith-builders on to someone else.

Elizabeth Sherrill

Introduction

From the earliest days of Youth With A Mission (YWAM), I've enjoyed hearing the stories of its young evangelists. Each one seemed to be a faith builder, challenging me to trust God for the unbelievable.

In the past few years, over three dozen YWAM books have been published, yet numerous stories are still hidden in the hearts of thousands of YWAM workers—stories which continue to build the faith of those who hear them. You'll find some of those stories, and other nuggets of truth, as we journey together through this collection of readings.

The stories and devotions in this book come from the everyday lives of YWAMers; not just young people, but folks of all ages. We are part of denominations as varied as Anglican, Baptist, and Pentecostal; work places such as science labs, shepherd's fields, and college classrooms; from places like Canada, the island of Tonga, European inner cities, Asian rice paddies, and Amazon villages. We share in common our love for Jesus and a desire to make Him known to others.

Youth With A Mission has more than 7,000 permanent staff at 425 centers in 110 nations. Each year, an additional 15,000-20,000 are involved in short-term mission projects; many thousands more attend YWAM-related events.

Perhaps you would like to pray each day for the YWAMer whose devotion you read. We've included, where possible, the home country, type of work, and his or her place of ministry.

Most of our contributors are not writers, but ordinary people with something they've learned from God to share with folks like you. You may find some of the accounts hard to believe. We've attempted to verify the facts. These are personal experiences, some without witnesses.

We'll see many facets of God's character throughout these pages: our guide, protector, teacher, healer, and much more. Often we'll see Him as our provider. This is to be expected in a faith mission where each worker seeks God for his personal finances. A single thread seems to run throughout: when we take steps in obedience to God, He's always there to meet us.

In any new ministry, mistakes are made. Lessons must be learned, usually the hard way—by experience. YWAM is still a relatively young mission. We still release young people into pioneer situations. We consist of young people—and old—who are "daring to live on the edge," and trusting God for whatever seems necessary for the situation. We hope as we have grown, and become more structured (with properties, ships, a university, etc.), and gained acceptance by our brothers and sisters in Christ, that we will never lose that sense of daring. We want to remain a people of daily faith.

We hope your faith will be challenged and that you'll find these stories and devotions to be faith builders.

Beverly Caruso
Senior Editor

Sunday

Meditation

Fear not, for I have redeemed you;
I have called you by name; you are
mine. When you pass through the
waters, I will be with you; and
when you pass through the rivers,
they will not sweep over you. When
you walk through the fire, you will
not be burned; the flames will not
set you ablaze. For I am the Lord,
your God, the Holy One of Israel,
your Savior....

Isaiah 43:1-3

Monday

Even though I walk through the valley of the shadow of death, I will fear no evil, for you are with me.   *Psalm 23:4*

In early 1984, doctors discovered a tumor growing rapidly in Johan's brain. It was in the speech center and memory bank, and was pressing on his optic nerve. Johan was only 36 years old.

Since our marriage eleven years earlier, we had been involved in Christian ministry as youth pastors, and Johan was dean of a Bible school. We often took our students to join Youth With A Mission in Amsterdam. We had three small children and a fruitful ministry, but now death was so close. *How could God be glorified in Johan's death?* I wondered.

Yet God was at work. Johan survived the five-hour operation to remove some of the tumor, but he remained unconscious. He remembers being in the presence of the Lord and being sent back to this life. He developed traumatic epileptic seizures. After 13 days, Johan began to awaken. My joy mingled with despair when I realized that he didn't recognize me. Could God ever use us again?

God's grace sustained us during the ensuing months. Johan studied hard to relearn Dutch, English, and the Word of God. As an added help, YWAM Amsterdam allowed him to attend, for a second time, a Discipleship Training School. Six months of immersion in God's Word revived him. The neurologist gave us the go-ahead to join YWAM staff.

The Lord has established our family in mercy ministry to addicts and street people in the heart of Amsterdam. We live in a wonderful old home where we offer hospitality to those needing refuge.

So much has been restored. God has given us the grace to persevere. He walked through the valley right beside us.

Carolyn Ros, an American married to a Dutchman, works on YWAM staff in Amsterdam, Netherlands.

Tuesday

I tell you that in the same way there is more rejoicing in heaven over one sinner who repents than over ninety-nine righteous persons who do not need to repent.

Luke 15:7

I first learned about Mario while working with Info/Action SIDA, a YWAM Montreal ministry designed to encourage Christians' involvement with AIDS victims. I agreed to pray for Mario, but soon realized that prayer was not enough. One afternoon, I called and offered him my friendship.

Soon after, he was admitted to the hospital with pneumonia. I visited regularly, and a close friendship formed. The physical anguish of his disease was heightened by the emotional trauma of isolation and loneliness. He knew he was too weak to care for himself, yet once he was released from the hospital, he had nowhere to go.

Here was an obvious need I couldn't ignore. Before I could offer my home, however, my family would have to agree; already five of us were cramped into a small space. I was even more concerned about their reaction to living with someone dying of AIDS. I needn't have worried. We welcomed Mario into our home.

The doctor instructed me in Mario's care. But it wasn't just his body that needed tending; it was his soul. Haunted by thoughts of death, he confessed he'd been pondering the things I'd said about Jesus. After living with us a few weeks, Mario made a commitment to Christ.

The changes in his life weren't always obvious. At times, I doubted his faith. Then one day Mario asked if I'd read the Bible and pray with him. We continued this practice daily.

One evening, Mario asked me to forgive his impatience and anger, and told me he'd asked God to take him home. The following morning, I found him comatose on the bathroom floor. Two days later, I was by his side when he slipped into Jesus' arms.

Story of Claudette Girouard, as told to Pierre LeBel, a Canadian who serves with Info/Action SIDA (a ministry to AIDS victims) in Montreal, Quebec, Canada.

Wednesday

Be very careful then, how you live...making the most of every opportunity, because the days are evil.   *Ephesians 5:15-16*

"What brings you to Sri Lanka?" the bank manager asked.

"I'm traveling with a group of Christians sharing our message," I replied. Then as naturally as possible, I went on. "Are you interested in spiritual matters?" He answered something about church, and I started searching for a way to make clear to him that, by itself, his church background was not enough to assure salvation. Suddenly I had an inspiration. "Would you say, then, that you're a friend of God's?"

I was quite unprepared for his response. Right there in the bank, this otherwise emotionless banker raised both hands and exclaimed, "I would give anything in the world to be God's friend and have peace of mind!"

I knew he should be interested in the Gospel, yet he didn't seem interested. When our business was finished, I hated to just leave. He had opened his heart to me. Shouldn't I ask if I could see him again? I decided to take the plunge.

The result was an invitation to his home for dinner; then in a subsequent meeting, he submitted his life to Christ. Later, he told me that at the time he met me, he was being cheated financially, and this had filled him with despair. Now Christ had given him the peace that he'd craved.

Melville has walked with the Lord for 23 years and has enthusiastically witnessed at home and abroad. How wonderful that the turning of a purely mundane conversation to a spiritual one resulted in his coming to Christ!

Ross Tooley, a New Zealander, serves at large on the staff of the College of Christian Ministries of University of the Nations, Kona, Hawaii, USA.

Adapted from *We Cannot But Tell,* by Ross Tooley, revised edition. Copyright © 1993 by Ross Tooley. Published by YWAM Publishing, Seattle, Washington. Used by permission [from pages 13-16].

Thursday

Then I heard the voice of the Lord saying, "Whom shall I send? And who will go for us?" And I said, "Here am I. Send me!"   Isaiah 6:8

I had always dreamed of being a television producer. My dream had come true, but I wasn't satisfied. The money and glamorous lifestyle seemed suddenly meaningless. I had a yearning to please the One I loved—the One who had given me more love, peace, joy, and forgiveness than anyone I'd ever met before—Jesus Christ.

He had a plan for my life. A relationship with me! Finally I dared to ask Him, "Lord, what do You want me to do? Where do You want me to go?"

Secretly I was hoping to hear, "Stay where you are." But I heard clearly, "Brazil, Rio!" I grabbed a map to find out where that was.

That night, I heard Loren Cunningham, founder of Youth With A Mission, challenging people to go into missions. Almost reluctantly, I stood with others to indicate my willingness to become a missionary.

After the meeting, I wondered how I could leave my job, my apartment, my family, and my friends. Yet six months later, I still could think of nothing else. Every time I opened the newspaper or turned on the radio or television, I seemed to hear about Rio!

I prayed often for Brazil. I asked God what I could possibly do for that country. It was as though God had been waiting for me to ask. A picture formed in my mind of many children following me through the streets, dancing and singing.

I had no idea that there were children on the streets of Rio de Janeiro. Later, I met someone who confirmed that many children lived on the city's streets, dying of hunger, and even being killed.

I couldn't stay in England. I had to obey. It was important to God. I'm so glad I did, for I have never known such joy.

Sarah de Carvalho, from England, works with street children in Brazil.

Friday

The man who plants and the man who waters have one purpose, and each will be rewarded according to his own labor.   *I Corinthians 3:8*

The Canary Islands, off the west African coast, served as port of call for Russian vessels to refuel and replenish their provisions. During their shore leaves, the sailors had little to do.

We couldn't evangelize in their home country, but we could reach them in this neutral location. So a group of us went to the Canary Islands to share Christ with them.

At the zoo in Las Palmas one day, a young Christian asked a sailor, "Can you believe that some people think we came from these monkeys?"

The sailor answered, "Don't you believe that? What do you believe?" In the next few moments, he heard for the first time about God's creation and His plan for mankind.

We weren't discouraged at the small number of conversions we witnessed. We knew we were tilling the soil and removing rocks in order for others to plant seeds and bring a harvest.

Years later, we received a letter from the son of a long-term missionary to the Canaries who had just returned from visiting Russia. Our friend introduced himself to a Russian pastor, and the pastor was astounded to hear that he was from the Canary Islands.

"That's amazing," the pastor said. "I was a sailor in Las Palmas. A group of young people shared Jesus with me there. They gave me a Bible, which I read from cover to cover on the way home from that trip. Once home, I found believers who helped me grow in God."

Al Akimoff, an American, directs YWAM's Slavic Ministries.

Saturday

You who make mention of the Lord, do not keep silent.

At an arts and crafts exhibit in China, I listened as a young man named Hu played beautiful classical piano. I asked if he knew any music by Tchaikovsky. He played part of Swan Lake, followed by a symphony—all from memory. Then I asked if he knew any Christian music "about Yesu Dijo," I said, using the Mandarin words.

"My father, who believed in Yesu Dijo, died when I was young."

"Then your father is in heaven with Shan Dei," I assured him.

"Yes," he agreed. "During the Cultural Revolution we were not allowed any music, but before my father died, he taught me one song." He began to play "Silent Night," then stopped abruptly and said with distress, "But I can't remember the words!" I sang them for him in English.

Hu then pulled a yellowed songbook from the piano bench. "My father gave me this book and I hid it so it wouldn't be destroyed by the officials," he said, turning the pages. He opened the book and began to play "What a Friend We Have in Jesus."

"But I can't read the words," he said, pointing to the old-style Chinese characters.

I told him, "I have a book which talks about this friend, Jesus, that is written in New Chinese." His eyes lit up when I handed him a Bible. He grasped it eagerly, then quickly hid it in the piano bench. When I asked, "Hu, do *you* believe in Yesu Dijo?" he paused for a long time before answering.

Then, with resolve, he replied, "Yes. Yes, I do." More than a response to my question, it seemed like a decision.

I prayed quietly for Hu before I left. As Hu walked me to my bus, I told him, "Hu, God loves you very much."

"Yes," he smiled and agreed.

Dawn Gauslin, an American, is the International Coordinator for YWAM's field-based Leadership Training Schools. She is also assistant to Darlene Cunningham.

Sunday

Meditation

You are my lamp, O Lord; the Lord turns my darkness into light. With your help I can advance against a troop; with my God I can scale a wall. As for God, his way is perfect; the word of the Lord is flawless. He is a shield for all who take refuge in him. For who is God besides the Lord? And who is the Rock except our God? It is God who arms me with strength and makes my way perfect. He makes my feet like the feet of a deer; he enables me to stand on the heights.

II Samuel 22:29-34

Monday

*How can anyone enter a strong man's house and carry off his possessions
unless he first ties up the strong man? Then he can rob his house.*

Matthew 12:29

In this passage, the *strong man* is simply the predominating
demonic influence in any situation, and we are to eliminate that
influence. It can mean the difference between life and death.

Some years ago, Darlene Cunningham, wife of YWAM's founder Loren Cunningham, had an experience which drove home
the importance of this. While living in YWAM's first center in
Switzerland, Darlene was standing on wet concrete in their laundry room, unloading her clothes from the washer to the dryer—
both industrial size. In Europe, the current for such machines is
350 volts.

When an article of clothing fell behind the dryer, Darlene
reached for it, not knowing that workers had removed its pro-
tective panel to repair it earlier. When her hand touched an exposed wire, her whole body convulsed. She found herself pinned,
helpless as 350 volts shot through her. "God help me! Jesus help
me!" she cried out, but still the surges coursed through her body.

Knowing she was seconds away from death, Darlene prayed
again. "Why isn't it working, God?" she cried. "Why aren't You
answering me?" Instantly the Lord responded, "Bind the devil,
Darlene." The moment she spoke out against Satan, Darlene was
hurled off the live wire and slammed against the opposite wall.

It took several days for the rhythm of Darlene's heart to return
to normal, but she was okay. Even the inch-wide hole burnt into
her palm by the live wire eventually healed without scarring. But
Darlene never forgot the lesson of that day in the laundry room.

Dean Sherman, an American, is an international Bible teacher living in the USA.
From *Spiritual Warfare for Every Christian* by Dean Sherman. Copyright © 1990 by
Dean Sherman. Published by YWAM Publishing, Seattle, Washington. Used by
permission [from page 184].

Tuesday

Think of what you were when you were called. Not many of you were wise by human standards; not many were influential; not many were of noble birth. But...God chose the weak things of the world to shame the strong...so that no one may boast before him.　　　　　*I Corinthians 1:26,27,29*

As a leader of a YWAM school, I have the opportunity to see changes in many people's lives. I will never forget an Australian woman in her early twenties who joined our school in Hawaii. "Timid" seems like an understatement to describe her personality. She was terrified to speak in front of even a small group.

This young woman's class was on an outreach to the Philippines. Each day, they asked God what ministry He had for them that day. One day, they felt they should go to the local hospital.

In front of the hospital, they again prayed and asked God where in the hospital they were to work. All the team members felt they were to go to the children's ward, except the shy Australian student. She felt she was to go to the Intensive Care Unit (ICU).

She walked alone to the ICU, and stopped at the door to pray again. She believed God wanted her to pray for a certain man she saw lying on one of the beds. Although she was certain she had heard from God, she was terribly afraid, yet willing to obey.

The man's family and three doctors surrounded the man's bed. He had been in an automobile accident three weeks earlier and was still in a coma.

The young woman walked in and got permission to pray for the man. She laid her hands on him and prayed a simple prayer. The man, who knew no English, sat up and said, "I'm healed."

This healing opened doors for the team to return to the hospital and lead other patients to Christ.

Randy Thomas, an American, is Director of the King's Mansion Discipleship Training School in Kailua-Kona, Hawaii, USA.

Wednesday

Praise be to the God and Father of our Lord Jesus Christ, the Father of compassion and the God of all comfort, who comforts us in all our troubles, so that we can comfort those in any trouble with the comfort we ourselves have received from God.   *II Corinthians 1:3-4*

A team of young people work with homeless street kids in Belo Horizonte, Brazil. During the day, they minister at one of YWAM's three house ministries: House of Refuge (for AIDS patients), House of Rescue (drop-in center), or House of Restoration (recuperation home). At night, they visit the kids where they "live" on the streets.

One night, a team of eleven had attracted about 30 kids. A group of policemen ran up and began beating team members. Mati, a Samoan YWAMer, was accused of being a gang leader and was hauled off in a police car. The kids scattered. They knew that capture by police meant certain torture, even sometimes death.

The shocked team members quickly returned to the staff house and awakened the others. While several interceded for Mati, others got on the phones to call Brazilian friends who might help. A Christian lieutenant colonel in the military police set to work immediately. After many anxious hours, through his help and influence, Mati was released.

Severely beaten, Mati was taken to the hospital. In only one week, he was home. In another week, he was back on the streets. The children welcomed him as a hero.

Mati now looked at the children with new eyes of love and understanding—a gift born out of his own suffering.

Jeannette Lukasse and her husband, Johan, both from the Netherlands, are the leaders of YWAM's urban ministry base in Belo Horizonte, Brazil.

Thursday

The King will reply, "I tell you the truth, whatever you did for one of the least of these brothers of mine, you did for me."   Matthew 25:40

When I was a young boy in El Centro, California, we lived across the street from the city park. Those were hard times, and the park usually had a hundred or so homeless men sleeping there. Often, they came to our back door, standing hat in hand and asking respectfully if we could give them something to eat. I never saw my mother turn one away. We had meager fare ourselves, living off the weekly tithes and offerings of the church folk. But Mom would give them something to eat and perhaps lend a man a quilt to keep him warm as he slept in the park.

There are many ways to help people, some of which have a more lasting effect. We should try to enable the poor to become self-supporting. But the most important thing is that we must not harden our hearts, nor rationalize away our responsibility to do something to help.

The Lord has many promises in the Bible for those who give to the poor. The Lord also said that when we stand before Him in judgment, our treatment of the poor will be one of the criteria by which we are judged (Matthew 25:31-40).

Jesus did not tell us to give only to the deserving poor. He did not say, "Give to him who asks of you...unless, of course, he is a welfare cheat or has been unwise in handling his finances." No, He said, "Give to him." Giving is an act of mercy, and mercy is never deserved.

Loren Cunningham, an American, is founder and president of YWAM. He lives in Hawaii, USA.

From *Daring to Live on the Edge* by Loren Cunningham with Janice Rogers. Copyright © 1991 by Loren Cunningham. Published by YWAM Publishing, Seattle, Washington. Used by permission [from pages 81-82].

Friday

Repent, then, and turn to God, so that your sins may be wiped out....

In 1981, two Christians, one an Indian and the other a Chinese YWAMer, knocked at a devout young Hindu woman's door. After being invited in, they noticed idols everywhere. Undeterred, Sam Yeo Le Hok began sharing both his testimony and the Gospel. Sashikala, the young Hindu woman, was soon asking what she needed to do to receive salvation, and the two patiently explained her need to repent of sin and receive Christ as her Savior and Lord. Sashikala understood and was willing to be ostracized to follow Jesus completely. Soon a bonfire raged in the backyard as the Hindu deities Shiva, Hanuman, Krishna, along with other idols, were burned.

Dietrich Bonhoeffer, the German theologian, warned of the dangers of offering cheap grace. He has this to say about the price God places on His grace:

> Such grace is costly because it cost a man his life, and it is grace because it gives him the only true life. It is costly because it condemns sin, and grace because it justifies the sinner. Above all, it is costly because it cost God the life of His son. "Ye are bought with a price," and what has cost God so much, cannot be cheap for us.

In our witnessing, we must be careful not to compromise the Gospel message for the sake of increased numbers of converts. This can happen when we neglect to preach repentance. By watering down the Gospel, we can rob a prospective convert of the joy of sins forgiven.

Danny Lehmann, an American, directs the YWAM base in Honolulu, Hawaii, USA, and travels extensively in a teaching ministry.
From *Bringin' 'Em Back Alive* by Danny Lehmann. Copyright © 1987 by Danny Lehmann. Published by Whitaker House, Springdale, Pennsylvania [from pages 67-68].

Saturday

The words I say to you are not just my own. Rather, it is the Father, living in me, who is doing his work. John 14:10

Bill, a 19-year-old Canadian, wanted to discover truth. This search led him to the Far East and to experimentation with various drugs and the occult.

When I met Bill, he had just become a Christian and had embarked on a basic discipleship program at a YWAM center in Kathmandu, Nepal.

In the foothills of the mighty Himalayas, Bill was starting his "journey with Jesus." I asked him what had led him to Christ. He responded that his travels had taken him to Tibet, to the very "roof of the world," where he met two travelers with a very different agenda. They had already discovered the truth.

The two travelers were young people who believed God wanted them to travel to Tibet to do intercession and spiritual warfare for that closed nation.

When they met Bill, he asked them what they were doing. They responded that they were there for spiritual warfare. Perhaps for any other person this wouldn't have made sense, but because Bill understood spiritual warfare from the side of the occult, it was his first step toward salvation.

Bill's ventures into the occult and the world of mind-altering drugs had brought him directly into a spirit realm that was in chaos, and had only brought frustration to his life. The two travelers were able to point Bill to Jesus, who would set him free and give him life.

Peter Jordan, a Canadian, leads YWAM Associates International, a ministry to YWAM alumni. He lives in Vancouver, B.C., Canada.

Sunday

Meditation

Blessed is the man who does not walk in the counsel of the wicked or stand in the way of sinners or sit in the seat of mockers. But his delight is in the law of the Lord, and on his law he meditates day and night. He is like a tree planted by streams of water, which yields its fruit in season and whose leaf does not wither. Whatever he does prospers.

Psalm 1:1-3

Monday

Delight yourself in the Lord and he will give you the desires of your heart.
Psalm 37:4

I went to Samoa as a bride of only two weeks. As base leaders, Dave and I cherished our times alone together. About eight months after our wedding, we went to the beach near the village of Fagalele. From the shade of a coconut tree, I watched Dave snorkel.

After several hours of relaxation, we packed up our gear and headed home. When we reached the pickup truck, I noticed Dave's wedding ring wasn't on his finger and asked him about it. Our rings were a matching set, with a tiny cross of diamonds on each one. We knew that finding a lost ring was unlikely in the pounding surf, the coral, shells, and sand. But we had to at least look.

After half an hour, we gave up and left with sad hearts. We struggled with the loss of this small, yet precious token of our love for one another. We knew it was only symbolic, that a ring doesn't keep a marriage strong, but....It seemed God wanted to teach us something new about surrender.

Two weeks later, we returned to the same beach. I kept thinking, *Somewhere in that big Pacific Ocean is Dave's ring. Only God knows exactly where.* After the guys snorkeled for about an hour, Dave brought me a handful of pretty sea shells. Secretly I wished it were his ring that I was admiring.

Then he brought his other hand forward. In it lay his wedding ring! He said all the guys had looked for the ring for over an hour. At last they gave up. He told me he prayed that if God wanted the ring to be found, to please put it right in front of his eyes.

Just before he got out of the water, Dave saw a pretty shell and reached below the water's surface to pick it up. While putting the shell in his pocket, his eyes seemed glued to what his mind was having difficulty believing. Just as he had prayed, the ring was right before his eyes—underneath the shell he had picked up!

Lydia Hall, a Hollander, leads Women's Ministries in Kona, Hawaii, USA.

Tuesday

Your Father knows what you need before you ask him.   Matthew 6:8

I sold my business and house to clear my debts and attend a YWAM training school. After careful calculation and planning, I had $2,000 left, just enough to cover my outreach fees to Asia.

A few weeks into the class, David Boyd told of plans for new construction on campus. He suggested that we ask the Lord if we should give to that project. To me, the Lord's voice usually sounds much like my conscience, just a quiet thought I know is right. This time, a new type of thought popped into my mind: *Give your $2,000.*

But Lord, I argued silently, *that's my outreach money! If I give it away, I won't be able to go.*

Again, I heard, *Give the $2,000.* I tried to ignore it, thinking that when I received some money owed to me in a couple years, I would be able to help with an offering.

Trust Me, the Lord seemed to whisper. I didn't dare disobey God, so I wrote the check, not mentioning it to anyone.

Our class regularly prayed and planned for the outreach. I was still confident I would be going, but had no idea how. My spending money dwindled. Once I pinched 82 cents for nearly two weeks. The day I *had* to wash clothes, a check from my church arrived in the mail. This was a whole new way of life for me.

The calendar inched toward the deadline for paying our outreach fees. Still, there was no clue about where mine would come from. I continued to pray.

Three days before the money was due, I got a surprise call from the man who had bought my house. He said he wanted to pay me off early. Could he send me $20,000?

You bet, Lord!

His check arrived in the mail at 3:00 p.m. the day of the deadline. I handed over my outreach fees an hour later, eager to see what the Lord would do next.

What was I worried about?

Shirley Walston, an American, is a freelance writer for YWAM, living in Washington State, USA.

Wednesday

And if he finds it, I tell you the truth, he is happier about that one sheep than about the ninety-nine that did not wander off. In the same way your Father in heaven is not willing that any of these little ones should be lost.

Matthew 18:13-14

Our outreach team had just finished performing a drama at the coffee house in Brussels when I was asked to witness to a young man sitting in the corner. He obviously lived on the streets. I was happy to have the opportunity to share with him—until I got close enough to smell the foul air that hung about him.

I watched in disbelief as he lowered his face to the cup and lapped up his tea. *Just like an animal,* I thought. It didn't surprise me to learn that he had grown up on the streets as an orphan and was only recently released from jail. I was surprised, however, when he steered the conversation toward the topic of Christianity, then became increasingly antagonistic.

I found myself wanting to end the conversation because he seemed to be trying to provoke me. I was fully conscious of the foul odor emanating from the man when I prayed silently, *Lord, I really want to love the man, but I don't have it within me. Please help me to communicate Your love to him.*

Without warning, the man's eyes got watery. I stared at him in silence, wondering where all the belligerence had gone. His tears became sobs. Finally, slowly, he said, "I want to pray with you to become a Christian."

After the prayer, he turned to hug me. I held my breath as he latched onto me; I tried to hide my revulsion.

I knew I should hug him back; that only with God's strength could I demonstrate acceptance, much less love. He was so unlovable.

Help me, Lord, I prayed. He did.

David Caruso, an American, works in the mission field of the film industry in Hollywood, California, USA.

Thursday

For...I was a stranger and you invited me in, I needed clothes and you clothed me....Whatever you did for one of the least of these brothers of mine, you did for me.
Matthew 25:35,36,40

I'd been ministering in a coffeehouse in Brussels, where a man who lived on the streets surprised me by asking me to lead him to the Lord. After our prayer, I had difficulty returning his hug because he smelled so bad. But with God's strength, I was enabled to share God's love with him.

Now I believed God wanted me to show the man our Father's love in a practical way. But how? Then I noticed again the tattered sweater he was wearing. My wardrobe had to last through the end of our outreach, but I decided to give him the sweater I was wearing. It was my favorite.

I pulled the sweater over my head, carefully folded it like new, and presented it as a gift. "I'm giving this to you in the name of Jesus. I want you to know that God loves you, and so do I."

His face beamed as he took off his sweater, folded it, and presented it to me as a gift. He put my sweater on, and motioned for me to put his on. I thanked him, but politely held his smelly, holey sweater on my lap. He again gestured for me to put on his sweater. After another silent request for God to grant me love for this man, I put on the sweater.

Nothing needed to be said when we returned to the main room of the coffeehouse. Our team had been together every day for many weeks; we all knew every item of one another's clothing. One glance our way, and our new brother was soon wrapped in arms of love, welcoming him into God's big family.

As I walked home that night, I felt the cold wind slip through the holes of my new, smelly sweater. I was warmed, though, by a new awareness: Whatever the sacrifice, nothing can compare with the joy of serving God. In some strange way, giving this man my sweater sealed his place in God's family. It was as if God was symbolically putting His robe of righteousness on him.

David Caruso, an American, works in the mission field of the film industry in Hollywood, California, USA.

Friday

Every place where you set your foot will be yours.   Deuteronomy 11:24

The torch flared in my hand as I picked up speed. Sweat glistened on the other runners as they passed beneath the street lamps of Century City. "I claim the resources of the west side for You, Lord! May the wealth, talent, and influence of this city be used to proclaim Your love."

The tiny cluster of runners moved on into the night, grateful to know the Pacific Ocean was only 28 blocks away, but dreading the thought that such a great adventure was coming to an end. Starting their journey at Plymouth Rock, they had run from the East Coast to the West Coast as an act of intercessory prayer, claiming America's new generation for Jesus. Along the way, they had been joined by thousands of children and teens who ran with flaming torches symbolizing the light of the Gospel.

I passed the torch to my 13-year-old son, David. *Does he really understand what we are doing?* I thought. *Is he beginning to comprehend the vast love of a heavenly Father who longs to pour healing, justice, and mercy into the earth if we simply humble ourselves and ask for it?*

A man exited a bar, stood on the sidewalk, and stared at the runners in amazement. After all, it was after midnight. "We're running for Jesus," shouted a teenager, and an amused smirk crossed the face of the bar patron. I could almost hear him thinking, *Those crazy Christians, what do they hope to achieve?*

God's people sometimes do crazy things, things that only make sense when seen with the eyes of faith. The infinite meets the finite in the simple obedience of a believer's life.

John Dawson, a New Zealander, is YWAM's International Director of Urban Missions.

From *Taking Our Cities for God* by John Dawson. Copyright © 1989 by John Dawson. Published by Creation House, Lake Mary, Florida. Used by permission [from pages 17-18].

Saturday

For the pagans run after all these things, and your heavenly Father knows that you need them. But seek first his kingdom and his righteousness, and all these things will be given to you as well. Matthew 6:32-33

After two years on board the m/v *Anastasis,* I transferred to Mercy Ships' port office in San Pedro, California. After several months in Los Angeles without a car, I wrote on the prayer request sheet of a supporting church that I was praying for a car.

Three months later, I received the first answer to my prayer—a check for $25 from a man I'd never heard of "to help you with your need for a car." A few days later, another man I'd never heard of, Paul Wojtkowski, called and said, "My wife and I feel the Lord wants us to support you. If that means helping you buy a car, we'd like to do that." He and his wife were interested in Mercy Ships and wanted to learn more about the ministry. They invited me for Sunday dinner, and mentioned that their neighbor was selling a little red car for $600.

During dinner, we talked about missions and life on board the m/v *Anastasis.* Then we looked at his neighbor's 1978 Honda Accord. It had over 130,000 miles on it, but had a rebuilt engine. The man reduced the price to $500, and Paul bought the car for me.

I set out to raise the deposit for the insurance, Paul did some minor repairs on the car, and his brother paid the registration fee. Two weeks later, Paul handed me the keys, and I drove off in the answer to my prayer. After many faithful miles of service, the car has required minimal repairs and has taken me from California to Mercy Ship's new Port Office in Texas.

The Wojtkowskis not only provided the car, but also supported me for the next year and helped with unexpected medical bills. The family eventually attended a Discipleship Training School on board the m/v *Anastasis.* God truly is faithful to provide.

Lucy Allen, an American, is on staff with Mercy Ships' Home Office in Lindale, Texas, USA.

Sunday

Meditation

This is how God showed his love among us: He sent his one and only Son into the world that we might live through him. This is love: not that we loved God, but that he loved us and sent his Son as an atoning sacrifice for our sins. Dear friends, since God so loved us, we also ought to love one another.

I John 4:9-11

Monday

Let your light shine before men, that they may see your good deeds and praise your Father in heaven.
Matthew 5:16

An upper-class Hindu named Rajan arrived alone in Calcutta at the age of 17. Rajan settled in to life as a tea seller in a local restaurant. Soon an unusual group of young, new customers aroused his interest. Some were Indians, but most were from various countries. They were talking about Jesus. The group returned to the restaurant several times.

Rajan's years of Catholic education had laid a foundation for an interest in Christianity. At his first opportunity, Rajan introduced himself and asked if he could visit the team during his time away from work.

Rajan learned that the young people were with YWAM, and lived nearby. The group's purpose was to start a base for evangelism and training. Each day after work, Rajan walked from the restaurant to the center to learn more about Jesus.

Rajan's hunger for God was deep. He asked many questions. In fact, the young people began to wonder if he were a spy for the police. However, Rajan's interest was sincere. After several weeks, they asked him if he would like to receive Jesus as his personal Lord and Savior. He responded eagerly.

The Lord stirred Rajan's heart to be reconciled with his parents. He visited them in South India. Shocked and disappointed to learn that he had abandoned his Hindu religion for a new faith, they hired a Hindu priest to convince Rajan to recant his faith in Jesus.

After several interviews, the priest told Rajan that he should definitely keep that which he found in Christ. He advised Rajan's parents to follow that way also, because he said he could see it had brought Rajan such peace.

Following his training school, Rajan joined the full-time staff of Youth With A Mission. He continues to declare the greatness of the Lord.

Steve Cochrane, an American, is Regional Director for YWAM in South Asia.

Tuesday

In all that has happened to us, you have been just; you have acted faithfully.
Nehemiah 9:33

I was rocking our first baby and idly singing, "Your father's gone away...boo hoo, boo hoo, boo hoo."

Suddenly my spirit heard, "Is this what you want your child to grow up with?"

I gasped. "No Lord, I don't." I felt God speak to me about the privilege of being married to a man of God, and the joy of releasing him to be all that God wants him to be. I wanted my child to grow up viewing our missionary life as a privilege.

I believe in the justice of God. One particular separation had been especially difficult. There were many pastoral problems to deal with, and Loren was away longer than usual. I stood at the kitchen sink where I'd just finishing washing the dishes.

"Well God," I said. "This has been a particularly difficult situation. Loren will be home tomorrow, and I just want to tell You that I'm looking for a little of Your justice." I went on with my duties. It wasn't a big cry. Just chatting with God.

About two months later, Loren and I were given a beautiful 27-foot trailer. I had thought God would provide a little trailer for our traveling, but this was gorgeous. The children had a separate little room with bunk beds. We had a room with a big bed. It was as though it was tailor-made just for us. In my joy I said, "God, this is wonderful. I never expected anything like this."

Clear as a bell I heard in my heart, "Darlene, remember the conversation at the kitchen sink? This is part of My justice for you. I'm going to make it that much nicer for you and Loren and the children when you can be together."

Darlene Cunningham, an American, is the YWAM International Director of Training. The wife of YWAM's President, Loren Cunningham, she also helped found Youth With A Mission. Loren and Darlene live in Kona, Hawaii, USA.

Wednesday

For He whom God has sent speaks the words of God; for He gives the Spirit without measure.
John 3:34 NASB

I wasn't sure what to do with my hands except wipe the sweat off them, but I wished I could grab the butterflies in my stomach. I was about to walk onto a stage before 1,800 students at the University of Central America in El Salvador.

The students, El Salvador's brightest, were attending this rally to raise money for the refugees of the civil war. Since I'd come to El Salvador with a YWAM mobile team to minister to the refugees, I was given an opportunity to speak. I didn't like speaking in public, and all I knew to share was my testimony.

"A few years ago," I told them, "I was a student of astronomy at the University of Arizona.

"I was shy and had few friends. I wanted to spend my life in an observatory, away from people. And though I had everything I wanted—a car, money, a good education—I was unhappy. I had the whole world ahead of me...but I needed answers.

"Looking in my telescope, I saw a decaying universe. Looking around me, I saw a decaying world. I looked in the Bible, and it said, 'The grass withers, the flower fades, but the word of our God stands forever.'

"I'm not here to represent my country," I told them. "I am a citizen of another Kingdom, one that will last forever. Peace will only come to this country, and this world, when we give up ourselves and our nations, and serve Jesus Christ."

I looked at the intent faces. Many were Communists, hostile to anything American, but they listened and applauded. Somehow I had brought the right message for the right audience.

So many times I have felt like a fish out of water, and have wondered why God called me into missions when I had so little to offer. That day, I learned that God had given me a message and had prepared people to hear it.

Jim Shaw, an American, is the editor of YWAM's *Personal Prayer Diary,* and is an editor with YWAM Publishing in Lindale, Texas, USA.

Thursday

A gentle answer turns away wrath, but a harsh word stirs up anger.
                                                              Proverbs 15:1

Forty of us were running across the United States, carrying a torch, representing the light of the Gospel of Christ. Our goal was to run from the Atlantic to the Pacific Ocean.

One evening, we pitched our tents in a city park, with the permission of the city manager. We awoke in the middle of the night to the sound of harsh profanity and threats.

Our co-leader, Tom, muttered a prayer and stepped from his tent. In a sleepy daze, he looked for the intruders, but could find no one.

Suddenly, from across the park, four huge figures appeared, heading straight for Tom. One man stared down at him with wild eyes. Blood dripped from a deep gash above his eyebrow.

"Who gives you the right to camp in the middle of our park? Just who do you think you are?" he demanded with slurred speech.

"We're running a torch across the country for Jesus," Tom calmly explained. Three of the men were visibly shaken. The wounded one was unimpressed.

"You bunch of Jesus freaks!" he screamed. "If it was my park, I wouldn't let you near here."

Tom kept a gentle attitude, and prayed silently. The man lunged toward Tom, but his friends grabbed him by the shoulder. "Leave him alone!" one shouted.

Tom watched with amazement as the four mammoth figures suddenly turned and walked behind some bushes a short distance away. Then they came back. As they approached this time, a peaceful attitude was evident. The man of intimidation came close to Tom's face. "I am really sorry for what I did," he whispered. "When you're running with the torch, could you pray for me?"

Four engulfing hugs later, Tom promised to pray for them.

Eric Olson, an American, works as administrative assistant on special projects in Georgia, USA.

Friday

How can they believe in the one of whom they have not heard? And how can they hear without someone preaching to them? Romans 10:14

On the Sundays when Mom said, "Set the big table," we knew there would be guests. It might be the pastor's family. It just might be missionaries who had left families and homeland to take the Gospel across the sea. It might even include nationals from another land.

My two brothers, my sister, and I grew up without the usual misconceptions about missionaries being super-humans. To us they were folks "with skin on," with stories to tell of trekking through soggy underbrush to a remote village, of eating strange food prepared by grateful converts, of praying for rescue from under a capsized canoe after taking the Gospel to outlying islands.

Mom served in many areas of church life. But no activity produced in her more enthusiasm than missions. Supporting our missionaries meant more than financial support and sharing a meal now and then. She was active in many missions-oriented groups.

Should anyone be surprised, then, that all of Mom's children have become missionaries? We never felt Mom clinging to us or her grandchildren as we boarded a plane for distant lands. We knew she'd like us living close by, but she let us go.

Some of Mom's now-grown grandchildren are ministering, as well. We gathered recently from Asia, the Pacific Islands, Europe, and the United States to celebrate Mom's seventieth birthday. Among the great-grandchildren present was one recently born in Belgium.

Others might not consider Mom a missionary. But she planted the seed of missions in us and exposed us to others who watered and nurtured it. I have no doubt that there are laid up for Mom many treasures in heaven.

Beverly Caruso, an American, is one of the daughters of Dorothy Hall, who works part-time as a church secretary in California.

Saturday

How precious to me are your thoughts, O God! How vast is the sum of them!
Psalm 139:17

In Shatin, Hong Kong, far from family and friends in the U.S., our first child was born. My husband and I had lived in Christian communities during most of our marriage; in Shatin we shared a home with three other couples. They had become our family.

We had decided as a group that it would be best for us to live as individual family units. Now, five days after our son was born, we had to move. This was a faith stretcher for us—starting out alone with a new baby. Because we had lived with others, we had little furniture. Now we needed baby items, too.

Little by little, we saw God provide everything from a washing machine and furniture to dishes and baby clothes.

One day, as I looked at my scraggly hair in the mirror, I wished I could have a permanent. I quickly dismissed the thought as frivolous. We still needed a refrigerator.

But I talked to my Father about it. "Lord, I'd like to have a permanent."

He said, "I'd like to give you one."

"But how, Lord? How can I justify spending so much when we have so little? Send it through my mom, Lord, then I'll know it's okay."

My husband agreed.

The next week, I received a letter from my mother. Out fell a check with a note attached: "This is specifically for you to get a permanent."

God knew exactly what I needed, and it was not too small for Him to care about.

Terrie Koller, an American, works in discipleship and as a homemaker in Hong Kong.

Sunday

Meditation

I will praise you, O Lord, with all
my heart; I will tell of all your wonders. I will be glad and rejoice in
you; I will sing praise to your name,
O Most High.
The Lord is a refuge for the op-
pressed, a stronghold in times of
trouble. Those who know your
name will trust in you, for you,
Lord, have never forsaken those
who seek you.

Psalm 9:1-2,9-10

Monday

The steps of a man are established by the Lord; and He delights in his way.
Psalm 37:23 NASB

In preparation for a YWAM outreach in 1988, my wife, Rocha, and I set out with a friend to go from Recife, Brazil, to Montevideo, Uruguay. We had enough money to reach our first stop in Rio de Janeiro. We went from one city to another, and in each shared about our outreach. We hoped for enough contributions to go on to the next city. Our resources were depleted by the time we reached the border town of Rivera, between Brazil and Uruguay.

Montevideo was some eight hours away from Rivera. We decided to go to the town square about 9:00 that morning and pray about money to reach Montevideo, and for Uruguayan visas. We all felt at peace as we searched for the government office to apply for visas.

As we left the building, a car pulled up beside us. The driver introduced himself as Mr. Wilson of the Brazilian consulate. He said, "I was praying at 9:00, and the Holy Spirit instructed me to get in my car and drive toward the consulate, where I would meet three young people who need help. Are you the ones?"

We told our story, and praised the Lord together. When Mr. Wilson left, he told us to return to the consulate at 3:00 that afternoon.

When we returned, we found three visas, three airline tickets to Montevideo, and some extra money waiting for us.

We were still awed as we boarded the plane—the first commercial plane trip for my wife and me.

We were able to give a generous thank-offering at the YWAM base in Montevideo, and still had enough for our journey back.

Written by Tony Santana.

Tuesday

But God chose the foolish things of the world...so that no one may boast before him.
           I Corinthians 1:27,29

Our team members asked God for creative ways to share Christ in China. One of the unique methods He gave us, we now refer to as "group photo evangelism."

Tourists are expected to take pictures when visiting significant historical sites. So we clustered before the walled city of Shanghai, Dr. Sun Yat Sen's mausoleum, and even the Imperial Palace, waiting for our designated team photographer to snap shots with our varied assortment of Canons and Pentaxes. While posing we would break into joyful singing. Sometimes we'd even do a brief drama presentation.

Naturally our singing attracted the attention of people nearby, and soon a curious crowd had gathered to watch the peculiar sight. By the time our photographer, who was never in a hurry, finally took the last shot, there were usually other tourists, or even local Chinese, eager to engage in conversation. We saw this normal tourist custom as one of God's methods to communicate the Gospel in a country closed to open evangelism.

Sometimes it feels strange doing something odd to attract attention in a public place. Yet it was equally odd for Peter and John to heal the lame man at the temple gate and for the apostle Paul to stand on Mars Hill and talk about the unknown God. God wants to use our circumstances for His purposes. We need only to be willing.

Dawn Gauslin, an American, is the International Coordinator for YWAM's field-based Leadership Training Schools. She is also an assistant to Darlene Cunningham.

Wednesday

And everyone who has left houses or brothers or sisters or father or mother or children or fields for my sake will receive a hundred times as much and will inherit eternal life.   Matthew 19:29

Moving and making new friends was a regular occurrence for our Air Force family. My brothers and sisters were my only permanent friends. We had our sibling rivalries, but when we were old enough to be on our own, we all settled near one another. Our families frequently ate and played together. We even did household projects together.

When God called my husband and me to be missionaries in the Philippines, I felt both excitement and dread. I wondered how I would ever survive apart from my family.

I cried out to God for His grace and peace. How many times had I said I would go wherever He directed, and do whatever He asked? Now I wanted to obey Him joyfully.

It has been over four years since that original departure day. God has filled to overflowing the hole caused by family left behind. In our very first month in the Philippines, we shared a big old house with people from Panama, Brazil, the United States, Malaysia, Indonesia, Hong Kong, England, Netherlands, Germany, France, and the Philippines! God has made our lives rich in relationships with many precious people.

Although it is still a sacrifice to live apart from family, there is little time or opportunity to feel homesick.

Bobbie Hamm, a Canadian, and her husband are Discipleship Training School directors and leaders in Baguio City, Philippines.

Thursday

As the heavens are higher than the earth, so are my ways higher than your ways and my thoughts than your thoughts.   Isaiah 55:9

We had been ministering for several weeks in Germany. Our hosts were my in-laws, Ken and Peggy, who pastor U.S. military personnel in Nurnberg, Germany.

I had been praying about what God wanted me to do during the two weeks my wife would be in Switzerland leading a Writer's Seminar, but God seemed to be silent. I knew that Peggy regularly spent an hour each night in prayer. Peg believed God was saying I should minister in Czechoslovakia.

Ken and Peggy's home in Nurnberg is only four hours from Pilzen, Czechoslovakia. They arranged for me to speak the next weekend to the leadership of a church in Pilzen.

After the long drive, my in-laws returned to Nurnberg. How refreshed I was to share with Czech brothers in Christ, so newly freed from communism. Afterward, I had the opportunity to speak to the entire congregation.

I planned to sleep in the church building and ride the train back to Nurnberg the next morning if God didn't open doors for further ministry. But God had other plans.

At the end of the evening service, a young professor from England offered me his extra bed. He had been in Czechoslovakia only a few weeks, but already was highly respected by his fellow teachers at Pilzen University. He quickly gained a grasp of the Czech language, and his students were learning English speedily.

"We're going to study religious words today," he told his students the first day when he introduced me. In class after class, tears coursed down the students' faces as they heard, most for the first time, of Jesus, who could forgive their sins. This truly was harvest time for the Lord.

God knew when my wife left for Switzerland what He had planned for me. He simply waited to unfold it in His time.

Peter Caruso, an American, pastors in the USA, and travels often to preach and teach in churches and missions.

Friday

Each man should give what he has decided in his heart to give, not reluctantly or under compulsion, for God loves a cheerful giver.   II Corinthians 9:7

For years, I watched my husband give generously. I wasn't a giver. I was the one who asked, "Are you sure we can afford to give this?" Now, at the age of 54, I was a recent widow on staff with YWAM. God would soon challenge me in the area of generosity.

A young man felt God wanted him to give away his guitar, and asked the staff to pray with him for a new one. The Lord spoke to my heart to buy it for him. Thinking I had a good idea of the cost, I answered, "I'm open to that, Lord."

I went to talk to the young man, and he told me what he needed. Since he was a songwriter and recording artist, he needed a custom-made acoustical guitar—and I was shocked at the price.

It wasn't that I lacked the money to give, although it was a significant amount to me. I was concerned about being a responsible giver. Understanding that a widow should seek confirmation from spiritual leadership in such a matter, I explained the situation to Loren Cunningham.

"Loren, do you think it would be good stewardship for me to give someone that much money for a guitar?"

Loren knew about acoustical guitars, and explained that this young man needed that particular kind for his ministry. "It will last forever, and will be a tremendous boost to him and his career," he said.

I ended up giving the money anonymously, and the young man was thrilled. His response was a confirmation to me that I had heard from God.

It wasn't until mid-life that I learned firsthand the truth that it is more blessed to give than to receive. Now I understand that because God is the greatest giver of all, He loves to share this joy with us. It's just part of His character.

Marcella Goulding, an American, is now retired and living in Washington State, USA.

Saturday

Love never fails.   *I Corinthians 13:8*

It was love at first sight. As Michelle and I spent time together, we discovered we had a great deal in common. On the first day that we talked about our feelings for one another, we prayed, and the line that I will always remember was, "Lord, whatever happens, please preserve this friendship."

In the weeks that followed, we grew closer together, loving one another's company, discovering 101 ways to date on a YWAM budget. Several people commented to me that we made a wonderful couple, and we even began to discuss the possibilities of marriage.

It's hard to pinpoint where the first cracks appeared, and by the time we noticed what was happening, our relationship was plummeting in an uncontrollable nose dive. Inevitably, there was a lot of pain, anger, and questioning. We asked, "God, what's happening? Where did we go wrong?"

As we had to deal with the reality of living and working at the same ministry center, we both clung to that first prayer, "Lord, preserve this friendship."

Slowly the healing came as forgiveness, grace, and understanding were expressed and received. I learned in a whole new way what it was to be forgiven, as well as the true meaning of love: It is to prefer another and to die to one's own desires. As the flames of our romantic love died, I developed a deeper love for Michelle, a love not born of this earth.

Michelle has moved on from the YWAM base now, but we still see each other from time to time. We are both secure in the knowledge that there is nothing more than friendship between us, and yet that friendship is stronger than when we were dating...because of answered prayer and a revelation of true love.

Trevor May, an Australian, works in the art and editorial departments at Last Days Ministries in Lindale, Texas, USA.

Sunday

Meditation

Clothe yourselves with humility toward one another, because, "God opposes the proud but gives grace to the humble." Humble yourselves, therefore, under God's mighty hand, that he may lift you up in due time. Cast all your anxiety on him because he cares for you. Be self-controlled and alert. Your enemy the devil prowls around like a roaring lion looking for someone to devour. Resist him, standing firm in the faith, because you know that your brothers throughout the world are undergoing the same kind of sufferings.

I Peter 5:5-9

Monday

"For I know the plans I have for you," declares the Lord, *"plans to prosper you and not to harm you, plans to give you hope and a future."*

Jeremiah 29:11

I met Cynthia while caring for a sick team member on an outreach in Madras, India. I had taken my ill colleague to a missionary medical facility where Cynthia, another American, was also awaiting treatment.

We struck up a conversation, and Cynthia told me she was seeking spiritual truth. She had been befriended by a guru, who was instructing her in Hinduism. I told her that there is only one God: Jesus. She listened politely, but explained that she was in the process of converting to Hinduism.

When Cynthia left to be examined, I prayed silently for her, asking God to give me the words which would pierce her heart. I felt impressed with the above Scripture from Jeremiah.

When Cynthia returned to get her medicine and say goodbye, I shared the verse with her. Her eyes grew wide, but she didn't say much. She just left. I never expected to see her again: Madras is a huge city.

The next day, I felt impressed to return to town with some of the others on our team. As I waited for them outside the store, I heard someone calling my name. It was Cynthia!

As we talked, Cynthia's story tumbled out. Her mother had told her about Jesus, but a painful experience in church had alienated her. We shared lunch that day, and I told her more about Christ's personal, planning love.

Cynthia started weeping. She was afraid of being hurt again and had felt that God had forsaken her. I reminded her that God loved her so much that He sent His Son to die for her. He also sent me halfway around the world to tell her about His great love.

With tears of joy, Cynthia accepted the Lord. She later returned home, having found the truth she'd been seeking.

Theresa Aragon is a member of an evangelism team in India.

Tuesday

Unless you change and become like little children, you will never enter the kingdom of heaven.   Matthew 18:3

I was about ten years old during the Los Angeles Olympic Outreach; I was part of a King's Kids performing group. We had been doing several performances a day, but were given a day off. We went to a park to celebrate the birthday of one of our youngest team members.

During the festivities, a scraggly man about 40 years old emerged from nearby bushes. He was looking through the trash can for something to eat.

Someone called him over and invited him to join us for birthday cake. I innocently asked him where he lived. He was homeless. Then I asked if I could pray for him. He seemed pleased by that. Then he asked if I would sing for him. Another girl joined me. I was amazed when he began crying. After several worship songs, I asked him why he was crying. He said he had never heard such pure, sweet things before.

Some of our leaders entered the conversation. We learned his name was Kevin, and that he had ruined his life with alcohol and bitterness. His wife divorced him, and he hadn't seen his child. Yet, he said, he hadn't cried for 35 years.

He said he was impressed that I wasn't afraid of him, and that my childlike softness, innocence, and genuineness touched his spirit.

We were all blessed when he asked, "Can I serve you guys?" He came back to the church where we were staying and helped, cooking our food and washing our dishes.

Kevin didn't come to the Lord right away. But after some time, he came back and asked us to pray for him to become a Christian.

Later, Kevin attended a Discipleship Training School on the m/v *Anastasis*. I saw him a number of times after that. Each time, he told me, "You've turned my life around; you've blessed me." But I reminded him that it was Jesus, not me.

Kiersten Kauffman, an American, is finishing her high school education in Norway.

Wednesday

May the God of peace...equip you with everything good for doing his will, and may he work in us what is pleasing to him, through Jesus Christ....

Hebrews 13:20-21

One of the most freeing truths the Bible teaches is that God provides everything we need to do His will and to please Him. Many years of my life were spent attempting to appease God through working hard and staying busy serving. I failed to grasp the simplicity of what truly brings joy to His heart.

If you seem to be always striving, yet never quite achieving that sense that He is pleased, then perhaps you also have missed this simple truth. His greatest joy is for you to know the joy that He has over you, and also that "you can indeed be pleasing to Him."

Most of my life I tried too hard, believing that my praise was never pure enough nor my service worthy enough. My prayers began with, "Lord, forgive me," because I was sure that I had grieved Him in some way. What freedom came when I began to understand that my repentant response to His correction when I sinned was pleasing to Him. Because of His sacrifice, it was as if I'd chosen not to sin in the first place.

I have learned that obedience, praise, faithfulness in the small things, love for my wife and son, brokenness over sin, and indeed, awareness of His joy and love for me are what please Him. He is faithfully at work in you to produce the character that He desires. He is very pleased to call you His own.

Jim Mills, an American missionary in the German-speaking world since 1976, serves in the area of praise and worship and the creative arts.

Thursday

Anyone who has seen me has seen the Father.   *John 14:9*

"What does God look like, Daddy?"

I can remember struggling one night several years ago with how to answer the question posed by my then five-year-old daughter, Misha.

As I pondered Misha's question, I realized that in her childlike simplicity she had asked a question that many people want answered. Perhaps adults state it differently, but the basic question is still the same. *If there is a God, what is He like?*

The Bible says that God is not finite like you and me, but He has made Himself known to us in such a clear, understandable way that we can know what He is like. "No one has ever seen God, but God the only Son...has made him known" (John 1:18).

I told my daughter what God looks like. I told her that He looks like Jesus. Jesus is God in human form. We find many examples of how Jesus revealed the Father to us in the Bible. One example of this is found when some Jewish mothers wanted Jesus to bless their children. His disciples thought He was too busy, too important to be bothered by these mothers, but Jesus scolded His disciples and told them to bring the children to Him. He took the children in His arms and talked to them. He had time for them; He had time to listen to their stories and hear about their games. He didn't mind getting dirty from little kids sitting on his lap, runny noses and all. Through seeing how Jesus had time for the little children, we learn that God has time for people. He cares, even about the little things in life. He is patient. God the Father looks like His Son.

Floyd McClung, an American, directs Leadership Development Programs for YWAM. He lives in California, USA.

Taken from *The Father Heart of God* by Floyd McClung. Copyright © 1985 Floyd McClung, Jr. Published by Harvest House Publishers, Eugene, Oregon. Used by permission [from pages 18-19].

Friday

Leave your country,...and go to the land I will show you.   Genesis 12:1

From the first day I met Steven, I knew he was called by God to go to Poland. Now, not quite a year after our wedding, we had told all our wonderful friends at YWAM in Holland goodbye. We sat in our hotel room in Krakow, not knowing what to do next, wondering whether we had indeed heard from God.

The only legal way for foreigners to live in Poland was either to establish a business or to study in the university. We would become student-missionaries.

While still in Holland, we had applied to Jagiellonian University in Krakow, but had heard nothing for months. Eventually, we began calling the Polish Embassy regularly. They kept repeating, "We are sure you will be accepted, but we haven't heard from Warsaw yet."

After more prayer, we felt it was definitely time to go to Poland. On the designated date we still had not heard from the university. With tourist visas in hand, we left.

The registrar at the university was surprised to see us. "But I don't have your names," she said. "This is a problem." She checked with the Ministry of Education and said we should come back the next day.

We walked quietly through the rainy streets of the old town back to the hotel. Fear and doubt lingered through the longest day and night of our lives.

The next morning, our stomachs in knots, we climbed the stairs to ask the registrar for the decision.

"You can stay," she said, smiling.

Our hearts leaped with joy as we raced out into the square. "Thank You, God," we shouted, wondering how we ever could have doubted Him.

Only God knew the wondrous changes about to take place in Eastern Europe in the next few months of 1989, and why He wanted us there.

Lori Wallett, an American, is part of the leadership of YWAM Poland.

Saturday

So neither he who plants nor he who waters is anything, but only God, who makes things grow.   *I Corinthians 3:7*

When I first arrived in American Samoa, I had only one contact. Soon, I met a skinny young Christian cameraman named Sosene who worked at the government television studio. Sosene encouraged me to stay and start a ministry.

As the days and weeks passed, a question grew in me: *God, what am I doing here?* I had left an effective ministry in Hawaii as director of Teen Challenge on Oahu. The Holy Spirit was drawing many young people from drugs and rebellion. It was 1974, the height of the Jesus Movement. For me, Waikiki was a cross-cultural mission field.

I learned that Samoa had at least one church in every village, with more than 98% of the population faithfully attending church. *Am I really needed here?* I wondered.

Soon God answered that question, at least in part. I became aware of the widespread sin: immorality, alcohol abuse, anger, and violence. Everyone knew about God, but few knew God as their personal Friend, as their own Savior and Lord. I stayed five years to pioneer Youth With A Mission in Samoa.

Ministry in Hawaii had been characterized by much observable fruit. But observable fruit was rare in Samoa. More than once, I asked, *God, what am I doing here?* There was the occasional conversion. Our Christian bookstore, village film ministry, weekly radio broadcasts, and other ministries planted seeds and helped build bridges of friendship for future cooperation and ministry.

Sometimes fruit is only observable over long periods of time. That young, skinny Samoan I met has influenced many other Samoans with the Gospel. Today Sosene is director of Island Breeze, and is the Pacific Regional Director for YWAM. Other Samoans are leading YWAM ministries in at least a dozen countries. More than 50 Samoans are now in full-time ministry around the world.

Dave Hall, an American, serves on base council in Kona, Hawaii, USA, and is General Manager of YWAM's radio station, KFSH-FM on The Big Island.

Meditation

If you follow my decrees and are careful to obey my commands,...I will grant peace in the land, and you will lie down and no one will make you afraid. I will remove savage beasts from the land, and the sword will not pass through your country. Five of you will chase a hundred, and a hundred of you will chase ten thousand, and your enemies will fall by the sword before you.

I will look on you with favor and make you fruitful and increase your numbers, and I will keep my covenant with you. I will walk among you and be your God, and you will be my people.

Leviticus 26:3,6,8-9,12

Monday

In your hearts set apart Christ as Lord. Always be prepared to give an answer to everyone who asks you....   *I Peter 3:15*

Our team from the south of England was ministering in Ghana, West Africa. My partner and I were taken to the Ahinsin Methodist Church outside the city of Kumasi. We were to preach and pray for the sick.

We enjoyed the African praise and music. Then we gave a message about trusting God's love.

First, a woman was healed of heart problems. This prompted almost the entire congregation to move toward the front for prayer. Others also received healing.

Through an interpreter, a pregnant woman explained that her doctor told her the child she was carrying had been dead for two days. He planned to remove it surgically the next day if it didn't come naturally. She didn't seem to believe for a healing; simply that God would extend His love to her through our prayers.

I thought of Peter's words in his first epistle. *Am I ready to give a defense or testimony of what God will do?* I wondered.

When I prayed for her, nothing seemed to happen. I prayed again. This time, I somehow sensed the Holy Spirit's work.

As she was returning to her seat, I felt an incredibly intense love for her. I knew it had to be God sharing a part of His love and hurt for her with me.

I called her back to the front. I had such a sense of assurance that I was willing to stake my reputation on what would happen next.

With a faith only God could provide, I spoke life to the child within her womb.

Her excitement made the results obvious. The child was moving and kicking inside her. Her gratefulness and excitement were a joy for all present.

Within hours, the child was born alive, and is now healthy and thriving.

Stephen Jones is director of YWAM in Southwest England.

Tuesday

Guide me in your truth and teach me, for you are God my Savior, and my hope is in you all day long.

Psalm 25:5

After four years of running a bed and breakfast inn, I longed to have a home just for our family. After discussion and prayer, my husband and I decided to get out of the business.

So in the early spring of 1987, we began house hunting. We looked at both property and houses, trying to decide whether to build or buy. Nothing seemed right.

In May, YWAM's Mercy Ship the m/v *Anastasis* docked in Sacramento. We took our daughters, Kari (15) and Kristen (11), to tour the ship. I listened to the guide describe the ministry of the ship. I was surprised to feel again a long-buried desire to work in missions.

"I think I could do this," I said excitedly. My husband's eyes grew wide with surprise. He knew my desire to have a home of our own.

His own interest was growing, despite our first disappointment with missions. Years before, we had served a short time with YWAM. Family and friends had promised financial support, but it never came. After seven months we left, disillusioned with God and with faith missions.

God's love continued working in us. During the following 12 years, we grew in our understanding of Him. He worked on our doubts and hurts. In the process, we realized it had been our choice to work in missions, not one made after prayer and seeking God's will. Now, with fresh vision, we sought God's desire.

It took 16 months of family prayer and preparation before we entered a school especially for those in mid-life, called Crossroads Discipleship Training School.

As we shared our plans with others, money came effortlessly for school fees and its subsequent cross-cultural outreach! As we were faithful to follow God's direction, He was faithful to provide our needs.

Sandi Wagner, an American, works as manager of the bookstore at YWAM's University of the Nations campus in Kona, Hawaii, USA.

Wednesday

Behold, I am doing a new thing; now it springs forth, do you not perceive it?
I will make a way in the wilderness and rivers in the desert.

Isaiah 43:19 RSV

We had to leave India every six months, then reenter under new visas. After several years and much prayer, we went to the local immigration office to plead for a long-term permit. The form asked why we were in India. I couldn't write "missionary work." I wrote that I wanted the permit "to continue doing volunteer work." When six months passed with no answer, I got worried. I was directed to another immigration office 70 kilometers away.

"Where does your mother live?" the officer asked. Puzzled, I answered, "Chicago."

Throwing the paper at me, he demanded, "Then why did you write this?" Following the words, *to continue doing volunteer work,* in the same color ink and in my handwriting, I read, "and to live with my mother." I couldn't believe it.

"I didn't write that," I protested. He stared at me accusingly. He took a large rubber stamp, slammed it on my paper and thrust it at me. In, bold black print I read, "We find no reason to object to the foreigner seeking residence in India."

I had tried to tell them the truth. I decided that if they wanted me to stay in India with a mother I did not have there, it was their problem.

I learned later that piece of paper was shuffled from office to office for the next four years seeking official approval. All that time we freely stayed in India. We were warned, however, that if we left the country, we might not be allowed to reenter. This was fine with us. We went about our work with zest.

Eventually, a family emergency arose and we had to leave India. When we returned, we submitted a fresh application with tremendous trepidation. This time they immediately accepted our application granting us long-term residency, and didn't ask a thing about my family. We could live in India indefinitely, and we wouldn't even have to live with my mother.

Tim Svoboda, an American, is National Director of YWAM in India.

Thursday

The fruit of the righteous is a tree of life, and he who is wise wins souls.
Proverbs 11:30 NASB

Some people are mistakenly waiting to be sent to the mission field before they witness regularly at home, and are missing out on many opportunities to lead people to Jesus Christ.

As we walk with the Lord, we grow in our ability to be sensitive to His leading in our life, both in day-to-day matters and when we are out sharing our faith with others. A good practice is to schedule a time into our weekly routine that we use specifically for sharing the Good News about Jesus with the lost. We schedule and discipline every other area of our life—going to work, recreation, entertainment, Bible studies, prayer meetings, and so on. So why not schedule a weekly time to spend with non-Christians in whatever type of outreach or friendship evangelism that seems applicable?

Don't just wait passively for it to happen, but passionately pursue "divine appointments" that the Holy Spirit arranges in the course of your day. Often we are so engrossed in our daily affairs that divine appointments just seem like another interruption. We must be alert and actively seeking them.

On a recent plane trip, an elderly man sat next to me. I was physically tired, and was not really "in the mood" for witnessing, but before long, I struck up a conversation with him. Soon he was pouring his heart out to me in regard to his health, having recently been diagnosed with terminal cancer and given only three months to live. I asked him about his relationship with God, and he admitted that his recent diagnosis had awakened spiritual hunger within him.

On that flight, I had the privilege of leading him to Christ.

Danny Lehmann, an American, directs the YWAM base in Honolulu, Hawaii, USA, and travels extensively in a teaching ministry.
From *Bringin' 'Em Back Alive* by Danny Lehmann. Copyright © 1987 by Danny Lehmann. Published by Whitaker House, Springdale, Pennsylvania. Used by permission [from page 90].

Friday

If any of you lacks wisdom, he should ask God, who gives generously to all without finding fault, and it will be given to him.   James 1:5

While Loren and I were expecting Karen, our first child, I thought through our needs. We're called to be a traveling family. We wanted our children to be a part of the team and to enjoy being a missionary family. I also didn't want to have frequent separations from them, or to have to leave them with babysitters. As I sought God's wisdom, He gave me strategies that worked well for us.

I bought child-sized sleeping bags and pillows, and sewed the children's names on them. Karen and David each had small backpacks for their personal things. By keeping these with us, the children could be at my feet wherever I was sitting, whether at a cathedral in England, the back of a tent in Germany, or at a YWAM meeting. They were able to participate in the worship time, then go to sleep.

Our mobile lifestyle could have resulted in no routine for the children. So I established a routine within the lifestyle we had. I knew that most children go to bed at about 8:00, so no matter where they were, ours did, too. They got their rest, but were not left out of our lives.

During most of our early years, all four of us slept in one room, often a different room every week or two. To provide a sense of permanence, I bought suitcases with lids that lift up, not suitcases which split in the middle and lay flat. Inside the lid I attached pictures of family members back home, and sometimes pictures the children drew themselves. With their own bed and pillow and the bag of toys, they only had to open their suitcase wherever they were to be in "their bedroom" within the bigger room they shared with us.

Darlene Cunningham, an American, is the YWAM International Director of Training. The wife of YWAM's President, Loren Cunningham, she also helped found Youth With A Mission. Loren and Darlene live in Kona, Hawaii, USA.

Saturday

Train a child in the way he should go, and when he is old he will not turn from it.
Proverbs 22:6

I was born into a missionary family serving God in West Africa. I grew up loving God while struggling with pride and a desire for independence—a battle between flesh and spirit for my soul.

How my parents must have prayed for me! They certainly loved me unconditionally. I remember one particular battle with my parents. I wanted to go to a night club in the city with some friends, and I wanted to use my father's car to get there. The argument, which seemed to me an attack on my freedom, lasted a long time. I did not trust my parents' motives. They probably distrusted mine.

Perhaps to bring the argument to an end as well as to make a point, my father reminded me that I had my own set of keys to his car. He told me I must decide for myself whether to go; whether to disregard my parents' concern for me. It would be my decision.

Their love won out. I decided that I would not go without their consent and blessing.

A news flash later that week caught my attention. A young man my age had gone to that same night club the night I intended to go. While minding his own business, not making any trouble for anyone, he was knifed to death in the parking lot.

That could have been me! I thought. My parents could very well have saved my life, although they did not know it. My pride and independence could have cost me my life if it hadn't been for my loving parents.

Stephen Jones is director of YWAM in Southwest England.

Sunday

Meditation

When he saw the crowds, he had compassion on them, because they were harassed and helpless, like sheep without a shepherd. Then he said to his disciples, "The harvest is plentiful but the workers are few. Ask the Lord of the harvest, therefore, to send out workers into his harvest field."

Matthew 9:36-38

Monday

God isn't interested in shortcuts. Have you ever really thought about Jesus' temptation in the wilderness? What was the devil trying to get Him to do? I believe it was to take a shortcut, to avoid all the pain and humiliation of the Cross by going after God's will the devil's way.

The devil promised to give Jesus all the kingdoms of the world if He would worship him. God's goal in sending Jesus to earth was to give His Son all the kingdoms of the world. One day, it is predicted in Revelation, the kingdoms of the earth will be the kingdom of our Lord. In a smaller way, this Kingdom is already coming through the Church of Jesus Christ. But someday, it will be finally and completely fulfilled when Christ returns to earth.

Satan was promising Jesus the instant achievement of that goal, sidestepping the pain and suffering of the Cross and the obedience of Christ's followers for many hundreds of years afterward.

What do we learn from this story? Jesus refused Satan, and we must refuse him, too. We have to learn to discern when the devil is offering us a shortcut—when he is tempting us to do God's will the devil's way.

Loren Cunningham, an American, is founder and president of YWAM. He lives in Hawaii, USA.

From *Winning, God's Way* by Loren Cunningham with Janice Rogers. Copyright © 1988 by Loren Cunningham. Published by YWAM Publishing, Seattle, Washington. Used by permission [from pages 95-96].

Tuesday

For whoever wants to save his life will lose it, but whoever loses his life for me will save it.   *Luke 9:24*

I remember holding the foot of the baby and thinking, "She can't die; she is so young." I started to cry. I had never been so close to death before. We could hear the bullets passing over the tin roof in every direction. The four of us lay flat on the damp mud floor of the small hut. We were caught in the middle of a gun battle between rival drug gangs.

People in Borel, one of the most dangerous shanty towns in Rio de Janeiro, were fighting against their rivals from Casa Branco, another shanty town on the opposite side of the mountain.

This was my new home, and it was a far cry from London! But God had called me here to share His love, especially with the children. As the shooting continued, I was gripped by fear. One of the gangsters was standing on our roof. The mother of the baby told us that a bullet had come through the roof the night before. I was sure that if another bullet came through, one of us would die.

My friends and I started singing to God. Instead of crying, we began laughing. Someone read from the Bible. I felt a Presence— a warmth went right through my body. I knew God was telling us that we were going to be all right.

After thirty minutes, the shooting stopped. No bullets had hit the hut.

The next day, I found myself too scared to even think about going outside. I prayed and God answered, "I want you to be prepared to die for Me." It was the hardest prayer I ever prayed, but I did it: "Okay, God." Immediately, the fear lifted. It seemed that because I had released my life to God, Satan couldn't use the threat of losing it against me anymore.

Sarah de Carvalho, from England, works with street children in Brazil.

Wednesday

He restores my soul.   *Psalm 23:3*

As I was walking toward the classroom, I felt tired and low in spirits. My husband had left the day before for a month-long outreach to Albania. I was staying in Texas to work with a children's summer discipleship camp. We'd never been separated that long; I missed him already.

I had worked hard all day with administrative duties. I really enjoyed what I was doing, but it had been a long day. I took a message to the classroom and turned to go back to my office.

Just as I came around the corner of the building, a strong gust of wind blew over me. Although it had been stormy that morning, the sky was now clear. The tree ahead was shaken with the force of the wind. As I felt the wind on my face, it was as though God was shouting, "I love you!" I felt refreshed. Within ten minutes, I was no longer sad and tired; I was joyful.

Later I thought of the Scripture, "The joy of the Lord is your strength." I realized my strength was not in my ability to carry out my duties. Nor was it in my husband's love, which seemed so far away.

God was teaching me that my strength was in His joy. He was pleased that I had chosen to follow His direction to work in Texas while He led my husband across the ocean. I believe He used the wind to convey His joy to me. He loved me and was pleased with me. In that truth lay the strength for the task before me.

Sandy Falor, an American, teaches at YWAM's Christian Heritage School in Tyler, Texas, USA.

Thursday

For this is what the Lord, the God of Israel, says: "The jar of flour will not be used up and the jug of oil will not run dry until the day the Lord gives rain on the land."   *I Kings 17:14*

We had been staying at Slavic Ministry's West European Co-ordinating Center in Austria for orientation. The van we planned to take on a six-week outreach to Bulgaria, Albania, and Yugoslavia had developed steering problems. Our command of the German language wasn't any better than our mechanical ability. We didn't have any idea what it would take to fix the problem.

A neighbor who sometimes worked on cars told us which car part we needed, but when we found it, we were horrified to learn the price was $600! That certainly wasn't in our outreach budget! Since we were scheduled to leave early the next morning, we had no choice. We knew that God is bigger than budgets, so we prayed that He would make up the difference.

Throughout the trip, we continued to pray that our funds would hold out. We did all the little things we could, like taking side roads through Yugoslavia to avoid expensive toll roads.

Equipped with a guide to Yugoslavian campgrounds, I sought for directions to our night destination. After driving all day, our team was tired and very anxious to eat.

Instead of finding a campground at the given address, we found a hotel! Inside, we were told the campground wasn't yet completed. One day, they told us, there would be a beautiful campground with full facilities out back. Today, however, it was only a dirt field covered with cottonwood trees.

The hotel managers felt so bad about turning away two vans full of hot, dusty people that they offered to let us put up our tents for free! We stayed a week, using the hotel's toilets and showers. They charged us only a nominal fee for electricity.

By the end of the trip, we had money to cover every single expense!

Sandy Oestreich, an American, works with Slavic Ministries.

Friday

My dove in the clefts of the rock, in the hiding places on the mountainside, show me your face, let me hear your voice; for your voice is sweet, and your face is lovely.   Song of Solomon 2:14

My husband, Floyd, and I place a high priority on spending time together. We often plan in enough time to walk together to our various meetings or appointments. We use that time to talk and share together. The exercise is great, too! You might find it enjoyable to cook a meal together and talk as you work, or do the weekly shopping as a team.

I read an article about a pastor's wife who said she had "a marriage on wheels." Her time with her busy husband was scarce. One day, she had an idea. She suddenly realized how much time he spent behind the wheel of the car visiting members of their congregation, so she decided to be with him in the car. With no phone or doorbell to intrude, they had plenty of opportunity for peace, privacy, and growth in their relationship. She took along little things to do while her husband made pastoral visits and ran errands for the church.

Floyd and I often can't be together because of his travel schedule. I like to send cards ahead to greet him at his various destinations. In this way, we can be together even while we are apart. I also have a special little bank where I regularly put some of my loose change to save for doing special things together when he is home. It's amazing how quickly the coins add up. We have enjoyed some very special times together, thanks to that little bank.

It is easy to become so busy with outside interests that we start taking each other for granted. We don't take the time to be together that nourishes our relationship. I once had someone tell me that spending time together with our marriage partner was "an extravagant waste of time." If so, it's a necessary extravagance!

Sally McClung, an American, has a ministry of hospitality and speaks internationally. She lives in California, USA.

From *Where Will I Find the Time?* by Sally McClung. Copyright © 1989 by Sally McClung. Published by Harvest House Publishers, Eugene, Oregon. Used by permission [from pages 42-43].

Saturday

Behold, you will call a nation you do not know, and a nation which knows you not will run to you, because of the Lord your God, even the Holy One of Israel; for He has glorified you.　　　　　*Isaiah 55:5 NASB*

When I first joined the staff of YWAM in my home country of Canada, I wasn't sure what God wanted of me. I wondered, *What is my niche? What are my giftings? Have I missed God somewhere along the line?*

During one time of private prayer, I asked God, "What country should I pray for today?" I was surprised by His answer. Into my thoughts came the name: Greenland.

Like most Christians, never before had I prayed for Greenland. I went to the world map on the wall. There it was, that huge mass of land to the east of Canada.

Are there any people there? I thought. *There must be. God doesn't usually ask us to pray for rocks and snow.* So I prayed. Greenland stuck in my mind, and I became curious. Before long, the "G" encyclopedia was pulled off the shelf, and new information about this remote place was filling my mind. I made a three-week visit there and discovered the largest island in the world to be a place of rugged and treeless beauty. Its small population of 54,000 is scattered along the barren coastline. There are only 70 towns and villages.

Eventually, we moved to Greenland and began a ministry to its people.

That first prayer was ten years ago. Over 120 people have participated in YWAM outreaches in Greenland. God has allowed us and other ministries in Greenland to see a tenfold increase in the number of believers. There is much yet to do to bring these precious Greenlandic people to a new life in Christ. I've found my niche. More importantly, I see God's immense faithfulness and love to every people group of the earth.

Errol Martens, a Canadian, is coordinator of YWAM-Greenland, and lives in Qaqortoq, South Greenland.

Sunday

Meditation

I love you, O Lord, my strength.
The Lord is my rock, my fortress
and my deliverer; my God is my
rock, in whom I take refuge. He is
my shield and the horn of my salvation, my stronghold.
He reached down from on high and
took hold of me; he drew me out of
deep waters. He rescued me from
my powerful enemy, from my foes,
who were too strong for me. He
brought me out into a spacious
place; he rescued me because he delighted in me.

Psalm 18:1-2,16-17,19

Monday

If from there you seek the Lord your God, you will find him if you look for him with all your heart and with all your soul. Deuteronomy 4:29

I was doing street evangelism with a group of YWAM students in the homosexual district of San Francisco. Two students and I got into a conversation with three homosexual guys hanging out on the street.

I started to tell one guy named Phil about Jesus and His love for us. Phil told me he was desperate for a change in his life. Everything was going bad: he had no money, no job, and was about to get kicked out of his apartment.

He said that under normal circumstances, he wouldn't have listened to a thing I had to say. But as he was walking down the street that night, he had said, "God, if You're really real, please prove it." Ten minutes later, I was talking to him about Jesus.

Right there on the corner of Castro Street, Phil accepted Jesus into his life. He repented of his sins and asked for forgiveness. After praying, he said he felt like a huge weight was gone.

Phil chose to make changes in his lifestyle, including going to church. He wanted to join a support group for people leaving the homosexual lifestyle.

That night, God showed me once again how much He loves sinners.

Becky Hilbert, an American/Polynesian, serves on staff with YWAM-San Francisco, California, USA.

Tuesday

Taste and see that the Lord is good; blessed is the man who takes refuge in him.
Psalm 34:8

Our extended family lived on a farm, and often entertained house guests, including European hitchhikers. Some of these guests stayed as a part of our household for several months at a time. One such was Mauri, a disillusioned French girl.

During the year she lived in our home, Mauri learned basic English and became a Christian with a call on her life to evangelize in Asia.

"Wonderful!" I told her. But I explained that to become a missionary, she must first graduate from a four-year Bible school, then apply to a mission board. "If accepted," I added, "you'll spend about two years raising financial support."

"No," she protested. "I need to go sooner than that."

One day while I was sewing and praying for Mauri, the Holy Spirit directed me to turn on the television. Reluctantly I obeyed.

On *The 700 Club,* Pat Robertson interviewed a man named Loren Cunningham. This was the first time I had heard of Youth With A Mission. After the interview, I sensed God telling me that this was what He had wanted me to hear.

I didn't want to mislead this "foster daughter," so I began to inquire about YWAM. I learned that a young couple who work with YWAM would be visiting our area soon. I made arrangements to meet with them and Mauri.

Although I anticipated language problems for Mauri, God had everything worked out. The couple spoke fluent French. In fact, they were leaders of the French-speaking YWAM school in Switzerland. They answered every question Mauri and I fired at them.

Mauri has since graduated from a Discipleship Training School in California, done evangelism in several countries, served for several years in Asia and, together with her husband, is currently a leader of YWAM in France.

Beverly Owen and her husband, Walden, both Americans, serve as directors of YWAM in Miami, Florida, USA.

Wednesday

So let us know, let us press on to know the Lord. His going forth is as certain as the dawn; and He will come to us like the rain, like the spring rain watering the earth.   *Hosea 6:3 NASB*

It was spring 1992, and New Zealand was experiencing a major water crisis. A lengthy drought was drying up the hydro lakes. As the crisis worsened, hot water use was limited to the early morning hours. Mandatory blackouts were threatened.

As we braced for the worst, we received a call from a local Christian businessman. God had been speaking to him about the need for New Zealand Christians to pray for water. He and others realized that God might be allowing this crisis to capture the nation's attention. God was calling New Zealand to repentance.

Sensing a need to call Christians to prayer, our friend asked us to design a full-page ad for all major newspapers. He agreed to help provide the necessary funds for the venture.

We accepted the job and sought God earnestly for a design. The result was simple, yet powerful. The New Zealand national anthem, a song with meaningful lyrics and recognizable by everyone, became our headline. In the background were ominous storm clouds representing God's response to our prayers.

The ad kicked off the four-week Prayer for the Nation Campaign. A committee set up a toll-free hotline, organized regional prayer coordinators, issued press releases, and arranged radio interviews. It is estimated that over 20,000 Christians prayed and fasted each Wednesday of the month.

God brought rain, but we believe God had higher purposes in mind. We believe that through the prayers of His people, God will also begin to reign more in New Zealand.

Mark Lee, from New Zealand, serves on staff of Media Plus in Hawaii, USA.

Thursday

But in fact God has arranged the parts in the body, every one of them, just as he wanted them to be.   *I Corinthians 12:18*

The family of God is incredibly diverse, yet many sincere believers are ignorant of the importance of having many ministries. During a conversation with a Christian leader in a youth ministry, he said to me, "If the local church was doing its job, we wouldn't need to have special ministries like this." What an incredible pressure we put on local churches to be the whole Kingdom of God represented in one place. No wonder pastors feel such stress. They feel obligated to meet everybody's expectations. The result is disappointment and discouragement.

There is no absolute model for what a local church should be. I once spent an afternoon with over one hundred spiritual leaders from several denominations. We tried to come up with a universal definition of a biblical local church. You may think that it was an easy task, but if you consider all the cultures and circumstances of people on the earth and you examine the diversity of models in the Bible, you will begin to understand our frustration. After many hours of discussion, we had produced many good models, but no absolute definition other than "people moving together under the lordship of Jesus."

The great blessing of the Kingdom is not sameness and uniformity but creativity and diversity. A local church will never do the job of Wycliffe Bible Translators, and Wycliffe will never do the job of Campus Crusade for Christ. Praise God for that!

We don't need to compete. We must be honest about our weaknesses, contribute with our strengths, and celebrate with joy the great diversity of ministries given to our generation by God.

John Dawson, a New Zealander, is YWAM's International Director of Urban Missions.

From *Taking Our Cities for God* by John Dawson. Copyright © 1989 by John Dawson. Published by Creation House, Lake Mary, Florida. Used by permission [from pages 108-109].

Friday

But he said to me, "My grace is sufficient for you, for my power is made perfect in weakness." Therefore I will boast all the more gladly about my weaknesses, so that Christ's power may rest on me.   *II Corinthians 12:9*

In a giant rubbish dump, I discovered that nothing in life is ever wasted when placed in God's hands. As a single mother from Australia, I have spent the past five years working among the poor Filipinos living at Smokey Mountain, Manila's city dump.

My initial response when asked to lead a Bible study for women living at the dump was, "I've never held a Bible study in my life." But I felt the Lord wanted me to do it, so I trusted Him and took the step of faith.

For our first Bible study, God impressed me to tell them about the importance of being a woman. But five minutes after I started, one of the women walked out. I told my story of a broken marriage, single motherhood, and the loss of a child.

They said, "But you're from Australia."

I said, "The problems are no different there, except that I didn't live on a garbage dump. The change came from within, and the healing came from Christ. I had to be willing to trust God."

From that time, I had their attention. They asked to hear more about marriage, children, families, and divorce. This was a challenging subject for women from a desperately poor community where alcoholism, violence, and immorality are rife.

By the end of the study, they were in tears. No one had ever shared with them that women are important.

Barb Carr, an Australian, serves in the Philippines.

Saturday

I have come that they might have life, and have it to the full.

John 10:10

Joe has a great relationship with his five-year-old son, Nick. It's the sort of relationship that makes me smile when I see them together with their heads bent over an anthill they've come upon, or running and laughing while flying a homemade kite in a field.

I once commented to Joe that I admired the way he took so much time out from his already-crowded schedule to spend time with his son. His response was interesting. He told me he wanted Nick to grow up and embrace his ideals—to love serving the Lord and to care for the world around him. Joe felt that for Nick to enter into his world, he first had to enter into his son's world, and so he worked at becoming his son's best friend. Joe built bridges into Nick's life through playing games with him, talking, listening, and caring.

Joe's desire to reach out to his son is very much like God's desire to be our friend. Jesus entered our world to show us the Father. He came as a friend to those who needed Him. In John's gospel, Jesus tells us "As the Father has sent me, I am sending you" (John 20:21). Jesus wants us to reach out to others as He reaches out to us. This is one of the signs of wholehearted commitment.

Floyd McClung, an American, directs Leadership Development Programs for YWAM. He lives in California, USA.
From *Basic Discipleship* by Floyd McClung. Copyright © 1990 Floyd McClung. Published by InterVarsity Press, Downers Grove, Illinois. Used by permission [from pages 153-154].

Sunday

Meditation

This is what the Lord says: "Let not the wise man boast of his wisdom or the strong man boast of his strength or the rich man boast of his riches, but let him who boasts boast about this: that he understands and knows me, that I am the Lord, who exercises kindness, justice and righteousness on earth, for in these I delight," declares the Lord.

Jeremiah 9:23-24

Monday

Your word, O Lord, is eternal; it stands firm in the heavens. Your faithfulness continues through all generations.　　　　*Psalm 119:89-90*

As our team distributed Bibles to the teachers we were meeting with in the former Soviet Union, I saw the joy on each face as they realized they had a Bible in their own language. I wondered how many of these teachers had even seen a Bible before.

We told the teachers that since all the Bibles looked alike, they should write their names on the covers. Those in my group refused; they felt it would be defacing this precious gift. So our team leader suggested that they write their names on the inside of the front cover. "The cover is not the Bible," he said. Reluctantly, they agreed.

A short while later we started to teach the group a song with hand motions. When the teachers were told to put their Bibles down so their hands would be free, they looked puzzled. With no chairs, they had no place to put the Bibles except on the floor, and they weren't about to put that precious Book on the floor.

At last, one young woman came up with an idea. She placed her lesson materials on the floor, then put her Bible on top. The others smiled and did the same.

May we treasure God's Word and handle it with reverence as those precious Russian teachers did!

Frances Bradley, an American, is a freelance writer who lives in Austin, Texas, USA.

Tuesday

Do not use vain repetitions as the heathen do. For they think that they will be heard for their many words.   *Matthew 6:7 NKJV*

During my School of Evangelism outreach, I was part of a small team in Belize, Central America. One day, we hiked to a remote village of Kekchi Indians. These are Mayan descendants of the Aztecs who live a simple lifestyle, carving out their existence through farming.

I worked with another student doing child evangelism. He entertained the children trying to demonstrate basic Bible truths through pictures and gestures. The children were captivated by the brightly colored pictures.

While trying to teach a Bible verse, my friend began: "First John, four, eight." The children mimicked him. He continued with "God is love."

Again the children repeated his words. He gave the children who correctly repeated the verse a colorful sticker. Each child tried hard to be heard above the others.

I realized that the children had no idea what they were saying. They were only repeating the phrase so they could get a prize. My friend had overlooked the importance of bringing true understanding to the children.

How often do we as Christians settle for reciting the right words in our effort to please others and get our reward?

David Dickson, an American, serves as an administrative assistant in Tyler, Texas, USA.

Wednesday

Then you will know the truth, and the truth will set you free.   John 8:32

Jesus states in the book of John that He came into the world to testify to the truth and that everyone on the side of truth listens to Him. Over and over, He proclaims that He is telling us the truth.

His truths are as meaningful for us today as they were when He first spoke them. The principles stated in the Bible will never change. They remain the same today as they were yesterday and always will be, because they come directly from God.

At times, I have let myself be carried along by my feelings or by whatever seemed good to me at the time. In doing so, I became a slave to my own desires and lost the freedom I had found in Christ. In the Kingdom of God, there is no place for slaves.

Whenever I have followed my own dictates, I have found myself in an even worse condition than I was before. However, whenever I have chosen to follow the truths of the Bible and have listened to and obeyed those whom God has put over me for my own good, I've experienced true freedom, victory, and that peace which Paul talked about in his letter to the Philippians, the peace of God which transcends all understanding.

True freedom doesn't come from doing whatever we want, but in choosing to do what is right. Everyone who lives according to the truth is set free.

Pilar Barriga, a Spaniard, is working as a bilingual secretary in Spain.

79

Thursday

If a man of peace is there, your peace will rest upon him; if not, it will return to you.   Luke 10:6

We had been praying for guidance about where our Far East Evangelism Team (FEET) should go. We believed God was leading us to Sikkim, a former Tibetan Buddhist kingdom. It had been a state of India for 15 years. While still in India, people discouraged us from going to Sikkim because of the restrictions against spreading the Gospel.

We had no contacts in Sikkim, yet several of us were impressed with Luke 10:6 which speaks of "a man of peace."

During the five-hour bus ride through the foothills of the Himalayas, we prayed silently, yet desperately, for God to provide the "man of peace." I also asked God to break through the normal resistance of the people toward the Gospel.

After we arrived, we started taking our things from the top of the bus. A man asked, "Are you the YWAM team?"

Uncertain of his intentions, I asked, "What YWAM team?"

"The YWAM team from Hong Kong."

When I admitted we were, he said, "Please follow me; I have rooms ready for you." His name was Solomon, meaning "peace." I'm still not sure how he found out about our arrival.

During our four days in the city of Gangkok, we preached to more than 4,000 people, about 14 percent of the population. Solomon said he found it hard to believe the openness he saw.

Joe Rystrom, an American, is a member of a FEET team in Hong Kong.

Friday

Before they call I will answer; while they are still speaking I will hear.
                                                        Isaiah 65:24

Work, work, work became the order of the day at the newly acquired YWAM base in France. Like the children who once lived there, the old orphanage buildings needed dedicated care and attention.

One by one, the buildings took shape as workers repaired what could be repaired, and replaced what could not.

Occasionally, an old repaired part gave out. Thus, in the coldest part of winter, the central heating broke down. We dressed in layers, and tried to work in the cold. I was sitting in my office, dressed in my heaviest winter coat, when the phone rang.

I recognized the voice of a friend who asked bluntly, "Are you cold?"

"Well, yes, but how did you know?"

"My wife had a dream, and she saw you all shivering. Are you out of fuel?"

"No, our central heating is not working," I answered.

"Call in a repairman, and send me the bill," he said.

A few hours later, he called again to ensure that we had followed through. As we hadn't yet been able to do so, he asked us to get him all the information on the type of burner we had. I did, and he said that he'd take care of it. Not long afterward, a workman arrived with all the right parts. Warm air was soon circulating throughout the building.

Daniel Schaerer, a Frenchman, leads YWAM's ministries in France.

Saturday

My sheep listen to my voice; I know them, and they follow me.

John 10:27

We had the wrong address. We were three Westerners on our way to deliver Bibles to a pastor for his underground church, and were now lost.

The next morning after praying, we decided to try another address. We knew that the pastor went there briefly once a week to pick up his mail. The chance of hitting the 15-minute window of opportunity and finding him there was small. We waited for the evening twilight, then, with some trepidation, we hailed a taxi.

We looked for the address, but the street was blocked short of our number by a maze of lanes and paths. We begged the driver to wait for us and set off into the labyrinth of darkening lanes. Once we left the main street and were wandering through the small lanes, we became hopelessly confused and were just about to give up when an angel appeared, or so he seemed to us.

Riding a bicycle, he loomed out of the gathering darkness and indicated he would help us. After reading the address on a slip of paper, he motioned for us to follow him and rode off into the tangle of alleyways. We soon spotted a six-story apartment building. It was the address we were looking for.

Upon clambering and stumbling through murky darkness to the top floor, we spotted a slit of light under a door. This was our destination. Wheeling around, we found that our angel-guide had disappeared. We were on our own. After a hesitant knock, the door swung open to reveal an elderly couple. As we asked how we could find the pastor, a figure came into view from the back room. He had arrived only five minutes before, received his mail, and was already preparing to leave as we knocked.

God had led us unerringly to the appointment.

Peter Jordan, a Canadian, leads YWAM Associates International, a ministry to former YWAMers.

Sunday

Meditation

I am not ashamed of the gospel, because it is the power of God for the salvation of everyone who believes: first for the Jew, then for the Gentile. For in the gospel a righteousness from God is revealed, a righteousness that is by faith from first to last, just as it is written: "The righteous will live by faith."

Romans 1:16-17

Monday

Let it be known today that you are God in Israel and that I...have done all these things at your command.   *I Kings 18:36*

It was a travesty—the TV documentary I was watching. Before me was secular man's interpretation of how we should bring up our children. I have taught and written from a biblical perspective on this subject, and felt that the distortion presented could not go unchallenged. After all, it wasn't spanking that was evil; it was spanking in anger that was wrong.

I was on sabbatical in my native New Zealand at the time. The next day I typed out a Christian response and addressed it to the biggest newspaper in the country—something I had never done before.

Two weeks later I had given up believing it would ever be printed. But one Saturday (the day the paper has the greatest circulation), there it was. The editor had made it distinct from other letters and assigned to it a four-column heading!

Several days later while alone with God, I felt a clear impression to do something I would never have thought up myself. I was to send that letter to other newspapers all over New Zealand. I knew that newspapers don't usually like to reprint what has already appeared in other papers. But if this was the Lord—well, then good would come of it.

To my amazement, of the sixteen largest papers I sent that letter to, fourteen of them published it, some under big headlines (like one which was six columns wide in the nation's capital).

Ross Tooley, a New Zealander, serves at large on the staff of the College of Christian Ministries of University of the Nations, Kona, Hawaii, USA.

Tuesday

All men will know that you are my disciples if you love one another.

Before I became a Christian, I wandered around on the "hippie trail" for several months. Then I met a couple who invited me to visit The Ark, a place of ministry in Amsterdam.

There I spoke with others about my life and their Christian commitment. Even as we discussed Christianity, I didn't feel threatened. These were people with an authentic, functional faith, and they were relaxing to be around. I found myself impressed by them. After about an hour, I followed my hosts into the dining room for dinner. As we entered, the rest of the people were sitting down at tables adorned with tablecloths, flowers, and candles. Their faces were not somber, but full of life and laughter.

Soon a large man (6-feet, 6-inches tall) with a long ponytail and beard greeted us. His name was Floyd McClung, and he was leader of the community. Still a little uneasy, I was taken by surprise when Floyd introduced me as their dinner guest. The community responded warmly. It was a welcome contrast to the impersonal ways of the hippie trail. After prayer, community members served a hearty meal family-style to each table. By the time dinner was over, I knew there was something real about these people.

After several weeks of mingling with these Christians, I made my first tentative steps toward following the Lord Jesus Christ, and soon became an active member of The Ark community.

Looking back over my own conversion, what attracted me to the person of Jesus Christ was not words or systematized Gospel presentations. Rather, it was the practical demonstration of genuine care and concern a small group of Christians showed toward me.

Andrew Jackson, an American, is pastor of world missions and evangelism at a large Evangelical Presbyterian Church in Virginia Beach, Virginia, USA.
From *A Heart for Others* by Andrew Jackson. Copyright © 1992 by Andrew Jackson. Published by YWAM Publishing, Seattle, Washington. Used by permission [from pages 117-118].

Wednesday

So shall they fear the name of the Lord from the west, and His glory from the rising of the sun; when the enemy comes in like a flood, the Spirit of the Lord will lift up a standard against him.   *Isaiah 59:19 NKJV*

So this was where the men were condemned to death! I had watched a movie of the Nazi war crimes trials many years before. Scenes flooded my mind. Horrible scenes. What atrocities mankind had committed upon other humans!

We had a few days free during a teaching trip to Europe, so we decided to visit some of the places in Nurnberg made famous by Adolph Hitler. Nothing about the building distinguished it as having historical importance. Our hosts, American missionaries stationed in Germany, had learned its location.

The man in the small office where we were directed led us down a hallway into a modest-sized room. To the left of the judge's bench were the seats where jurors had listened intently. Beside him, the witnesses had poured out their stories. In front was the table where the men on trial had sat.

As I grieved over what had happened, my sorrow gradually turned to joy. Our missionary friends told an unusual story, taken from a book, *The Sword and the Swastika.*

During the trials, an American military chaplain had been assigned to work with the accused men. He spent hours...weeks... months with them. He listened to them, and told them of God's love and forgiveness.

When the end of his tour of duty drew near, the accused men wrote to his wife, begging her to agree to an extension of his tour of duty. She and the children had longed for his return, but with agony of heart, she complied. The chaplain stayed on until the end of the trials and the execution of those condemned to die.

Of the ten put to death, eight had received forgiveness for the terrible things they had done. Our loving Father's forgiveness has no limits.

Beverly Caruso, an American, is a Bible teacher and author who leads YWAM Writer's Seminars. She lives in California, USA.

Thursday

Jesus replied, "What is impossible with men is possible with God."

Luke 18:27

God's word to us was simply, "Go," so we left our native New Zealand and arrived in the United States with our two children. Our step of faith had not been without incident. We had faced many hindrances. But the most troubling of them was affecting our nine-year-old daughter, Michelle.

The day before we left New Zealand, Michelle developed an ear infection. Over the next month, her hearing grew worse. A doctor said it would get better on its own.

A few weeks later, Michelle awoke in intense pain. A local pediatrician referred us to an ear specialist. One of Michelle's eardrums had ruptured. Substantial hearing loss had occurred because of fluid behind the eardrums. The specialist said it would not drain naturally. There seemed no way other than surgery.

But we were to face another hindrance. The cost of the operation was to be $2,500, a lot of money for any YWAMer. We were very anxious. We prayed for healing and for God's highest purposes in the situation.

The next day we noticed that Michelle's hearing seemed to have been restored. Could God really have healed her? Were we experiencing God's provision just as we had heard other YWAMers had? We immediately went back to the specialist.

Hearing tests confirmed that Michelle now had perfect hearing. The stunned, previously articulate doctor could only say, "It seems to have gone." Contrary to his previous statement, there *was* another way to correct the problem—nothing is impossible for God!

Many months have passed. Michelle has experienced no more infections or deafness. But more than that, long after this young girl becomes a woman, she will remember God's faithfulness to her when there was no other way.

Bruce Sparey, a New Zealander, serves as accounting manager for University of the Nations in Kailua-Kona, Hawaii, USA.

Friday

May your ways be known on earth, your salvation among all nations.

Psalm 67:2

"Who, me? A grandmother go to Russia?" That was my response when I first heard about the trip for Christian educators. The invitation had come from the Russian Education Ministry wanting us to share materials on morals and ethics with Russia's public school teachers. I wanted to be in on what God was doing there. After much prayer, I flew with a group to Yaroslavl.

I was amazed by the words of Nickoliovitch, the Deputy Head of the Regional Administration, "We are only too glad to turn our backs on the dogmas that have permeated our society."

The Minister of Education in Yaroslavl, Olga, said, "It is time to examine the monument of the Bible as we study our past and future. We welcome the blending of minds from an atheist background of 70 years to the examination of a way of life based on historical Christianity."

I didn't see any Russian smile during the first day of our visit. I was told they didn't understand why we had come such a long way to help them. We told them that the best guidelines for government, education, and the home are found in the Bible. We assured them that we wanted them to know from us personally the meaningful things of our lives. This meant personal sharing.

My 21-year-old translator is a good example of the changes we saw. At first she was frightened, but after a few days she absorbed love like a dry sponge.

On the last day she told me, "I've never known anyone who believed there is a God...not my mother or father...friends or relatives. I now believe He is real, and I want to know Him."

Frances Bradley, an American, is a freelance writer who lives in Austin, Texas, USA.

Saturday

*Every good and perfect gift is from above, coming down from the Father of
the heavenly lights, who does not change like shifting shadows.*

James 1:17

Early in 1985, a typhoon struck the lower islands of the Philippines. My wife, our two young daughters, and I went with a
team to help the injured and homeless.

We were accomplishing much in ministry areas, but I wasn't
taking much time for my family. One day, while communing with
the Lord, I felt impressed to take each of my daughters out for a
treat once each week.

We kept our pesos in a jar in the house, and when I reached
in the jar the first week, I only found 50 pesos (US$2.50). I
pocketed the money, and six-year-old Rita and I walked to a cafe
where I bought two ice cream cones for about 38 pesos. We sat
together, licked ice cream, and talked away the afternoon. When
we got back home, I dropped the change back into the jar.

I planned to take four-year-old Mary to split a candy bar the
next day—that's all the remaining 12 pesos would buy. But when
I reached into the jar, I again found 50 pesos! Mary and I walked
to the cafe and enjoyed ice cream together. Back home, I again
dropped the 12 pesos into the jar.

We stayed four weeks on the island helping the typhoon victims. Each week, I took my daughters out for a treat. I dropped
the change into the jar, and each time, there was more when I
took it out later. God cares about things like candy bars and ice
cream cones, too.

Randy Thomas, an American, directs Discipleship Training School at King's Mansion, Kona, Hawaii, USA.

Sunday

Meditation

Shout for joy to the Lord, all the
earth. Serve the Lord with gladness;
come before him with joyful songs.
Enter his gates with thanksgiving
and his courts with praise; give
thanks to him and praise his name.
For the Lord is good and his love
endures forever; his faithfulness
continues through all generations.

Psalm 100:1-2,4-5

Monday

I am making a way in the desert and streams in the wasteland.

Isaiah 43:19

It had been five years since God spoke the words to her heart. "Go to Yeravan and tell them I love them." "Teresa" knew that Yeravan was in Armenia, but didn't understand why God had told her that. Nevertheless, she determined to obey as soon as God showed her the way.

Teresa was now a member of a team going to Armenia. However, because of nationalistic demonstrations, the road to Yeravan was closed. All along the way, the team watched as tourists were turned back. Guards also refused to let the team enter. The girl remembered something she thought was significant.

"Please," Teresa begged the guards, "let us go through. I saw a documentary on television about Yeravan saying that its people are world-famous for their hospitality. Ever since then, it has been my life's ambition to meet those people. Please let us through."

The officer relented.

In the town, Teresa talked to an Armenian woman on the street. She felt God wanted her to tell the woman the circumstances of the team's visit there.

Wide-eyed, the woman asked, "Are you a believer?"

"Yes."

"So am I," said the woman.

She then took the entire team to visit her small, struggling fellowship of believers. They had despaired because of the upheaval in their country, wondering if God had forgotten them. They were emboldened after hearing of God's specific instructions to this special group to come to them. The congregation made a banner to carry in the nationalistic demonstration, boldly proclaiming: "People of Armenia, this is not the way. Turn back to God. He has not forgotten us. He sent people to tell us He loves us. This is our only hope."

Sandra Oestreich, an American, serves with Slavic Ministries.

Tuesday

By faith in the name of Jesus, this man whom you see and know was made strong. It is Jesus' name and the faith that comes through him that has given this complete healing.   Acts 3:16

Most people avoided this part of town. But this was where I spent most of my time, taking medicine, food, and when possible, clothing to the children living on the streets of Rio de Janeiro, Brazil.

I was ministering with a few friends when I heard my name being called. My friend Rose, a prostitute, came running toward us. Only thirty, she looked much older. She had spent most nights on the streets. Frightened, she pleaded with us to come and help. I started to pray silently as she led us up a dark alley. Water from the recent rain was still pouring off the tin-roofed huts on either side of us.

I didn't know what to expect as she opened the door to a small wooden hut. My heart pounded. The smell of dampness and human sweat filled the air. Dim light fell on a body of a young boy lying on a small bed.

Anderson's face was covered in blood. He was delirious with pain. An enemy had stuck a knife in his cheek and forehead, sliced half his ear off, and then stabbed him in the neck. Anderson refused to go to a hospital because of the police. First aid didn't help him much; he was losing blood.

Three of us gathered around Anderson and prayed as Rose looked on. Suddenly an incredible sense of the power of God filled the room. Rose started crying.

I was surprised when I saw Anderson a few days later. His deep wounds were nearly healed. There was only a scratch on his ear. He was telling everyone, "Jesus has healed me!" God had heard and answered our prayer.

Sarah de Carvalho, from England, works with street children in Brazil.

Wednesday

I have learned to be content whatever the circumstances.

Philippians 4:11

My circumstances were getting the best of me. My husband, Kip, and I were in Belize, Central America, on a YWAM outreach. While Kip shared in a Bible school, I did what I could to bring order to our living conditions.

Our three children were young and energetic, and it was almost a full-time job just taking care of them. I had to prepare all our meals from scratch, with no "convenience" foods. In the tropical climate, our many insect bites wouldn't heal, and ants were *always* in the food. I didn't need anyone to spur me to prayer!

I prayed and cried out to God to remove these uncomfortable situations. But things got worse! Two of our children got sick, a dog chewed up our few disposable diapers, and animals came into our kitchen and ate our food. But God performed a miracle.

No, the circumstances didn't change—I did. God showed me that my hope and trust had to be in Him. I couldn't just serve Him and be happy when everything was going right. I had to trust that He would give me grace in the midst of chaos.

Diana Gaines and her husband, Kip, both Americans, lead YWAM training programs in Tyler, Texas, USA.

Thursday

He told them, "The harvest is plentiful, but the workers are few. Ask the Lord of the harvest, therefore, to send out workers into his harvest field. Go! I am sending you out like lambs among wolves."   Luke 10:2-3

I remember an encounter I had with a member of a worldwide cult. During a door-to-door witnessing outreach in Seattle, my partner and I walked up to a house and were met at the door by a square, balding man in his thirties. To our surprise, there was none of the usual "sales resistance." He eagerly ushered us in, offered us a seat and settled back to talk.

My friend opened his Bible, but first the man fired a question. "What do you think about the Trinity?"

I shot a look at my partner. He gave me a little smile, for now we knew who we were dealing with. We asked him if he was in such-and-such a group, and he admitted proudly to being one of their local leaders.

We settled back and got into serious debate. It was a great debate, and after an hour or two, I noticed the man was wilting. He was out-gunned. Finally, all his geniality disappeared. Angrily, he stood and asked us to leave.

My friend and I walked down the street with our Bible, laughing and congratulating ourselves on how we had won out over the well-honed argument skills of this cult leader.

I remember that afternoon and drop my head in shame. I thought I had won, but I know I lost. That particular cult is known by its aggressive, arguing spirit. It is controlled by the spirit of religious controversy. Instead of meeting that spirit with the opposite one, humility, I had entered into it and embraced the same spirit. We had won the argument that day in Seattle, but had left behind a man who was humiliated and further alienated from the Gospel.

Loren Cunningham, an American, is founder and president of YWAM. He lives in Hawaii, USA.

From *Winning, God's Way* by Loren Cunningham with Janice Rogers. Copyright ©1988 by Loren Cunningham published by YWAM Publishing, Seattle, Washington. Used by permission [from pages 99-101].

Friday

Whatever you ask for in prayer, believe that you have received it, and it will be yours.   Mark 11:24

My wife, Marcia, and I arrived in Belo Horizonte, Brazil, to attend a YWAM Bible school in the latter part of 1988. Marcia was about six months pregnant, and like many pregnant women, often craved certain foods.

One night about 10:20, Marcia developed a craving for pepperoni pizza. I tried to be patient and understanding, but knew there was no way on earth we could get pizza at that time of night. We were an hour away from the city by bus, and had to be up the next morning for classes.

We had been taught that God can satisfy our desires, so we called out to Him. I encouraged Marcia that God could satisfy the craving, even though she couldn't have the pizza.

Ten minutes later, there was a knock on our door. Sueli de Souza, the base secretary, had three pieces of pizza for us! We started crying—God *did* satisfy Marcia's craving.

Written by Paulo Cesar Banthar.

Saturday

How can they believe in the one of whom they have not heard? And how can they hear without someone preaching to them? Romans 10:14

I worked with YWAM's mercy ship, m/v *Good Samaritan,* docked in Santo Domingo, Dominican Republic. One afternoon, my partner and I walked to town. We were stopped by a young shoeshine boy. I often let him shine my shoes, because it afforded me a captive audience for the Gospel.

While Gary and I were witnessing, we were interrupted by Miguel, who seemed eager to talk to us. Pleased with the progress of my conversation with the boy, I grew impatient with Miguel. I tried to ignore him. *"Si, si,"* I said to each of his questions.

Gary stopped me. "No, Robert. This guy is trying to sell you a woman, and you keep saying 'yes' to every word."

Angrily, I turned and told him we were Christians, and as such, we do not do such things. As I rebuked him, the gentle voice of the Holy Spirit stopped me. *Tell him why. Tell him he is breaking the Father's heart.*

My message of condemnation quickly turned to the message of the weeping Shepherd, heartbroken over the condition of His sheep. To my amazement, the pimp, with whom I was annoyed and had discounted, began crying softly. When I asked if he wanted to be forgiven by God, he quickly said, "Yes."

Right there, he prayed to receive Jesus Christ as his Savior!

Robert Fountain, an American, serves on YWAM staff in Florida, USA.

Sunday

Meditation

Though the fig tree does not bud and there are no grapes on the vines, though the olive crop fails and the fields produce no food, though there are no sheep in the pen and no cattle in the stalls, yet I will rejoice in the Lord, I will be joyful in God my Savior.

Habakkuk 3:17-18

Monday

See, I have placed before you an open door that no one can shut.

Revelation 3:8

I was one of fourteen YWAMers from seven nations traveling overland to Calcutta, India. We divided into two groups of seven. The first group would start the trip about a week before the other. I was in the second group.

Stephanie, a young woman from South Africa, was in the first group. We had been told that she would not be allowed into the Communist countries the team would travel through. In fact, officials in the American consulate told us that she would never be allowed into Afghanistan.

After much prayer, and despite the warnings, we felt God wanted Stephanie to remain in the group, and they started the journey. We prayed each day for Stephanie, and received a phone call from Bulgaria: Stephanie had been allowed in! We continued praying as we started traveling, though we heard nothing further for another three weeks.

During an intercession time one Friday evening, we felt God leading us to pray for the first team's entry to Afghanistan. This didn't seem to make sense, because the schedule said that the team should already be in the country by then. But we went ahead and prayed.

Two weeks later, when our two teams were reunited, we asked the others, "Where were you two Friday nights ago?"

"We had been delayed, so we had only gotten to Tehran, Iran," they responded. The morning after we had prayed for them, God impressed the team leader to take Stephanie to apply for her Afghan visa. She asked for a ten-day transit visa, but within ten minutes, they came back—with a one-month tourist visa.

Stephanie was given several visa extensions in Afghanistan, doing medical relief work with the Afghan people.

As told to Paul Hawkins by Stephanie Teubes Van der Westeizen, a South African who now works in Colombia.

Tuesday

The Spirit of the Sovereign Lord is on me...to comfort all who mourn.

Isaiah 61:1-2

Our team was visiting Shanghai University where we hoped to share Christ with students. Because many of the Chinese people are eager to practice speaking English, it was easy to engage in conversation with them. On the lawn we sang and did a drama for a spontaneous crowd of several hundred.

My friend Nuala and I talked with a young man named Hang. After telling us he had no religion, Hang mentioned that one of his best friends had recently become a Christian.

"I could see positive changes in my friend," said Hang. "Before this, he had no religion, no beliefs. Now he has joy and seems at peace. He's been inviting me to visit his church."

Hang watched our drama, but later told us that several people close to him had died recently and that he had trouble accepting life's suffering.

Nuala told him about Jesus' tears with Martha when her brother Lazarus died, and about her own husband's recent death. Hang listened as she explained about the comfort God gives to His own.

Hang asked many questions of members of our team. Before we left, he accepted a copy of the Gospel of Mark, saying, "Maybe I will become a Christian, too."

Sally Jarvis, an American, is involved in a worship and dance ministry at Church of the Hills in Austin, Texas, USA.

Wednesday

Feed my sheep.   *John 21:17*

Top chef Brad Hansen switched from preparing meals to preparing messages when God placed missions on his heart. The Australian turned his back on a well-paying career to join a volunteer group of young Christians who share their faith through open-air drama and music.

For four years, Hansen had studied to be a chef. After graduating from college, he worked at several top hotels and restaurants, and was cited in a national magazine article as one of the country's leading new young chefs. But in 1989, he decided to give it all up and become a missionary.

Brad Hansen has traveled thousands of miles to three continents. His work has taken him from a women's high security prison in the United States, where he prayed with an inmate who had murdered her husband, to Moscow's famous Arbat walking street, where he and his friends were filmed for Soviet television.

"I realized that I could have stayed in the industry and probably made quite a lot of money, but there was something inside me that was quite empty despite all the high living," Brad said.

Following a six-month Bible training school, Brad moved to Holland to join the YWAM staff. Now Brad works as a youth pastor to the young adult children of staff members in Amsterdam, a city famous for its liberal attitudes about sex and open drug use.

Brad says, "Young people face real pressures growing up in this kind of an environment. I want to help them realize that they can stand against the trends, and make a difference in the world by serving God." Today, Brad is fulfilled by feeding God's lambs the Bread of Life.

Andy Butcher, from Great Britain, directs the Press & Media Services Department of YWAM's International Operations Office, and lives in Colorado Springs, Colorado, USA.

Thursday

Whatever you do, work at it with all your heart, as working for the Lord, not for men.
Colossians 3:23

A pastor friend of mine once told me, "I believe one prospers as a result of what he does with the opportunities God gives him."

For the better part of three years, while I was in Seattle directing a ministry called Gleanings for the Needy, that's exactly what God had given me: plenty of opportunities. Those opportunities involved use of the mental and physical gifts that He had already given me.

The ministry's expenses were mostly for fuel and maintenance to keep our old van running six days a week on its daily assigned route. We collected two to three tons of food a week which would otherwise have been thrown away. The discarded food was still nutritious, but had passed its prime. We then delivered that food to groups which fed hungry people or redistributed it to needy people who could prepare it themselves. We had no regular financial donors, but the opportunities to apply entrepreneurial gifts were plentiful.

For thirty months, many volunteers from various churches were faithful to keep their appointed days to drive our old unheated van, even on days of freezing cold. At one point, the ministry had three vehicles and a bank account large enough to keep the ministry financed for several months. The ministry was finally turned over to a local church in the area and is still in operation today.

Opportunities are like miracles. They often appear, but if you are not looking for them, you'll miss them. To see an opportunity and to act upon it may determine your prosperity and success.

To keep our focus, we must remember that we are called to faithfulness, not success. Success must never become the barometer of our ministry, but let us also not discard God-given opportunities which are placed in our path.

Cleon Harper, an American, is the director of Love, Inc., a ministry of World Vision.

Friday

The King will reply, "I tell you the truth, whatever you did for one of the least of these brothers of mine, you did for me."   Matthew 25:40

I first noticed her when a friend and I came bounding down the gangway of the Mercy Ship m/v *Anastasis* for a late night walk. She shuffled on alone, clutching a battered, old shopping bag. I noticed the large hump on her shoulder, and, peering closer, could see the painful lines the years had carved into her face.

My heart went out to her. Sorrow and loneliness seemed etched into her creased face. Vacant eyes stared lifelessly at the ground. My heart prodded me to offer help, yet I ignored the nudge and continued on our walk. I looked back to see her gazing up the steep gangway to the light shining behind the closed doors.

Later, my friend and I spied the same hunched figure shuffling toward us. My heart sank, and I began to weep. Although she passed within a few feet of us, I still resisted the urge to reach out. Instead, my friend and I prayed.

The next morning, my friend handed me a note. She had just read this old Quaker saying in her devotional: "What am I to do? I expect to pass through this world but once. Any good work, therefore, any kindness, or any service I can render to any soul, be it man or animal, let me do it now. Let me not neglect or defer it, for I shall not pass this way again."

My friend continued, "As I read this last night, I thought of the old woman trudging home in the dark. I know that I'm forgiven for my slow compassion, but still...."

I often think of this old woman, too. And I know I missed out.

Nancy Grisham, an American, works as Assistant to the Vice-President of Operations at the Mercy Ships Home Office in Lindale, Texas, USA.

Saturday

In the same way, the Spirit helps us in our weakness. We do not know what we ought to pray, but the Spirit himself intercedes for us with groans that words cannot express.   Romans 8:26 NASB

We had been in France for nearly one year, trying to establish a YWAM ministry. The work was far more difficult than I could have imagined. As I lay in bed, somber thoughts as dark as the night surrounded me.

"Lord, why did I ever think I could get this ministry going? Where is my support? Where are all the people who said they would pray for me and this work? Lord, is there one person in this whole world who is interceding for me?"

I heard an inner voice in my spirit. *Yes, Daniel, Me.* Cares fell away; my shoulders raised along with my spirit and voice.

Daniel Schaerer, a Frenchman, leads YWAM's ministries in France.

Sunday

Meditation

Rejoice in the Lord always. I will say it again: Rejoice! Let your gentleness be evident to all. The Lord is near. Do not be anxious about anything, but in everything, by prayer and petition, with thanksgiving, present your requests to God. And the peace of God, which transcends all understanding, will guard your hearts and your minds in Christ Jesus.

Philippians 4:4-7

Monday

When I called, you answered me; you made me bold and stouthearted. Though I walk in the midst of trouble, you preserve my life; you stretch out your hand against the anger of my foes, with your right hand you save me.

Psalm 138:3,7

We had several times of intercession in preparation for an outreach to the city of San Francisco. During one particularly good prayer time, my thoughts were directed to the above Bible passage.

On the second day of the outreach, we split into groups of four. Each group went to a different neighborhood to intercede for it. My group went to the Tenderloin, known for prostitution, gangs, and drug abuse.

In Bodecker Park, we thought we would simply walk quickly through, praying blessings on the people there. About halfway through the park, a drunk man wound up like a baseball pitcher and threw a quart-size whiskey bottle at me. As I stared at the glass at my feet, he cursed me. Then he yelled, "I'm gonna kill ya, I'm gonna kill ya, I'm gonna kill ya!"

The hair on the back of my neck stood on end. It was as though a blanket of fear had been spread over me. Then I remembered the Scripture, "Though I walk in the midst of trouble...."

As I remembered God's Word, peace filled my heart. Backing away from the man, I shared the Scripture with our group. The Lord seemed to be saying, "Be bold."

On through the park we walked, in the direction of the man. As we approached him, his countenance changed. As we got closer, he sat down peacefully and didn't bother us any more.

God showed me that spending time before Him is necessary. Then I can expect Him to take care of me in every situation.

Paul Wood, an American, is on staff at YWAM-San Francisco, California, USA.

Tuesday

A man...called his servants and entrusted his property to them...each according to his ability.   Matthew 25:14-15

I sat on the porch swing watching yet another magnificent East Texas sunset. The sky seemed afire with reds, oranges, pinks, and purples. The puffy clouds reflected the colors, casting shadows onto themselves and causing new hues to merge with the others.

"God," I said, "I wish I could paint like You."

But I have created you to paint with words, came the words in my mind, quick and unbidden in the way I had come to recognize God's quiet voice.

I thought on this for a while. I thought of the YWAM School of Illustration in session just a few hundred yards from where I sat, and of the incredibly talented artists whose work we "oohed" and "aahed" over. How many of us, I wondered, secretly wished for their talents?

I thought of Richard, our chef, a man who had given up a successful career in the restaurant business to feed Jesus' "sheep" at our base. We were certainly blessed, and part of me wished I could cook like that man.

But God has created me to paint with words. I may not be Tom Clancy (my writing hero), but what is important is that I do the best with what God has given me. If I am a good steward of the talents He has given me, I will receive His reward when my work is done.

It would not matter if I was a painter, a plumber, a chef, or a mechanic. My responsibility is to be the painter, plumber, chef, mechanic, or writer that God has created me to be.

Nothing else matters.

Trevor May, an Australian, works in the art and editorial departments at Last Days Ministries in Lindale, Texas, USA.

Wednesday

He raises the poor from the dust and lifts the needy from the ash heap.

Psalm 113:7

I watched as a very thin, tired-looking mother quieted her baby while my husband preached to a small group of Mapuche Indians in southern Chile. It was her first time at one of our meetings. As my husband, Fernando, talked about our loving heavenly Father, I wondered how the woman would respond.

She put the baby to her breast. After a few seconds, he cried again. Her malnourished body just couldn't produce enough milk.

Later she told me more about her family. Her husband had been sick and out of work for several months. Their overwhelming poverty made my "God loves you" seem shallow, yet she accepted my suggestion of prayer for her husband.

Later Fernando visited the man at his hut. The man's chest heaved as his damaged lungs attempted to take in oxygen. "God can heal you right now," Fernando explained. "But first He wants to heal your soul." The family listened intently as he shared the Gospel. Together they prayed to invite Christ into their hearts. Then Fernando prayed for Juan's healing.

Our rejoicing over their salvation was dampened by their extreme poverty. We wondered if God's love would remain real to them in the midst of such misery.

The answer came quickly. The next day, Fernando saw someone walking briskly toward him, carrying a bag on his back. It was the man he had prayed for the day before. Juan joyfully explained that soon after Fernando left, he suddenly felt better, and was instantly healed. "Jesus is so powerful and so wonderful," he exclaimed. "Now I am walking to town to seek work to support my family. Next Sunday I will come to church to give testimony of how God healed me."

Juan found a permanent job and kept his promise to be in church. Little by little, with God's help, his family climbed out of the poverty that had swallowed them.

Carol Sue Ossandon, an American, is married to a Chilean, and they work in evangelism and church planting among the Mapuche Indians of Chile.

Thursday

We are labourers together with God.　　　　　*I Corinthians 3:9 KJV*

After our song and drama presentation at the Jeun Nam University in Korea, I asked a young man named Jeom Sik and a young woman named Hee Yun if they understood our message. "I want to know this God you talked about," Hee Yun replied.

This is too easy, I thought, *certainly she doesn't understand what I mean.*

I explained more fully the plan of salvation and the cost of discipleship, stressing that she would need to let Jesus become Lord over all areas of her life.

"I want to know God personally," she affirmed.

Just then a young Korean Christian joined our conversation. He translated as I led Hee Yun in prayer for forgiveness of sins.

I turned to Jeom Sik, who had silently stood by. "What are you going to do?" I asked him.

Using a writing pad and drawings he answered, "I believe in God, but I want to be in the middle." I used God's Word to show him that there is no middle ground where God is concerned. He grimaced outwardly as he thought it over. There seemed to be an inward struggle taking place.

Again, at just the right moment, another Korean Christian joined us. "I've been praying for Jeom Sik for a long time," he said. This seemed to deepen Jeom Sik's inward struggle.

But then he declared, "Okay, I'm going to do it!" This seemed to bring him release, and he confessed his sins and made a commitment to live his life for God.

Gail Maidment, an Australian, is director of the Small World Christian Kindergarten in Hong Kong.

Friday

Jesus Christ is the same yesterday and today and forever.   Hebrews 13:8

Often, things seem to be falling apart. During those times, it is easy to fail to look to Jesus. Consequently, we become depressed and discouraged. During such a time in my life, I read the above Scripture.

When I realized that Jesus has never changed, my heart was filled with encouragement. I saw the reality of Jesus' unchanging character. He is the same today as He was in the times of the New Testament. He will always be the same.

When I truly saw this, I thought of the words of Jesus, "I will be with you always, to the very end..." (Matthew 28:20). These words bring comfort again and again to our lives. We are not alone. He is with us.

John Kisamwa, from Kenya, is an evangelist, leader, and translator with YWAM in Kenya.

Saturday

Jesus, tired as he was from the journey, sat down by the well.   John 4:6

Hong Kong—where East meets West. Because of Hong Kong's location and political status, her people are more religiously diverse than perhaps any other Asian nation. And yet many residents have never heard of Jesus Christ. For years we were aware of the prayer and intercession of many Christians for this crowded island nation. We came to Hong Kong to share Jesus with as many people as we could, and we had asked God to lead us to those who were ready to listen.

One unusual opportunity came at a housing complex. The young people were uninterested in the beginning, so we asked them to join us for a game of basketball. They agreed.

After this act of friendship, they were eager to hear what we had to say about Jesus, and several opened their hearts to Him.

We were invited several times to return to play basketball with them. While some of us played, others stayed on the sidelines and talked with the spectators about Christ. There were a whole range of responses, from indifference to curiosity, from hardened rejection to open-hearted acceptance.

This type of friendship evangelism reminds me of the time when Jesus sat by Jacob's well in Samaria. In that natural setting He shared with a village woman the good news of eternal life. In the same way, we can share Jesus' love in a natural way with those around us.

Allana Hiha, a New Zealander, is the South Pacific Regional Coordinator for the University of the Nations College of Communications. She lives in Canberra, Australia.

Sunday

Meditation

Yet this I call to mind and therefore I have hope: Because of the Lord's great love we are not consumed, for his compassions never fail. They are new every morning; great is your faithfulness. I say to myself, "The Lord is my portion; therefore I will wait for him."

Lamentations 3:21-24

Monday

But whatever was to my profit I now consider loss for the sake of Christ. What is more, I consider everything a loss compared to the surpassing greatness of knowing Christ Jesus my Lord, for whose sake I have lost all things. Philippians 3:7-8

Jesus taught us to seek His kingdom first, and that includes submitting to Him the choice of who we marry. Christians must make the choice of a marriage partner while keeping their ministry and calling in mind. Otherwise, they could be robbing God of what is His due.

What if no suitable person is around? I heard of one young lady who trained at a missionary-sending base. "I'd like to get married," she said, "but I'm called to Pakistan. I'm going there even if I don't get married."

Later she went off to Pakistan to serve the Lord in obedience. Once there, she met the son of a missionary who had been raised in that country. They are happily married and serving God in Pakistan. Her story has a fairy-tale ending, but that cannot always be guaranteed.

I have to agree with the sentiments of a young lady who also said, "If the right man doesn't come along, I'd rather stay single than to marry the wrong guy." The last I heard, she was in Vietnam and still hadn't married.

God wants the very best for us, and we can trust in His wisdom—He knows just the right person to bring to us as a life partner.

Ross Tooley, a New Zealander, serves at large on the staff of the College of Christian Ministries of University of the Nations, Kona, Hawaii, USA.
Adapted from *We Cannot But Tell,* by Ross Tooley, revised edition. Copyright © 1993 by Ross Tooley. Published by YWAM Publishing, Seattle, Washington. Used by permission [from page 147].

Tuesday

Fear not, for I have redeemed you; I have called you by name; you are mine.
Isaiah 43:1

I was housesitting for friends and taking care of their dog, Frisky, when a severe thunderstorm hit. The thunder clapped and lightning flashed through the house. Frisky was so scared that she jumped into my lap. I held her close and talked to her soothingly until she stopped shaking and calmed down.

At that moment, it seemed as though God spoke a comforting message to my heart: *Just like you're holding Frisky to comfort her, I hold you close to comfort you.*

This made me feel good, secure, and cared for. Then I sensed that God had more to say. *But at least Frisky is afraid of a real storm— real thunder, real lightning.*

As if to emphasize the point, lightning struck right outside the house. I felt that God was showing me that I sometimes get just as scared with imaginary storms—the "what if's" and the uncertain future. God has promised to help me in real dangers—real water, real fire, real troubles. He could comfort and protect me, but I needed to learn to trust Him with imaginary storms.

Although Frisky wasn't even my dog, I was trying the best I could to ease her discomfort. I felt God whisper, *Do you think I would do less for you? It is you whom I love and have redeemed. Rest in My arms and do not fear for I am with you now and forever.*

Since that night, whenever I find myself beginning to travel into "what if" territory, I ask God to help me determine whether there is a *real* problem, then ask Him how to deal with it.

Ralene Jennings, an American, works in the accounting department in Tyler, Texas, USA.

Wednesday

Lead me in Thy truth and teach me, for Thou art the God of my salvation; for Thee I wait all the day.   Psalm 25:5 NASB

It was Saturday morning, and I decided to take a walk through the woods. The sky was full of gray clouds, but the sun was gleaming through in some places.

Waiting—it can be very long and difficult sometimes, I mused. We all wait for something: a letter, a visitor, the end of a difficult situation, an answer to prayer.

What am I waiting for? I thought. It had been two months since I had seen my parents, and I still had no word from them. *Why haven't I heard from them? Do they still love me?*

Every morning at 10:30, each student rushed to the letter box looking forward to hearing from relatives, friends, and those who love them. I always left disappointed, having found nothing for me. How many times did I come to my box focusing all my expectations on a letter from my parents? I did not know. I did not count.

I walked on, listening to the sound of my footsteps on the narrow country road. The walk offered me rest and refreshment.

Suddenly, big drops of rain mixed with snow began to fall. I pulled my hood over my head and walked swiftly toward the village. Still thinking about my parents, I prayed for them. Portions of Scripture came to mind: "Wait for the Lord, be strong," "My soul waits for the Lord," and, "In His Word I put my hope."

Then God planted a question in my heart. *Is not your purpose for coming here to wait only for Me?*

Anna Bombova, from Czechoslovakia, translates Christian literature.

Thursday

And whoever welcomes a little child like this in my name welcomes me.

Matthew 18:5

I was part of an outreach team in the Philippines working at Smokey Mountain, Manila's city dump. Thousands of poor people make their living and their home there. Like the other team members, I had children holding my hands and my clothing while we sang, played games, and laughed together.

A nurse pointed out a six-year-old boy standing by himself, holding a dirty dinner roll. "He needs a miracle," she said. She explained that while he and his mother were riding a public bus, his mother jumped off, leaving the boy to fend for himself. Abandoned, he aimlessly walked the streets, hungry and homeless. He became thin and ill.

A young mother living at the dump found the boy and brought him back to care for him. His stomach hurt too much to eat. It seemed he had decided that the pain of death was less than the pain of life.

The little boy didn't look up as I approached and sat beside him. I asked his name; he gave no response. A little boy ran up and called out, "His name is Randy." With excitement, I told him that we shared the same name. Still no response. It was as though he had not heard me.

Not knowing what else to say, I stood and reached down to pick him up. His response took me by surprise. Still holding the dirty dinner roll, Randy quickly wrapped his feeble arms tightly around my neck.

I cried as I held this child who was so close to death. For the first time, I felt Jesus' heart for another person. I prayed for Randy, then called the rest of the team over to pray with me. I held him in my arms for the remainder of our time there.

As we left the dump, I looked back. Randy was eating the dirty dinner roll. He has continued to eat since, and is gaining weight and health.

Randy Thomas, an American, is Discipleship Training School Director of King's Mansion, Kailua-Kona, Hawaii, USA.

Friday

"Because your heart was tender and you humbled yourself before the Lord...I truly have heard you," declares the Lord.   II Kings 22:19 NASB

I wanted to be a good soldier for Christ. But my concept of warfare came from history, comic books, and movies. I thought a soldier was a tough, hardened man who kept his emotions in check.

I worked with YWAM in El Salvador, doing evangelism and ministering to the refugees. Everywhere we went, I saw hurting people—children with burns, people with missing limbs, babies dehydrated and dying from diarrhea.

My co-workers comforted the wounded and embraced the dying, but I couldn't. I saw the hurts and couldn't cope, so I withdrew. I wanted to cry, but was afraid that I'd never stop. So I got angry at the injustice man's sin caused, and hardened my heart against the pain.

Over the years, my heart grew harder. I knew it wasn't right, but I seemed helpless to change. I wanted the tender heart I once had.

Then one Easter, I understood. I saw the hands of God—and they were wounded. I looked in His side and saw where His heart was pierced. Jesus sweat blood in His agony over the sins of the world, while I ran and hid. Soldiers of God have tender hearts.

Jim Shaw, an American, is the editor of YWAM's *Personal Prayer Diary*, and is an editor with YWAM Publishing in Lindale, Texas, USA.

Saturday

I have set before you life and death, blessings and curses. Now choose life, so that you and your children may live and that you may love the Lord your God, listen to his voice, and hold fast to him. For the Lord is your life....

Deuteronomy 30:19-20

There she stood, all 45 pounds dug in for the siege. Once again we squared off. What my six-year-old daughter wanted wasn't best for her, but with set jaw and taut muscles, she wanted it anyway.

"Lord, why is it so hard for her to be obedient? What do I say to get through?"

As my daughter and I faced each other in silence, she waited to see what I would do and I waited to know what to do.

Finally I asked, "Honey, do you know who is the only one who can make you mind me?"

She thought a moment. "You?"

"No, I can't make you mind." Her muscles started to loosen as she thought about my question.

"God?" she asked.

"No," I replied, "He won't make you mind."

Thoroughly caught up with solving this riddle, my daughter suddenly looked up with the light of discovery in her eyes.

"Me?"

"Yes, you. You're the only one who can make you mind."

Slowly a huge smile lit up her face, revealing two dimples. With a deep breath, she relaxed her stiff little shoulders and started swinging her arms back and forth. She would obey. The standoff had ended—by her choice.

As she skipped down the hall to her room, I stood amazed at the transformation. One right decision and she was free.

And so it is with us and our heavenly Father. By giving us the ability to choose, God gives us the power to create turning points in our lives.

Martha Hedge, an American, serves as secretary to the pastor of Tyler Christian Fellowship in Tyler, Texas, USA.

Sunday

Meditation

Do not let your hearts be troubled. Trust in God; trust also in me. In my Father's house are many rooms; if it were not so, I would have told you. I am going there to prepare a place for you. And if I go and prepare a place for you, I will come back and take you to be with me that you also may be where I am.

John 14:1-3

Monday

Go home to your family and tell them how much the Lord has done for you, and how he has had mercy on you.   *Mark 5:19*

When we answered God's call to enter missions full-time, we were still relying on our own efforts for our finances. When we reached Korea on our first outreach, God worked a change in us.

We planned to go from Korea directly to Tokyo to work in YWAM's coffee house, saving hundreds of dollars in airfare. So when my husband, Stew, said he thought God wanted us to go home to the States before going to Tokyo, I was puzzled. I said, "If this is true, I need God to confirm it to me so I can believe Him for the finances."

Late one evening, I picked up my Bible and read it. The words from Mark 5:19 seemed to bounce off the page.

We had been taught that God sometimes speaks this way, but it was a first-time experience for me. Since the Lord had healed my broken spirit and had become my deliverer, I knew these words were appropriate for me. I prayed that if this was His will, He would provide the necessary finances. I turned to Stew and told him what God had shown to me.

We returned to the campus in Hawaii and got our mail; it included $357 in checks. The next day, we bought two one-way tickets to Seattle, Washington.

I nearly fell off my chair when the travel agent told us the cost—$357. God has continued to supply all our needs: spiritual, physical, and financial.

Millie Lieberman, an American, serves on staff with YWAM in Kona, Hawaii, USA.

Tuesday

Charm is deceptive, and beauty is fleeting; but a woman who fears the Lord is to be praised.   *Proverbs 31:30*

When I was 15 years old, I was very embarrassed by my grandmother's ankle-length skirts, which had long since gone out of style. Her clothes were black, and she seemed unaware that her thick, cotton stockings wrinkled around her ankles.

I was already uncomfortable about Grandma's disregard for matters of appearance when she came to visit us in our small western Canadian town. But then she did something I'll never forget. Every spring, our high school organized a track and field day. Other schools from around the countryside came to compete. The only place large enough to serve lunch to this crowd was the basement of our church. I was there with my school friends.

Lunch was about to begin when my grandmother got everyone's attention, and ordered them to bow their heads for prayer.

Grandma climbed onto one of the big tables in her long, black skirt and wrinkled stockings, and held up her hands just like I always imagined Moses did. She said a long prayer, thanking God for everything she could think of. If I was uncomfortable before, this made me want to disappear through the floor!

Now, forty-five years later, I praise God for such a woman; for someone whose first thought was of pleasing God. She was willing to do whatever He told her to do. We need more people to stand up for what they believe, even if it means standing on top of a table.

My clothes probably seem out of style to today's young people. My stockings are slipping around my ankles—at least symbolically. But I want to have the courage to stand up for my beliefs in ways that matter.

Carol Fosdick, a United States citizen born in Canada, teaches in the School of Biblical Studies in Lakeside, Montana, USA.

Wednesday

But I, when I am lifted up from the earth, will draw all men to myself.
John 12:32

As we approached the coastline of the island of Roatan in Honduras, I called out over the rail of the ship, "Roatan, receive your King!" Our team of 54 young people aboard the mercy ship m/v *Anastasis* was eager to bring the Gospel to this island.

As our crew unloaded the mercy goods, a local missionary led the way down the muddy, unpaved road through broken-down shacks of tin and cardboard. Listless eyes stared at us. But smiles broke out when we told the people of our special message and the goods we had for them.

The only open place for our performance was a patch of muddy ground outside a bar, with rotting garbage and broken bottles littering the ground. The nauseating stench turned my stomach. Mangy dogs foraged for rotting tidbits as we set up our puppet theater, drama props, and portable sound system.

A curious crowd gathered when we started singing and giving testimonies. The children loved our puppet show and drama. Adults showed little response. Our choreography called for us to kneel. How could we kneel in that garbage? We made a last-minute change and had everyone remain standing during the dance.

At first, we carefully picked our way across our unusual stage, but soon our hearts were more set on lifting up Jesus than watching where we stepped. Halfway through, I looked out on the sea of beautiful, black faces. Tears were streaming down many cheeks.

When the people were invited to repent of sin and receive Christ, the derelict of the village came forward and fell to his knees, weeping. Others joined him one by one, and knelt in the garbage.

Roatan had received the King!

Fay Williams, a New Zealander, serves on staff in Hawaii, USA.

Thursday

Ask of me, and I will make the nations your inheritance, the ends of the earth
your possession.   Psalm 2:8

At a School of Missions in Oregon, I was challenged to work with preschoolers who had no opportunity for an education. Then for six months, I worked with such children in Guatemala while learning Spanish and getting practical training. Upon returning to Oregon, I continued to hear the still small voice of God saying, *Mary, what about the children?*

"Yes, Lord, I'm willing to go, and You promised to supply my needs, so I'm waiting." A friend told me she would pray for my desire. Later, she showed me an advertisement asking for one hundred people to teach English as a second language, and another person to set up a preschool in Uzbekistan, a former republic in Soviet Central Asia.

Imagine my disappointment when I broke my left foot in three places! *Lord, I know I heard You clearly, but how am I going to go without money...**and** with a broken foot?*

A month later, I received a fax inviting me to set up a preschool in Uzbekistan. Joy filled my soul! The Lord blessed me with gifts of money, but only enough to pay for my medical bills. Some Christian friends wanted to be a part in my ministry, so they took me shopping for new clothes and a suitcase. Then they paid part of my airfare. I wept tears of joy. Through the mail, I received a letter from my church, promising to pay the rest of my expenses.

God was faithful to meet every need I had in order to follow His call on my life.

Written by Mary Agostini.

Friday

Greater love has no one than this, that one lay down his life for his friends.
John 15:13

Dr. C. Everett Koop, former U.S. Surgeon General, has distinguished himself as a godly man and a servant of people. In three decades of service at Philadelphia's Children's Hospital, Dr. Koop treated more than 100,000 pediatric patients, many of them small enough to hold in one hand. Koop pioneered many techniques for saving malformed and premature babies. He treated countless numbers of deformed infants that other physicians wouldn't touch. One of his patients, who needed 37 facial and abdominal surgeries to correct birth defects, is now a university graduate. Another patient, for whom Dr. Koop fashioned a new esophagus out of a section of colon, went on to become a pediatric surgeon.

As Surgeon General, Dr. Koop became America's family doctor. Though his career was surrounded by controversy, Dr. Koop came to be respected as a man of great integrity. To a jaded general public hungry for integrity in their leaders, Koop became a genuine folk hero. Though Koop was often the bearer of bad news about cancer and AIDS, the public trusted him because they knew he was concerned for their health.

Sacrificial service, as exemplified by Dr. Koop, comes against the pleasure-oriented, self-indulgent spirit of the age permeating our society. I talk to pastors all over the nation who cannot motivate their people to sacrificial service. Many Christians insist, "My time, my money, and my energy are mine to use as I please. What right does my pastor have to tell me what to do?" They are caught up in the spirit of the age. They have adopted the world's attitude. Holiness in a fallen world doesn't mean that we retreat to the desert of selfishness. It means that we go into the world to bring the gospel of peace to those who so desperately need it.

Floyd McClung, an American, directs Leadership Development Programs for YWAM. He lives in California, USA.
From *Holiness and the Spirit of the Age* by Floyd McClung. Copyright © 1990 Harvest House Publishers, Eugene, Oregon. By permission [from page 171-172].

Saturday

Your path led through the sea, your way through the mighty waters, though your footprints were not seen.
                                                          Psalm 77:19

Winter that year touched more than the landscape around me. Before the last leaves had fallen, I felt its icy fingers drive deep into my heart. I'd experienced spiritual "winters" before, but never one like this.

Only months earlier, my time in Discipleship Training School had been so full of life and change. After much prayer, I'd decided to stay and work with the ministry center. Slowly, however, winter snows had fallen over my excitement, and my energy dropped to survival level. Spiritual warfare ground me down even further.

God was a patient teacher during those dark months, and my intimacy with Him deepened. I realized that the new lessons and perspectives had been worth the difficulty, and sensed that my long winter might be ending soon.

As February turned into March, announcements about an upcoming prophetic conference punctuated ministry gatherings. Would God speak to me there? My hopes were high, so it stung when I had to work during almost every session and was somehow overlooked by others when I sought out prayer.

During a quiet time after the conference, I sensed God asking me to pray out Psalm 86:17, "Give me a sign of your goodness, that my enemies may see it and be put to shame, for you, O Lord, have helped me and comforted me."

Four hours later, I met a girl who'd stopped by the ministry for a break during a trip of several thousand miles. "I feel like I'm supposed to pray for you," she said. Intrigued, I eagerly complied.

The ice began to melt as her words spilled out, many of them echoing promises God had given me earlier or prayers I'd cried out to Him—one just that morning.

Though spring hadn't arrived, I knew it couldn't be far away.

Marguerite Watson, an American, works in the editorial department of Last Days Ministries in Lindale, Texas, USA.

Sunday

Meditation

The heavens declare the glory of God; the skies proclaim the work of his hands. Day after day they pour forth speech; night after night they display knowledge. There is no speech or language where their voice is not heard. Their voice goes out into all the earth, their words to the ends of the world.

Psalm 19:1-4

Monday

He will cover you with his feathers, and under his wings you will find refuge; his faithfulness will be your shield and rampart. Psalm 91:4

I fought back tears when I learned that my friend Metrey's house had been the target of a grenade explosion the night before. Metrey's small bamboo house would be devastated!

I met Metrey upon my arrival at Site II, a Khmer refugee camp on the Thai-Cambodian border. This beautiful Christian woman was a medic in my clinic and often helped me translate and direct the weekly Bible study. I considered her my closest Khmer friend.

Now I cried out to God, *Please, God, not Metrey or her family. They've been through so much!* I tried to calm down enough to listen to my director's explanation.

"The injured were taken to Kao-I-Dang camp for surgery. Metrey and her husband are fine." I was relieved, but I had to see for myself, so I hurried to her house.

When I saw my friend standing in her doorway, tears filled my eyes. She was unhurt! She took me through the house to see the one small room which had been damaged. I saw the bloodstained bed and the shrapnel holes in the walls. In that household of five adults and two children, only one man had been hurt.

Outside, we found shrapnel in several directions, indicating a blast which could have injured the entire family. As tears formed in her eyes, Metrey said, "God put His hands over us."

Miriam Sjodin, a Canadian, served as a nurse on a medical team on the Thai-Cambodian border.

Tuesday

The living, the living—they praise you, as I am doing today; fathers tell their children about your faithfulness.   Isaiah 38:19

It is a joy for parents to share God's faithfulness with their children. Yet it's an even greater blessing when our children are able to tell their parents of God's faithfulness to them!

Three of us needed $1,500 each to get from our home in Sydney, Australia, to join Youth With A Mission's m/v *Anastasis* in Italy. The ship was being refitted to be used for mercy, evangelism, and training. I felt God wanted me to believe for double that amount so we could go by way of the United States to see our son Peter. I felt the above verse was God's promise to us.

Little did we realize that God had impressed our son in Los Angeles that He was going to do this very special thing. He even mentioned it in a lecture to the Discipleship Training School students he was leading.

The last week before our airfare was due, we were visiting the YWAM base in Goulburn, Australia. The leaders insisted we be included in an offering being taken for those with needs. One of the students heard that we had a need and said that she wanted to give us $1,500. However, the next morning the leaders told me they believed she was not mature enough to give such a large amount.

Was I disappointed! Yet I praised God for leaders who cared enough to protect students in such situations. On the third day, a student told me he had felt God tell him to give during the offering, but thought God was merely testing his willingness. He gave us the $1,500.

The Lord encouraged me to trust Him further. I bought three one-way tickets to Los Angeles. After we arrived, God faithfully provided the balance of what we needed.

Rix Warren, an Australian, works with Hispanics in the United States.

Wednesday

Even though I walk through the valley of the shadow of death, I will fear no evil, for you are with me.   Psalm 23:4

It was my first trip into what seemed like hell on earth. The foul stench of rotting garbage and human waste was inescapable.

This landscape of death was home to some 10,000 men, women, and children living a squalid existence in Manila's garbage dump—the place where our team worked.

We stood outside the shack of a grieving family that had no means to pay for a burial. I wondered how our regular team could face these conditions day after day.

A small, naked boy stood smiling at me. He thrust his filthy hand toward me in friendship. I dodged the threat of his approaching hand and looked away in shame.

My mind searched frantically for solace from my screaming conscience, but found none. Cold steel penetrated my heart. *What would Jesus do?* I wondered. But I knew.

I forced my eyes back to the little boy, and stretched out a tentative hand. He took it much as a hungry dog would snatch a scrap of meat. As I lay my other hand on his dirty, scabbed head, I prayed a short prayer of blessing. God filled my heart with love and compassion.

Then it hit me. This little boy cared more about love than about his surroundings. As I grasped this truth, I understood the key to my co-workers' ability to cope day after day. They walked with the Father and He provided all the grace they needed.

Rick Thompson, an American, is a writer and lecturer and serves as assistant to the Dean of the College of Humanities and International Studies at the University of the Nations in Kona, Hawaii, USA.

Thursday

Is not this the kind of fasting I have chosen:...Is it not to share your food with the hungry and to provide the poor wanderer with shelter—when you see the naked, to clothe him, and not to turn away from your own flesh and blood?

Isaiah 58:6-7

My friend and I were part of a group of 5,000 YWAMers witnessing in the streets of Los Angeles during the 1984 Olympic Games. We were excited about sharing our faith.

As we walked down the street, I saw some money on the sidewalk, and bent to pick it up. Just then, I noticed a young man who had also noticed the money and was headed toward it. As I unfolded the money, the three of us froze—it was a one-hundred dollar bill!

The young man fumed, "I could have used that money! I'm out of work and living in my car. I'm on my way to give blood so I'll have the money to eat!" I glanced at my friend, and could tell he was thinking the same thing I was.

"Can we buy you something to eat? We'd really like to help you out."

During the meal, this young man poured his heart out to us. It seemed he was grateful to find someone who cared enough to listen.

"I came to L.A. to make a new start after my marriage and my job went sour. Now I have nothing. What's there to live for?"

We shared with him how Christ had made the difference in our lives, and tears streamed down his face. He was eager to respond, and openly prayed to make Jesus the Lord of his life.

After prayer, he asked if he could join us in our witnessing. So the rest of the day, he shared his new faith with others on the street. That evening, we took him shopping, using the hundred-dollar bill to buy him some new clothes.

The money was quickly gone, but our new friend found a treasure that will last for eternity—friendship with God.

Ron Boehme, an American, is director of YWAM's Revive America Project, and lives in Washington State, USA.

Friday

How good and pleasant it is when brothers live together in unity!

Psalm 133:1

Conflict does not make a marriage good or bad—it is how we deal with it that is important. If not dealt with properly, it can destroy even the best of marriages. Learning how to disagree is a vital part of communication.

Ephesians 4:26-27 tells us, "Do not let the sun go down while you are still angry, and do not give the devil a foothold." We need to be careful that we do not store up our disagreements.

When we were newly married, because of my idea of a "perfect" marriage, I would not express any disagreements to Floyd. Instead I bottled them up inside and carried them around with me.

After we had been married about six months, that internal bottle was so full that it exploded at 2:00 a.m. We talked through the night until we had worked out what had happened and resolved our areas of conflict. It would have been much easier for both of us if we had dealt with the problems as they arose, "before the sun went down."

Sally McClung, an American, has a ministry of hospitality and speaks internationally. She lives in California, USA.

From *Where Will I Find the Time?* by Sally McClung. Copyright © 1989 by Sally McClung. Published by Harvest House Publishers, Eugene, Oregon. Used by permission [from pages 46-47].

Saturday

He will command his angels concerning you to guard you in all your ways.
Psalm 91:11

It was a clear desert night. We gazed out the restaurant window at the endless stream of lights. Holiday weekend traffic thundered by on a California freeway.

"Where's Matthew?" my wife, Julie, asked our son Paul.

"He went to the bathroom with David," Paul said.

A few minutes later, my oldest son, David, returned, but Matthew, two years old, was missing. We searched the restaurant. We searched the parking lot. After searching a nearby shopping center, we became desperate. Our greatest fear was that Matthew would stumble onto the freeway or the busy streets, all unfenced, on three sides of the restaurant.

I was searching the steep slope on the edge of the freeway when I found him. He was sitting in the dark, just a few feet from the speeding line of cars and trucks. "Hi, Matthew," I said, trying not to reveal the panic in my voice.

"Hi, Dad," he said. "The man tied my feet up, so I sat down."

"What man?" I asked.

"The nice man," said Matthew. "See, my feet are all tied up." I could see nothing on his little feet, but he acted as though he could not move them. And indeed, he could not move them until I reached down and caught him into my arms.

"Thank God for His angels!" I shouted into the night.

John Dawson, a New Zealander, is YWAM's International Director of Urban Missions.
From *Taking Our Cities for God* by John Dawson. Copyright © 1989 by John Dawson. Published by Creation House, Lake Mary, Florida. Used by permission [from pages 145-146].

Sunday

Meditation

The Lord does not let the righteous go hungry but he thwarts the craving of the wicked. He who heeds discipline shows the way to life, but whoever ignores correction leads others astray.

Proverbs 10:3,17

Monday

A father to the fatherless, a defender of widows, is God in his holy dwelling. God sets the lonely in families....　　　　　　　　　　　　　*Psalm 68:5-6*

We had given our five children and both sets of parents over to the Lord's keeping when we set out to become missionaries in the Philippines. We had no idea how God would use that relinquishment of our right to be near our families.

One Sunday, the pastor asked the congregation to turn to and pray for one another. I held out my hand to the young Filipina seated next to me and drew her close. I prayed fervently for God to meet her needs.

When I finished, she gazed up at me from her barely-five-foot stature and exclaimed, "I sense a mother's love in you!"

From that beginning, a lasting relationship grew that transcends all barriers. A loving Father brought us together.

Orphaned at eight months, Jo-Jo was reared by an older sister, referred to as *Aute* in the Philippine culture.

During our five-month tenure in this southernmost island of the Philippines, Jo-Jo expressed her love for me in various ways. At times, she nearly overwhelmed me with her adoration. One day, she knelt beside my chair and proclaimed, "You are my very own Mommy!" After that, we privately referred to her as "Mommy's girl."

Often I think of the Scripture verses in Mark 10:29,30 which speak of believers receiving up to one hundred times more than the children and family given up to follow Jesus. God has given back to us a hundredfold in this one young woman, whose needs have been met through a mother's love.

Our God is faithful to His Word. Letters between Jo-Jo and me continue to reach across the sea to encourage one another.

Betty Faux, an American, served on staff with YWAM Hawaii, and now lives in Florida, USA.

Tuesday

Ah, Sovereign Lord, you have made the heavens and the earth by your great power and outstretched arm. Nothing is too hard for you.

Jeremiah 32:17

When I am speaking to a group and challenge them from this Bible verse in Jeremiah 32, the response is revealing. It usually goes like this: I will say, "Is there anything too hard for God?"

People from the audience respond with a hearty chorus—"No!"

Then, I ask a second question. "Is there anything too hard for God to do...through you?"

Silence. A few grin, ducking their heads.

That is the way it is for all of us, isn't it? As long as we keep the principles of God's Word at a nice, comfortable, theoretical distance, we can believe it all. It's only when it comes to putting it into practice that we become disbelieving. Somehow, God gets smaller when we get involved.

God is a great God, and He wants to be great through you.

Loren Cunningham, an American, is founder and president of YWAM. He lives in Hawaii, USA.

From *Winning, God's Way* by Loren Cunningham with Janice Rogers. Copyright © 1988 by Loren Cunningham. Published by YWAM Publishing, Seattle, Washington. Used by permission [from page 113].

Wednesday

I will give you a new heart and put a new spirit in you; I will remove from you your heart of stone and give you a heart of flesh.   *Ezekiel 36:26*

I didn't know I had a heart of stone until my counselor showed me the chipped-off pieces: impatience, anger, and jealousy because my plans for my life weren't working. I saw that when my demands of God and others went unsatisfied, I submerged my feelings in the deep freeze of depression, and my heart became stone cold. And its chips became chunks too heavy to bear.

"Wounded hearts"—that's what they call those of us who have been sexually abused as children. My counselor took me back through my pain of betrayal and abandonment, through my helplessness as a victim, and through my rage for revenge. And while my reopened wounds were bleeding, I saw that I had new choices before me: forgiveness instead of bitterness, repentance instead of penance, and Christ's responses instead of my responses.

As I moved toward forgiving those who had wounded me, and left behind my sinful responses to those wounds, God gave me a heart of flesh. My heart of flesh is still wounded (the final healing will come in heaven), but it is alive and warm. My new heart knows the longings of a daughter for her father and the desires of the beloved for her Lover.

My new spirit sees that God has always loved me. That's why He sent His Son, Jesus, to take care of my wounds. The betrayal and the helplessness were taken care of at the Cross. He has given me a new heart for Him.

Teresa Link, an American, is a homemaker, college English teacher, and freelance writer who lives in Morenci, Arizona, USA.

Thursday

Now get up and stand on your feet. I have appeared to you to appoint you as a servant and as a witness of what you have seen of me and what I will show you.   Acts 26:16

It is easy to become so involved in our daily activities that we forget our purpose is to know God. Yet, it is in life's everyday situations that Jesus reveals Himself to us. The circumstances we find ourselves in are not coincidences. Rather, they are opportunities for understanding God's character and His ways.

Circumstances also expose our needs. He comes to that place of need and reveals Himself to us.

- In sorrow, He comes as our Comforter.
- In our weakness, He is our Strength.
- In temptation, He is our Savior.
- In loneliness, He is our Friend.
- In ignorance, He is our Teacher.

There have been times when I have been so concerned about a release of funds or the solution to a problem that I have missed the revelation of God's character He was wanting to show me. The solution is in Him. "His divine power has given us everything we need for life and godliness through our knowledge of him..." (II Peter 1:3).

Cheryl Knepper, an American, is pioneering children's ministries in Kenya.

Friday

Do not be overcome by evil, but overcome evil with good.   Romans 12:21

Until 1990, Albania was the world's only official atheistic country. I had ministered next door, in Yugoslavia, where over a million ethnic Albanians live. But Americans were forbidden even to travel to Albania.

I read about blood feuds and vengeance patterns common among Albanians and wondered, *How can God change values and mentalities so deeply embedded in any culture? How can He ever teach an entire nation to forgive?*

On November 9, 1989, the Berlin Wall fell and communism tumbled. A YWAM team and seven other mission groups planned an evangelistic campaign in Albania's capital. We held Bible studies and discussions in a city park each morning. In the evenings, we sang and preached in a stadium.

One who showed interest was Anastas, a man in his thirties. He told us that his sister, the gem of his family, had died at the hands of a man in East Germany.

For years, Anastas was tormented, not only by his grief, but also by the impotence he felt because he couldn't travel to East Germany to avenge her death. He needed to understand God's view toward responsibility.

I explained that the Bible tells us to respond to injustice with love and forgiveness; that vengeance is to be left to God. Despite his culture's belief that it was his responsibility to avenge his sister's death, Anastas tearfully accepted the spiritual truths about God's forgiveness.

Through Anastas' life, I saw that God knows exactly how to go about changing an entire nation— one person at a time.

Sandy Oestreich, an American, works with Slavic Ministries.

Saturday

Blessed is the man who finds wisdom, the man who gains understanding, for she [wisdom] is more profitable than silver and yields better returns than gold.
                                                                    Proverbs 3:13-14

Not every crisis is a crisis. We must continually ask God for wisdom to discern which people and situations need our attention, and which don't. The important thing is to be open and free in our spirits to adjustments along the way as the Lord directs. A crisis may hold blessing for us, as well. Someone explained that the Chinese character for the word *crisis* is made up of two parts: One is the symbol for danger, the other is the symbol for opportunity. An unexpected crisis can be an opportunity for growth. God wants us to be flexible and open.

Change is a way of life—always has been and always will be. "Blessed is the man who has discovered there is nothing permanent in life but change." We should not become so stuck into a rut of time management that we miss the unexpected that God brings or that we miss being open to change.

One particular way in which God brings the unexpected into our lives is in the form of people. People are more important than things. There is the schedule, there is the job that God has given us to do, but people should always come above these tasks.

There are times when I have a list of priorities that God has given me for the day, and someone comes along unexpectedly. My temptation might be to say, "What a bother!" Often God has said to me, "Wait a minute. That person is more important than all those papers on your desk. In fact, I have brought this person here for a special purpose."

At that point, I realize I must lay aside my schedule, my papers, and my plans, and give my attention to this person. We must remain flexible within a framework of planning.

Sally McClung, an American, has a ministry of hospitality and speaks internationally. She lives in California, USA.
From *Where Will I Find the Time?* by Sally McClung. Copyright © 1989 by Sally McClung. Published by Harvest House Publishers, Eugene, Oregon. Used by permission [from pages 72-73].

Sunday

Meditation

On the first day of the week, very early in the morning, the women took the spices they had prepared and went to the tomb. They found the stone rolled away from the tomb, but when they entered, they did not find the body of the Lord Jesus. While they were wondering about this, suddenly two men in clothes that gleamed like lightning stood beside them. In their fright the women bowed down with their faces to the ground, but the men said to them, "Why do you look for the living among the dead? He is not here; he has risen!"

Luke 24:1-6

Monday

When my heart is overwhelmed: lead me to the rock that is higher than I.
Psalm 61:2 KJV

The inner city of Amsterdam forms a hub of intrigue and delight. Tourists, refugees, and pilgrims of every description make their way to this "Venice of the North." Its ethnic mixture contains 44 major nationalities and countless subgroupings. This city of refuge has, for centuries, been the destination for those seeking a place where social and religious tolerance would triumph.

Amsterdam was once a haven of refuge, founded on Christian principles. Now it is filled with prostitution, drug trafficking, and addiction; child pornography has found an ample breeding ground along these picturesque canals.

Before joining YWAM, our family asked the Lord where we should live. We felt He said, "the heart of Amsterdam." With four young children, my heart's cry was, "Lord, how can our children grow up to be normal people in the center of such degradation?"

As I expressed my fear and apprehension to the Lord, the Holy Spirit brought peace and understanding. Only in the center of God's will is there true safety. With a deep assurance, we knew God was with us. He would be our source of wisdom in raising our children. He is concerned about their well-being.

My fears of raising children here are valid, but the Lord is asking me to look to Him. He gives us wisdom to nurture our children to be God-fearing, God-loving people.

Carolyn Ros, an American married to a Dutchman, works on YWAM staff in Amsterdam, Netherlands.

Tuesday

Being confident of this, that he who began a good work in you will carry it on to completion until the day of Christ Jesus.　　　　*Philippians 1:6*

I was only seven years old when I responded to a missionary challenge by kneeling at my seat and telling God I would go wherever He wanted me to. I still don't know how, but when I stood, I knew that one day I would go to China to do missionary work. When I told my mother about it, she wisely said, "If you've heard from God, it will happen."

After I married, we pastored for twenty years, taking trips to do missionary work every few years. On one trip, we'd been ministering in Singapore, Hong Kong, and the Philippines. Now we had a few weeks to spare, and we were so close to China. But we were told that there had been trouble at the border. No more trips were being allowed. We persisted in our request, and God came through.

Forty-eight hours later, we stepped from a hydrofoil onto the dock in Canton. As a Red Guard watched from a short distance away, my son whispered, "Mom, you're in China!" It had been 34 years since God had spoken to the heart of a seven-year-old girl, saying that one day I would travel as a missionary to China.

Beverly Caruso, an American, is a Bible teacher and author who leads Writer's Seminars. She lives in California, USA.

Wednesday

What a wonderful God we have—he is the Father of our Lord Jesus Christ, the source of every mercy, and the One who so wonderfully comforts and strengthens us in our hardships and trials. And why does he do this? So that when others are troubled, needing our sympathy and encouragement, we can pass on to them this same help and comfort God has given us.

II Corinthians 1:3-4 LB

As I walked down a dark, rainy street of the small Polish town that night, I saw a man lying motionless in the street and ran toward him. I placed my coat over him and called an ambulance. Upon examining him, the ambulance attendants informed me that he was dead. As I stood there, trying to take this in, I pondered the irony: it was five years ago to the day that my own husband had died.

He and I had been commissioned by our church as missionaries, and were waiting to hear where God would send us when my husband was "called home"—to heaven.

I had been a teacher at churches, retreats, and conference centers for 25 years, but wondered what God's plan would be now that I was alone. I wrote letters to every missionary organization I'd heard of. Youth With A Mission in Switzerland responded, inviting me to attend their Crossroads Discipleship Training School (CDTS). This is a school like their regular DTS, but for folks over the age of 35 who find themselves at a "crossroads" in life. I was 24 years past 35, and I was certainly at a crossroads!

After three months of training, I was closer to Jesus than ever before. Jesus and I became a missionary team, and I joined a YWAM outreach to France, Czechoslovakia, and Poland.

It had been a long journey to this dark Polish street, but as I wrote a letter of comfort to the man's widow, I realized that the Lord had brought me full circle—from being comforted by Him, to comforting another.

Mary Lee Ehrlich, an American, worked on staff in Switzerland and Hawaii. She is now on sabbatical in the USA, writing a book.

Thursday

Although [Jesus] was a son, he learned obedience from what he suffered.
Hebrews 5:8

The view of dead grass outside painfully reminded me of my circumstances. Our three-year-old daughter had a painful mouth infection; two other children and I had a stomach virus causing continuous, painful cramping and diarrhea. Despite this, my husband and I were writing final exams for the Introduction to Biblical Counseling School we were attending.

Added to this was the emotional trauma of living in a foreign country and dealing with a foreign language. The burden seemed too heavy to carry.

"God," I cried. "I don't know how I can manage another moment. Please help!"

Suddenly I heard someone singing, "Oh Come, Let Us Adore Him." The song made me think about the character of Jesus and His loving Father.

It struck me like a lightning bolt: Jesus had been born in a barn. It was in a dirty, smelly, lowly place that God chose to reveal His Son—a part of His very life.

I realized that it is in "barnyard" experiences that God sometimes chooses to reveal His life-changing truths.

Sharon Egert, a Canadian, serves on staff in Kailua-Kona, Hawaii, USA.

Friday

I can do everything through him who gives me strength.

Philippians 4:13

We were going door-to-door witnessing in Texas. At 17 years of age and only five feet, two inches tall, I was happy to let my partner do the witnessing. Nick had some Bible college training; I was just out of high school. I was content to be the silent prayer partner, listening to Nick share Christ with those we met.

As we approached yet another door, Nick said, "It's your turn."

"No," I blurted. "I like what you're doing. I like doing the praying."

Nick wasn't about to give in. "This is your door, Al. You take the lead."

We'd arrived at the door. There was no time to argue. I watched a man inside approach the screen door. He silently stood just inside. His huge size made me shake. I couldn't get words to come out, just stutters. He finally stopped me.

"Now, just calm down." He invited us inside to sit with him. "Okay, now tell me what's on your mind."

I did calm down, and was able to share the Gospel of Christ with him. He even helped me by encouraging me to talk and be calm. My weakness opened the way into this big man's heart.

We often think we must be strong in such areas to accomplish anything for God. The apostle Paul says that it's in our weakness that we become strong. We need only trust Him.

Al Akimoff, an American, directs Slavic Ministries.

Saturday

Whoever trusts in the Lord is kept safe. *Proverbs 29:25*

My first foreign outreach with Youth With A Mission was in Jamaica. My father and I discussed the prospect of my going, and while he was behind my desire to go, he made it clear that it was not going to be *my* faith and *his* finances that got me there! (Later, as I grew in my faith, I saw how wise his counsel was.)

After talking with my father, a phrase I'd heard came to mind, "If you do the possible, God will do the impossible." I set about raising as much money as I could. My friends and I collected used household items from friends and neighbors, and we had a garage sale. I even tried to sell my old basketball trophies, but I quickly found out that nobody wants secondhand trophies!

As I did this, God began to release the finances I needed. From a bus depot in Texas, I called my father, who told me excitedly of a non-Christian relative who had just visited him. He had told the relative about my trip, but made no mention of my financial needs since he assumed the relative would not be interested in helping. But to his surprise, the relative had offered to write a check for me. Neither of them knew how much I needed, so I was both surprised and excited when I found out that my relative's check covered my remaining travel costs and other expenses to the last penny.

I learned firsthand that God will provide if we just step out in faith. I did not step out presumptuously. I knew God wanted me to attend that outreach, and I did my part as well, so His provision was indeed a confirmation to me of His will. The principle of doing the possible and trusting God for the impossible had become real to me.

Floyd McClung, an American, directs Leadership Development Programs for YWAM. He lives in California, USA.

From *Basic Discipleship* by Floyd McClung. Copyright © 1990 by Floyd McClung. Published by InterVarsity Press, Downers Grove, Illinois. Used by permission [from pages 62-64].

Sunday

Meditation

And we rejoice in the hope of the glory of God. Not only so, but we also rejoice in our sufferings, because we know that suffering produces perseverance; perseverance, character; and character, hope. And hope does not disappoint us, because God has poured out his love into our hearts by the Holy Spirit, whom he has given us.

Romans 5:2-5

Monday

Then the Lord reached out his hand and touched my mouth and said to me,
"Now, I have put my words in your mouth."   Jeremiah 1:9

I have always trusted God to help me prepare my sermons.
But never had I come across a situation like this one that occurred
in India.

My family and I were in the city of Bangalore. We were neither
ministering in local churches nor accepting preaching assign-
ments. This was to be a time of rest for us.

One Sunday, we decided to attend a church where the pastor
was an acquaintance. The pastor spied me before the service began
and asked me to give a ten-minute testimony. I told him I hadn't
come to speak, but to be refreshed by his message.

He pleaded with me, "Just ten minutes." Again, I refused. At
his insistence, I finally agreed to a short account of the work of
YWAM in India.

When I was introduced, the pastor said, "It's so nice to have
Tim Svoboda with us tonight. Tim is the Director of YWAM
Madras, and he's come to deliver our sermon."

Shocked and surprised, I rose and walked slowly to the platform. When I passed the pastor, he whispered, "You go ahead
and give the message. I have to leave and go preach at another
church." Then he walked off the platform—and straight out the
door.

I closed my eyes and bowed my head. Never had I prayed so
hard. I whispered, "God, I can't do this. But You can. If You
don't speak through me, this is going to be a wasted 30 minutes
for a lot of people."

To this day I can't remember what I said. I wish someone had
taped it. For afterward, people crowded around and said it was
one of the best messages they had ever heard.

Someone even said they could tell it had been prepared especially for this church.

Tim Svoboda, an American, is National Director of YWAM in India.

Tuesday

A generous man will himself be blessed, for he shares his food with the poor.

Proverbs 22:9

"Oh, God, put me in an impossible situation so I can prove You to the world!" There I stood, with a thousand other zealous young people at the close of the Munich Olympic Games Outreach in 1972, responding to a challenge from Joy Dawson to let God use me to demonstrate His greatness.

He took me up on my request! Within a few months, I found myself trusting God for an airline ticket from Europe to Korea for a large international outreach we were planning for that nation. I needed about $1,000 for the ticket, injections, outreach fees, etc. I faithfully kept my list of itemized needs, and prayed fervently for God to meet them.

God provided from many sources. But every time I had nearly all the finances I needed, He would say, *Give some away.* It was never just a few dollars, but always a big enough chunk that I had to rally my faith for another large amount.

I sensed God saying, *Dawn, I don't care what your list of expenses dictates to you. I just want you to learn to listen to Me and obey, then trust Me to provide for your needs.*

God used that experience to break my bondage to money and release me to live in generosity and obedience to Him. He brought in all the finances, and I flew with 80 others from London to Brussels to Baghdad, then to Bombay and Hong Kong, then on to Taipei and Seoul, Korea.

Dawn Gauslin, an American, is the International Coordinator for YWAM's field-based Leadership Training Schools. She is also an assistant to Darlene Cunningham.

Wednesday

You who call on the Lord, give yourselves no rest, and give him no rest till he establishes Jerusalem.   Isaiah 62:6-7

Years ago I was part of a team who went to the southern Philippines to work with a church and share Christ.

My wife, Margaret, was impressed with today's Scripture. Inspired by that verse, our team began to maintain an around-the-clock prayer vigil. At the same time we continued to witness, and soon things began to happen.

One day a young college student who was totally committed to the philosophy of communism questioned me. As we talked, I felt an inspiration and asked, "If we were to take all the wealth of the Philippines and heap it here on the street, and then divide it equally, would that solve all the woes of this nation caused by corruption?"

I was to learn later that he went home to wrestle with that question until 2:00 a.m. Finally, he concluded that only Christ could solve the nation's troubles, so he gave his life to the Lord. Today he pastors the very church outside of which we talked 21 years ago!

There are others who came to Christ as a result of that around-the-clock praying we did over a two-month period (and all the witnessing that went along with it), who are going on well today. As I look back on what took place all those years ago, I learn a valuable lesson: Concerted effort in prayer can lead to remarkable conversions.

Ross Tooley, a New Zealander, serves at large on the staff of the College of Christian Ministries of University of the Nations, Kona, Hawaii, USA.
Adapted from *We Cannot But Tell,* by Ross Tooley, revised edition. Copyright © 1993 by Ross Tooley. Published by YWAM Publishing, Seattle, Washington. Used by permission [from pages 33-35].

Thursday

The eternal God is your refuge, and underneath are the everlasting arms.
Deuteronomy 33:27

Directing a Discipleship Training School is always a challenge, but nothing could have prepared us for the excitement we experienced on the opening day of our July, 1990, school in Baguio City, Philippines.

Everything was going according to plan when suddenly the earth was heaving and shaking with a major earthquake (7.7 on the Richter scale). In less than one minute, our mile-high mountain city was completely cut off from the rest of the world. All roads leading in were closed by landslides.

The airport runway had heaved and cracked—unusable. Telecommunication lines were down. We had no electricity and no water. Thousands of people lost their lives, and thousands more lost everything they had. It was a minute that changed our lives by rearranging our perspectives and priorities.

It was dangerous to enter our house, since buildings were collapsing in the hundreds of nerve-rattling aftershocks. Life became an adventure in prayer and perseverance. Where would we find food for our "family" of 35 people? Where would we find water, a place to sleep? What about sanitation?

Every day, we sent some of the fellows out to scout for food, with instructions to buy whatever they could find. We had some amazingly interesting meals in those first days! When our mealtime population grew to 50, time and again we saw God stretch what little we had and make it sufficient.

Each evening, we gathered in the dark on the driveway—our new meeting room, kitchen, dining room, and bedroom. We sang praises to God for His miraculous protection and provision. We experienced an incredible sense of God's comfort and peace-giving presence.

I hope never to repeat the experiences of those days. But I wouldn't trade them for anything.

Bobbie Hamm, a Canadian, and her husband are Discipleship Training School directors and leaders in Baguio City, Philippines.

Friday

Do two walk together unless they have agreed to do so?   Amos 3:3

How easy it is to fall aside from that special call of God on each of our lives: "to be conformed to the likeness of His Son."

Not only do I forget in the busyness of my daily activities that this is my destiny, but often I forget how much my destiny is woven into the destiny of others. If we find it hard to walk alongside God for very long, it may be because deep down inside, we haven't agreed with His purpose and direction for our journey together.

It is often easier to love the lost in Timbuktu than to love the people right beside us. Yet often, loving the people dearest to us means we may need to change something in our heart or life. There might be an area that needs repentance or healing.

God wants to create in us the image of His Son. This is exactly opposite to what the devil has for us. He would like us not only to forget the King, but the purpose of the Kingdom, as well.

If we are to be more like Jesus, we have to be careful not to get sidetracked waiting for a vision or looking for a particular ministry. Jesus was people-oriented, not project-oriented. If we let God change us into the image of Jesus, He will open opportunities each day to manifest His love for the world through us. We need only make ourselves available.

Scott Morey, an American, serves as a YWAM leader in Liberia.

Saturday

Before they call I will answer; while they are still speaking I will hear.

Isaiah 65:24

Our group of 120 had driven from Yaroslavl to Moscow; from there we would catch a train to Riga, Latvia for a conference. We would have four hours to see Moscow before catching the train.

Later we learned that our leaders had been quite concerned about what they would do with the truck carrying our luggage during our sightseeing time. They didn't have a place to park it and had no one to guard it. We had a glimpse of God's sense of humor when He answered their prayers.

We drove downtown, the truck carrying our luggage leading the way for our two buses. A policeman pulled up, motioning for the truck to pull over. We all pulled to the curb, and the truck driver got out to talk to the policeman. They argued, then both became angry. We surely didn't want to get delayed by the police in Moscow, so we all prayed. Our translator came to the rescue, and the policeman calmed down.

Unknown to us, trucks are not allowed on downtown streets in Moscow. A fine of $1,000 rubles (a little over one U.S. dollar) must be paid or the truck would be held at headquarters until it was paid.

Our leader told the truck's driver to take it to the police station. When the time came for us to board the train, he would pay the ticket and bring us our luggage.

Not only did God provide us a place to park the truck, but the police looked after it for us.

Frances Bradley, an American, is a freelance writer who lives in Austin, Texas, USA.

Sunday

Meditation

I sought the Lord, and he answered
me; he delivered me from all my
fears. Those who look to him are radiant; their faces are never covered
with shame. This poor man called,
and the Lord heard him; he saved
him out of all his troubles. The angel of the Lord encamps around
those who fear him, and he delivers
them. Taste and see that the Lord is
good; blessed is the man who takes
refuge in him.

Psalm 34:4-8

Monday

He who fears the Lord has a secure fortress, and for his children it will be a refuge. The fear of the Lord is a fountain of life, turning a man from the snares of death.   Proverbs 14:26-27

When I teach on evangelism, I like to ask, "Do you feel like witnessing on the streets tonight?" Usually, only a small percentage raise their hands, so I continue, "What if I guarantee that tonight each one of you will lead the first person you approach to the Lord—how many would feel like it then?" Almost without fail, every hand will shoot up. Everyone wants himself and his message to be accepted. No one relishes being put down, ignored, or looked upon as a fool.

The key to handling rejection is making sure we are getting all the acceptance we need from the Father and not looking for it in the world. By its very nature, evangelism means we are uninvited people taking an uncomfortable message to a Christ-rejecting world where many will refuse it. The glorious good news is, however, that some will accept it if we go out fearlessly, trusting that the perfect love of Jesus will cast out fear.

If we look to the Lord for our acceptance, placing our identity in Him and standing in awe of who He is, then the snare of the fear of man will fall away.

Danny Lehmann, an American, directs the YWAM base in Honolulu, Hawaii, USA, and travels extensively in a teaching ministry.
From *Bringin' 'Em Back Alive* by Danny Lehmann. Copyright © 1987 by Danny Lehmann. Published by Whitaker House, Springdale, Pennsylvania [from pages 76-77].

Tuesday

Cast your bread upon the waters, for after many days you will find it again.

Ecclesiastes 11:1

In 1940, I heard about the Lillian Trasher Orphanage in Assuit, Egypt. This single woman went out with nothing and began to take in orphans until, finally, she had the responsibility for up to 2,000 orphans and widows. Miss Trasher sent a representative to share at the church I was pastoring in El Centro, California. When we heard of the pitiful needs and what this woman was doing, I gave generously, as did many others in my congregation.

When Miss Trasher made her final trip to the United States, I had the privilege of having this great woman visit our church. Later, as a denominational leader, I helped promote the orphanage to all our churches. Over the years, I watched the orphanage grow; the Lord's hand was obviously on this work.

In 1979, I contracted some kind of ailment while in China. Just when I thought I had it licked, it came back again. I battled it for a year. Because I had picked up the bug overseas, my doctor was at a loss as to how to treat it. I decided to look for a specialist.

When I arrived at the clinic for my appointment, I noticed that I would be seeing Doctor Habib. In the Arab world, the name *Habib* is as common as *Smith* or *Jones* is in the States. I guessed I would be seeing an Egyptian doctor.

"Doctor, you wouldn't happen to be from Egypt, would you?" I asked when we met.

"Why, yes, I am. Why do you ask?" he replied. I told him I had traveled in Egypt, and asked if he had heard of the orphanage.

"I sure have. In fact, I lived in it for a while during my childhood." While he examined me, we exchanged memories of Miss Trasher and her work.

Forty years before, I cast my bread on the waters; it came back to me from one of the orphans I had helped. Through the skill of Dr. Habib, I was cured of the ailment which I had battled for a year.

T.C. Cunningham, an American, represents missions and missionaries internationally. He is also the father of YWAM's Founder and President, Loren Cunningham.

Wednesday

Now we who are strong ought to bear the weaknesses of those without strength and not just please ourselves.   *Romans 15:1 NASB*

There was a couple on my staff whom I treated as acquaintances. I didn't appear to have a lot in common with them, so my wife and I only mixed with them on a casual social basis. There were times when other members of the ministry tried to tell me that the couple was having some problems, but I was too busy, and decided to "let sleeping dogs lie."

It wasn't until the couple left the ministry abruptly and filed for divorce that I realized the gravity and seriousness of my mistake. I had not taken the time to involve myself in their lives. I really didn't know the couple beyond the social veneer of casual visits. As their leader, I had accepted them but had never challenged them. And in practicing the one without the other, I had failed them as their leader.

That which distinguishes biblically appropriate acceptance from unconcerned tolerance is compassion. Compassion, which literally means "to feel pain jointly," is the quality which allows one person to enter into the felt needs of another. It is a deep inner desire to identify with someone else in order to be a channel of healing to them.

Tolerance, on the other hand, is passive acquiescence, or a state of non-involvement. It is an outward attempt to give credibility to a heart that is inwardly unconcerned. It is sad but true that many in the Church today are tolerated, but few are properly accepted.

Denny Gunderson, an American, serves as North American Director for YWAM, and lives in Seattle, Washington, USA.

From *Through the Dust...Breaking Leadership Stereotypes* by Denny Gunderson. Published by YWAM Publishing, Seattle, Washington. Used by permission [from pages 50-51].

Thursday

His compassions never fail. They are new every morning.
Lamentations 3:22,23

About 200 Discipleship Training School students from various countries gathered for an outreach in Athens, Greece. Before dawn one morning, I walked up the hill and watched the sunrise over the Aegean Sea. Aware I was walking near the place where the apostle Paul walked, I sat down to read what he had written. I was having good fellowship with the Lord, feeling so close to Him. I sang to Him a new song which included the words, "I'll go anywhere for you."

Suddenly I stopped. *Do I really mean that?* I asked.

Following this outreach, some of my classmates would be going to work at refugee camps in Thailand. This was a dangerous work; war was a short distance away on the border. Would I do that? Would I go to a war zone?

God's Spirit reminded me that His mercies are new every morning. I sensed Him saying, "The same strength you are feeling as you fellowship with Me now is the strength I can give every morning. Wherever you travel, the sun is going to rise, and My mercies are going to be new every morning. I'm going to be with you."

I knew then that I would go anywhere He asked.

Karen Lafferty, an American, leads Musicians in Missions International, based in Amsterdam, Netherlands.

Friday

A little child will lead them. Isaiah 11:6

Our evangelism team was quite a presence as we rumbled across the wastelands of Siberia on the Trans-Siberian Railroad. The crew and other passengers listened with interest as we worshiped Jesus and tested our limited Russian expressions.

This phrase of Scripture had run through my mind prior to our team's outreach. I didn't know why at the time, but I had tucked it away for later use.

A little boy on the train started counting in English. I laughed and instinctively began to sing with motions, "One, two, three, Jesus loves me...." He was thrilled to learn a whole English song, and ran back to his compartment to sing it for his parents.

Later, his mother invited me to their compartment. I grabbed my Bible and bilingual dictionary and followed her. She knew no English, so our two-hour conversation was entirely by gesture and dictionary. In the privacy of the compartment, she began to ask questions, and soon reached the inevitable question: "Are you married?"

"*Nyet,*" I replied.

"How old are you?" she asked.

"Twenty-seven."

I smiled at her worried expression. She obviously thought I had "missed the boat." I explained that I had given control of that area of my life to God. (This through our friend, the dictionary.)

"I love Him, and He's my first priority," I explained.

She looked puzzled, and finally responded, "How did God propose to you?"

What an opportunity to share the message of Jesus! I retrieved my Russian Bible and opened it for her to read passages for herself. She held it tenderly and read aloud page after page. Later, I bid her farewell and exchanged addresses, leaving the Bible with her.

Barb Nizza, an American, serves on staff of the College of Early Childhood Education, University of the Nations, Kailua-Kona, Hawaii, USA.

Saturday

Be strong and courageous. Do not be terrified; do not be discouraged, for the Lord your God will be with you wherever you go.   *Joshua 1:9*

Two thousand drunken bikers watched as we performed the mime production of "Tale of Two Kingdoms." They hurled abuse at our team. Some staggered in their own dance. We knew we were not wanted there, but God had told us to do it, so we stayed.

One biker shoved his way onto the performance area and began to strip. One of our leaders tried to speak, but was drowned out by the crowd.

A big biker wrenched the microphone from the leader's hand, pointed to the girls and said, "I say, let's grab these Christian virgins down here, and show them what life is all about!"

We quickly escorted the girls onto the bus. While some of our guys guarded the girls, the leaders began to pack things away. A biker came over and said, "What you guys did took guts. What is it you were trying to tell us?" So one of our guys shared the Gospel with him.

Meanwhile, God spoke to my heart, *Go ahead and witness to them, two by two.* For the rest of the afternoon, we mixed with small bunches of bikers who listened to the Gospel! Even the girls moved through this once-hostile crowd, knowing that something had changed and they were now perfectly safe.

Although we came close to missing this work of God's Spirit, He was faithful. Our battle was not against the bikers, but against the powers of darkness that ruled over them. God used prayer, praise, and the declaration of the Gospel to render the powers helpless.

David Skeat, an Australian, serves as base director for YWAM Albury, New South Wales, Australia.

Sunday

Meditation

This is what the Lord Almighty says: "Administer true justice; show mercy and compassion to one another. Do not oppress the widow or the fatherless, the alien or the poor. In your hearts do not think evil of each other."

Zechariah 7:9-10

Monday

Jesus said, "Father, forgive them, for they do not know what they are doing."
Luke 23:34

I was a new Christian and was in New Delhi, India, on my first outreach. My team was performing a pantomime about Jesus on the lawn of Delhi University.

When we came to the part about the Crucifixion, the students became hostile. Pelting us with rocks and trash, they shouted angry words. We continued to present the visual picture of God's love.

I continued going through the motions of the drama, but inside, I was angry with the students. *How can they laugh at Jesus' death when He died for them? They're laughing at Jesus! They're mocking my Lord!*

I whispered to one of my friends in exasperation, "I can't believe this. It feels like we're at the actual Crucifixion." She nodded in agreement. As the garbage continued to hit us in the face, she whispered, "And to think that Jesus said, 'Forgive them, they know not what they do.'"

Realization poured over me as I thought about how Jesus must have felt dying on the Cross, then speaking those words. A new understanding of God's heart for the lost brought me to tears. My bitterness changed to forgiveness. It was a lesson I will never forget.

Nancy Vallese, an American, is the director of the Far East Evangelism teams in Hong Kong.

Tuesday

He cuts off every branch in me that bears no fruit, while every branch that does bear fruit he trims clean so that it will be even more fruitful.

John 15:2

Some years ago, I went to Israel to work on a kibbutz. My job was mainly to pick oranges. One day, I was sent to help two gardeners prune trees. I followed them with tar to seal the cuts they made. Tar keeps insects from entering the wood and damaging it, and prevents infection. It also prevents the sap from bleeding out.

I was amazed at the amount of wood the gardeners cut off the trees, leaving them looking naked. One of the gardeners explained, "If there are too many branches, the energy of the tree goes to produce foliage instead of fruit. In order to get as many good quality apples as possible, we remove unnecessary wood." He also explained that through pruning the tree, it is conformed to the desired shape.

As I walked behind the gardeners, sealing the wounded trees, God spoke to me. He was working in my life in a similar way, removing everything that hindered me from bearing fruit. Even though it meant some of my beautiful "foliage" had to go, God's plan for me was fruitfulness, that the Father may be glorified.

Where He made cuts, He gently sealed the wounds with His Holy Spirit, preventing the entrance of evil. By pruning, He rendered me closer to the likeness of Jesus.

Gitta Leuschner, a German, has a teaching ministry in Germany.

Wednesday

As a father has compassion on his children, so the Lord has compassion on those who fear him.   Psalm 103:13

We hadn't been with YWAM in Japan for very long when my husband, Martin, suddenly became ill. Within two weeks, he was paralyzed from the waist down. Doctors immediately operated to halt any further damage, and transferred him to a second hospital. He was then moved to a rehabilitation facility.

Japanese hospitals require 24-hour family care. Even though a friend flew in from Texas to help care for Martin, my presence was still required.

Our children and home were almost a seven-hour drive from the hospital. This forced us to make two difficult decisions: let the house go so I could live near the hospital, and send the children back to family in the United States.

We decided to take the children to visit Martin before they left. The trip was important to the children. It would be more than four months before they would see their dad again.

The cost of the train travel, food, and lodging for the weekend visit was nearly $700, or 100,000 Japanese yen. We had planned to leave for the hospital on Saturday, and return on Monday. By Wednesday morning, we still had no money. We prayed fervently for God's provision.

At noon on Wednesday, Alma, a missionary friend from a neighboring town, burst through our front door waving an envelope and shouting that she had the money for our trip. The envelope held 100,000 yen.

Our family never met the woman who gave us the money. She'd given it to Alma, who knew exactly what it was meant for.

Jennifer Cuthbertson, an American, served on staff of Crossroads Discipleship Training School in Kailua-Kona, Hawaii, USA.

Thursday

For nothing is impossible with God.   *Luke 1:37*

The Lord gave me this verse before I joined a team for an African field trip. By the time we were somewhere in the bush in Upper Volta, the tension within my team seemed to be increasing. Rebellion was very much a part of my life at that time, even though it was well disguised.

I had just complained, "We will never have unity on this team," when I was surrounded by a swarm of bees and stung more than 80 times. Usually, 30 stings cause a body's whole system to become poisoned, and chances of survival are slim.

The pain was so intense that it was indescribable. With considerable difficulty, members of my team endangered their own lives to come to my rescue. They managed to drag me to safety.

As they prayed for me, the peace of God flooded over me. I heard the words, "Nothing is impossible for Me." I had heard the Lord say these words to me before, and I knew that He was the Almighty God, the God of the impossible.

The Lord healed me. He also showed me the importance of being committed to Him and to others. I learned that I need others, and that I am responsible for my attitudes and actions toward them. My rebellion had played a big part in the problems our team was experiencing. Once I worked out the problems in my own life, God could start bringing unity to the entire team.

Lidia Giudice, an Italian, is involved in evangelism and public relations in Lausanne, Switzerland.

Friday

I will instruct you and teach you in the way you should go.   Psalm 32:8

The pressures were especially difficult. Loren was going back and forth to the South Pacific to sort out problems there while I stayed in Hawaii, trying to keep the work going there.

Then my mom telephoned saying that my father was desperately ill. It was not life-threatening, but he was very sick. Logically, I should have gone immediately. But with Loren away, I couldn't leave the children in Hawaii, and Dad was too sick for us to stay with my parents.

I walked along the beach in Hawaii, talking with God about all my responsibilities: I was a daughter, a mother, a wife, and a leader. "Father," I said, "I trust You to tell me exactly what day to go home, what to do about the children, and where to stay. You know the needs there, and those here."

One morning, I sensed the Lord telling me I'd be going in the next few days. I called some neighbors of my parents that I knew well, and asked if the children and I could stay at their home.

"Well, Darlene!" she answered with delight in her voice, "So you're the one we've been expecting. Two weeks ago God impressed me that we must finish the guest room we've been working on." Their guest room was completed the day we arrived.

The time with my father was just what I had hoped it would be. After he had recovered completely, his doctor told me, "It would not have done your father any good for you to come any earlier. That was when he really needed you."

Darlene Cunningham, an American, is the YWAM International Director of Training. The wife of YWAM's President, Loren Cunningham, she also helped found Youth With A Mission. Loren and Darlene live in Kona, Hawaii, USA.

Saturday

I was young and now I am old, yet I have never seen the righteous forsaken or their children begging bread.   Psalm 37:25

My wife, young daughter, and I were living in a tiny upstairs apartment to be close to the local Japanese people. Support had dwindled, and we'd received nothing in almost two weeks. On my birthday, our money and food were depleted.

Our postman always arrived at 2:30 p.m. We had checked the mail at the expected time, to no avail. I checked the mail one last time around 4:30. Still there was nothing.

Our faith was at its lowest ebb. We called our daughter to pray with us about what we should do for supper. We really didn't want to go to a friend and ask for a loan. The Lord had always called us to trust Him in the leanest of times. Nonetheless, we asked the Lord to show us if we should make our need known.

As we waited, we opened our hearts to the Lord, willing to do whatever He said. Neither my wife nor I heard anything definite, but our eight-year-old daughter said, "The Lord told me, 'Check again.'"

We figured that meant we were to pray again and see if the Lord was going to speak to the adults. As we prayed again and heard nothing clearly, we decided to go to our friend's for help. As we passed the mailbox, I peeked in one more time. To my great surprise, I saw a letter. It contained a gift of $200.

Then we understood our daughter's words, "Check again."

We went out that night, and had a birthday dinner with great rejoicing and thankfulness.

Written by James Foreman.

Sunday

Meditation

Then Jesus said to his disciples: "If anyone would come after me, he must deny himself and take up his cross and follow me. For whoever wants to save his life will lose it, but whoever loses his life for me will find it. What good will it be for a man if he gains the whole world, yet forfeits his soul?"

Matthew 16:24-26

Monday

When you said, "Seek My face," my heart said to You, "Your face, Lord, I will seek."   *Psalm 27:8-9 NKJV*

How do we approach the time we spend alone with the Lord each day? With what expectations do we come? Is our prime object or expectation that we will get something out of the time; that we will receive something? Or rather, do we come with the expectation of being able to give ourselves to the Lord, of ministering to the heart of God, and of expressing our love to Him?

I have a tendency to come with mixed motives. The Bible says, "Seek the Lord," not, "Seek the Lord for...." In John 6:27, Jesus exhorted the people not to come primarily seeking Him for fulfillment of their needs, but rather to seek Him—the "Bread of Life."

Oh, that our hearts would be filled with the same anticipation we experience when meeting a close friend at a busy airport after a time of separation. We eagerly search the crowd for the face of that one whom we long to see again. As we glimpse him from a distance, we press our way through the crowd to welcome and embrace him. Those things that were so much on our mind when we came are brushed aside in the excitement and sheer joy of spending time with our dear friend.

Let us learn to seek the face of the Lord. The fruit of this relationship will take care of our needs and problems. Indeed, as we seek God first, then "all these things shall be added unto us." God is faithful and true to His Word.

Sarah Gerhart, from Zimbabwe, served nine years with Mercy Ships, and now lives in Los Angeles, California, USA.

Tuesday

Then he said to them, "Whoever welcomes this little child in my name welcomes me; and whoever welcomes me welcomes the one who sent me."

Luke 9:48

Like many adults, I thought that only certain people can relate to little children, and others cannot. Most of us probably think we are in the second category. I did. As a child, I had the impression that children were not important until they grew up. It seemed that grownups had no time for children. I thought that having an adult friend was out of the question.

Despite these misconceptions, I became an elementary school teacher. After I joined YWAM, I felt the Lord was directing me to teach the very little ones. I often struggled with the feeling that my work was unimportant. Before long, however, I was convinced that instilling godly principles, developing friendships, and serving as a role model to children was far more effective than waiting until they are older.

God called me to focus not so much on the work as on the child. One day, I was praying with a co-worker. She asked the Lord to give me a friendship with a certain three-year-old child, soon to be promoted to my class. Although I had never given thought to the possibility of choosing a child for a friend, I knew my friend's prayer pleased the Father. I welcomed God's faith to bring this about.

A warm friendship developed. As a result, I realized that the enemy of our souls hates little children. Looking back, I can see the devastation he has brought to me and to countless others.

Only now am I beginning to understand why Jesus wants us to love and be a friend to little children.

Molly Young, an American, teaches school on the m/v *Anastasis*.

Wednesday

Oh, how I love your law! I meditate on it all day long.   Psalm 119:97

The small building sandwiched between two massive structures was barely visible. How glad I was that a Christian from Hong Kong had written out the Chinese address for us to give the taxi driver.

My husband, our son Dave, and I entered the Three-Self Patriotic Church (State-run) in Canton, China, with a sense of destiny. We sat on one of the low, straight-backed benches, and the melodies of the hymns reminded me that it was Palm Sunday.

Sitting next to Dave was a little woman who rubbed her arthritic hands throughout the service. Something must have happened in Dave's heart toward her as he watched her suffer.

When the sermon began, Dave took a small book from his pocket. This was one of ten such books carried across the border in my purse. They contained one of the gospels of the New Testament, with English on the left page and Cantonese facing it.

Using the English version, Dave found the page with the Palm Sunday story, and held it in front of the woman. At first, she pulled back slightly. When she recognized it as Scripture in her own language, she grabbed it from his hand. She eagerly devoured the words on the page. Then slowly, reverently, she closed the book. She gave Dave a loving smile and gently placed it back into his hands. He shook his head, and gently pushed the booklet back toward her. She continued to try to return it to him. At last he pulled open her coat, just far enough to push the book inside.

At last she understood! Her eyes, wide and unbelieving, asked if he really intended it to be hers.

"Yes," he nodded, and pointed to the book, then to her.

May we treasure God's Word as this precious Chinese sister did.

Beverly Caruso, an American, is a Bible teacher and author who leads YWAM Writer's Seminars. She lives in California, USA.

Thursday

The man who plants and the man who waters have one purpose, and each will be rewarded according to his own labor. For we are God's fellow workers.
I Corinthians 3:8-9

Before we left Hawaii for the Philippines years ago, the administrator of the YWAM base in Kona asked us to meet with his staff. They wanted to pray for us during our time away.

We met lots of challenges on that trip to establish a discipleship program for Filipino students: choosing the buildings for the program, recruiting and selecting the students, scheduling teachers, and overseeing the program.

Back in Hawaii, those office workers faithfully prayed for us every day during that eight-month period.

God answered prayer. The 25 students God drew to that school were eager to learn, to serve God, and to pray. In the classroom God moved among them in cleansing power. When it was time to go on outreach, they took the prayer blessing with them as they traveled among the churches on the island. Church members openly got right with the Lord and with each other as the students preached and shared what they had earlier learned in the classroom. Since that time six years ago, almost all of those students have been involved in full-time Christian work, and about half continue to serve the Lord in that way today.

Others were praying for us as well, of course, but special mention has to be made of those in that administration office who prayed every day before they turned to begin their own work.

Ross Tooley, a New Zealander, serves at large on the staff of the College of Christian Ministries of University of the Nations, Kona, Hawaii, USA.

Friday

Faithful is He who calls you, and He also will bring it to pass.

I Thessalonians 5:24 NASB

The sound of waves rolling onto the shore was soothing, and the sun felt warm against my skin, yet my body protested taking another step. After ten days of flu-induced fever and chills, the thought of putting on my 80-pound backpack and going anywhere was about as appealing as trying to eat again.

I had begun this trip with high expectations. Our School of Missions believed God had called us to minister to the Li people of Southern China. I had been confident He would show us how we could bring them the Good News of Jesus Christ. Now, ten days later, I wondered how a few days of illness and one too many bus rides shared with ducks, chicken, and fish could deal such a devastating blow to my confidence.

I searched for something to eat that wouldn't cause my stomach to revolt. After a mile hike up the beach, I found that the large hotel did not serve Western food. Walking back was more difficult than the trudge uphill, and my stomach still rolled in that hungry, sick way. Beside me, and in character, my optimistic husband was whistling a familiar tune, "He has all authority here in this place."

From behind us, in English, we heard, "Excuse me, but are you Christians?" We were instantly linked with the only people who could help us reach the Li people, English teachers at the minority university. They were Christians, and were interested in our mission. My stomach suddenly felt better.

In a matter of minutes, the God of the universe had jolted me back to reality. He was capable of carrying out everything that He had spoken to us in prayer concerning His heart for the Li people. He is faithful.

Charlene O'Connor, an American, works with the School of Frontier Mission in Kona, Hawaii, USA.

Saturday

A man who has friends must himself be friendly.   *Proverbs 18:24 NKJV*

We all need friends. We need the love that comes through friendship. Love is a basic human need. We all need it—no matter how self-sufficient, "macho," wealthy, or successful we may be. If we want this love and want friends, we must show ourselves friendly. Sometimes we struggle in this area of friendship. We say we're shy—we can't reach out to others. But we shouldn't use shyness as an excuse.

People often find it hard to believe that I am basically a shy person. Floyd has always been the outgoing one in our relationship. Shyness was something I had to overcome. It was—and still is—much easier for me to sit back and listen to others. But years ago, the Lord challenged me that I would never be all that He wanted me to be if I used shyness as an excuse. I chose to step out of my shyness and quietness. It was hard at first. I was scared. I was nervous. I was insecure. But the more I took those steps of reaching out to people, the easier it became.

If we want friendship, we can't just wait for it to come to us on a plate; we must begin by reaching out to those around us. We must look to those who are lonely. We must be a friend to others. In fact, the only way to have a friend is to be one.

Sally McClung, an American, has a ministry of hospitality and speaks internationally. She lives in California, USA.
From *Where Will I Find the Time?* by Sally McClung. Copyright © 1989 by Sally McClung. Published by Harvest House Publishers, Eugene, Oregon. Used by permission [from page 75].

Sunday

Delight yourself in the Lord and he will give you the desires of your heart. Commit your way to the Lord; trust in him and he will do this: He will make your righteousness shine like the dawn, the justice of your cause like the noonday sun. Be still before the Lord and wait patiently for him; do not fret when men succeed in their ways, when they carry out their wicked schemes.

Psalm 37:4-7

Monday

Though he brings grief, he will show compassion, so great is his unfailing love. For he does not willingly bring affliction or grief to the children of men.
Lamentations 3:32,33

What a comfort during a time of affliction or grief to know that it is not a light thing with God to allow any one of His children to suffer. Why suffering, then? Job, famous for his suffering, found no final answer to this question. A revelation of God in His magnificence brought his suffering to comparative insignificance. Then the release God intended for Job's life was realized. Job saw God, his understanding was enlightened, and his losses were restored to him doubled.

God, who loves me as no other, desires my eternal good. He is willing to sacrifice temporarily my health, comfort, provisions, friendships, or fulfillment for my eternal welfare. His purpose in allowing suffering in the lives of His children is release. I cannot choose whether I will suffer, but as a Christian, I can embrace the suffering God permits to enter my life, and see His purpose of release realized.

Jesus suffered for the release of all mankind. He knew the release the Father intended. "For the joy set before him he endured the cross...." I cannot usually see ahead the release that the Lord intends. But if, by His grace, I can endure, I am assured that release will come.

Deyon Stephens, an American, is helping prepare financially and logistically for YWAM to purchase a fourth ship. She lives in Texas, USA.

Tuesday

Jesus replied, "Go back and report to John what you hear and see: the blind receive sight, the lame walk, those who have leprosy are cured, the deaf hear, the dead are raised, and the good news is preached to the poor." Matthew 11:4-5

In this passage, our primary model and mentor, Jesus, communicates to us the essence of His ministry. He had just been questioned by John the Baptist and his disciples. They wondered, "Was Jesus really doing what He was supposed to be doing? Was He, indeed, the Messiah?" In other words, His ministry did not appear, to John the Baptist, to have the right focus.

Jesus responded in a way which shows us that our ministry is to be a "kingdom ministry." It requires a two-fold approach:

A. Ministering to the physical needs of the world around us—the blind, the lame, the leper, the deaf.
B. Proclaiming the Good News to those who have not yet heard.

Jesus gives a brief, thumbnail sketch of what He did that we should follow as our primary model. He cared for the physical through practical ministry, and at the same time, proclaimed in articulate vignettes, which we call parables, the essence of the kingdom of God.

Don Stephens, an American, pioneered and directs Mercy Ships. Don serves on YWAM's International Council and lives in Lindale, Texas, USA.

Wednesday

It is God who works in you to will and to act according to his good purpose.
Philippians 2:13

When God called us to leave the pastorate for missions work, it seemed impossible. For years, I had stomach problems. An even greater hindrance was the needs of our 26-year-old son, Steve.

Due to a birth injury, Steve developed cerebral palsy. During his infancy, doctors told us he might never walk or talk, but we saw Steve press beyond the unexpected in many ways. He learned to walk with canes. His speech is not clear, but those who take the time can understand him. Steve's kind, gentle spirit has made him many friends. Everyone who knows him seems to love him.

Although Steve graduated from high school, I assumed he would always live with Don and me. Steve desired independence, but could he really live on his own? I knew that if God truly was calling us to a ministry overseas, He would somehow make it possible.

We prayed. We also worked to help Steve become independent. He soon added shopping and banking to cooking and cleaning skills. Eventually, he learned to drive a car—modified for his disabilities.

Working together with Social Services, we were finally able to get Steve qualified for a supervised independent living arrangement. Each resident has a specially equipped apartment adjacent to the sponsoring church facility.

Steve's been on his own now for five years. As an additional blessing, he recently married a young woman whom he led back to the Lord.

During the months I was preparing Steve for a life on his own, God also took care of my other need. I learned of a doctor whose treatment eliminated my stomach problems. I've had no recurrence in any of the many countries where we've traveled.

Patti Hall, an American, serves with her husband, Don, in an international Bible teaching ministry.

Thursday

Before they call I will answer; while they are still speaking I will hear.

Isaiah 65:24

While serving with the mercy ship, m/v *Anastasis,* on a winter outreach, I worked as a nurse on the ward, as well as in the village clinics in Jamaica. Since I had paid the outreach fees and airfare in advance, I didn't anticipate any financial needs.

During the course of the outreach, I received a phone call from home. Someone in my church had anonymously donated $500 to my account. Even though I was pleased that someone thought that much of me and the work I was doing, I was puzzled. Why would God direct them to give to me so generously?

Toward the end of the outreach, I learned that the airline I had reservations with had declared bankruptcy! I prayed about what I should do. I was able to buy one-way tickets, but there was a mix-up in reservations, and I had to stay overnight in Miami at my own expense.

That night in Miami, I felt lonely and depressed. I wanted to be home. Why had things gone wrong? Suddenly, my mood turned to awe and thanksgiving as I realized God had foreseen my need and supplied it before I even knew to ask. The cost of the tickets and the room totaled exactly $500!

Jeanine Larsen, an American, serves as the food services manager and chief cook with YWAM Belize.

Friday

Very early in the morning, while it was still dark, Jesus got up, left the house and went off to a solitary place, where he prayed.   Mark 1:35

It is so easy to center our eyes on what Jesus did rather than on why He came. The miracles He performed and the messages He gave showed His authority. They leave us no question as to where He came from, but they were not His primary purpose.

Similarly, I find it easy to become more concerned about what I am doing for God than with the relationship I am building with Him. As the tensions and pressures of work build inside me, and I feel I cannot cope, I know the time has come to withdraw, to seek a "lonely place"; to call upon the Lord and relax in His presence. Only then will I be refreshed and renewed and able to tackle the activity of the next day.

Tension can be a spiritual thermometer for me; a measure of my relationship with God. As I walk close to Him and keep my eyes on Him, I can relax and walk calmly and peacefully in what He wants me to do. Sometimes I lose that closeness to Him, then I experience tension and turmoil. From my "lonely place," I know I can seek healing and renew the closeness of our relationship.

Dr. Christine Aroney Sine, an Australian, is a medical practitioner living in the United States.

179

Saturday

He who began a good work in you will carry it on to completion....

Philippians 1:6

Kathy leaned over the shiny bundle of purple material, and I held my breath as I watched her carefully pin the pattern pieces together, picturing the way the bridesmaid's dress had looked on the pattern envelope. It did look a lot more like a dress than it had when I first cut out the pattern pieces. We both knew, however, that there was still a long way to go.

As Kathy continued pinning, I reflected on the process the fabric had already been through. When I first laid it out, the fabric was beautiful—a rich, glossy sweep of color. To someone who didn't know how to sew, cutting it might have seemed ridiculous. Why destroy the fabric by making it into so many strange shapes? And that was only the beginning of a long, laborious journey. I knew, though, that without being "destroyed," the fabric would never be as beautiful—or as useful—as my dress pattern revealed it could be.

Then I thought of how our lives are like the fabric's journey toward becoming a dress. We're all in process, and sometimes God's work in us cuts, pierces, and seems incomprehensible. Once in a while we may even look back on who we were before He began the work and wonder if we're less "together" than we were then.

Yet the divine Tailor holds the pattern. He knows what kind of material we are made of, and how we will fit most beautifully and usefully into His plan. Even when we feel like we're turned inside out, with ragged seams and loose threads painfully exposed, we can be sure that it's for a reason.

Marguerite Watson, an American, works in the editorial department of Last Days Ministries in Lindale, Texas, USA.

Sunday

Meditation

For you did not receive a spirit that makes you a slave again to fear, but you received the Spirit of sonship. And by him we cry, "Abba, Father." The Spirit himself testifies with our spirit that we are God's children. Now if we are children, then we are heirs—heirs of God and co-heirs with Christ, if indeed we share in his sufferings in order that we may also share in his glory.

Romans 8:15-17

Monday

Be strong and courageous. Do not be afraid or terrified because of them, for the Lord your God goes with you; he will never leave you nor forsake you.

Deuteronomy 31:6

Perhaps my dreams were born from the stark reality that even making phone calls was difficult for me. During my teen years, I had visions of becoming another Joan of Arc or an Albert Schweitzer. These two vastly different individuals, who lived in different periods of history, portrayed uncommon courage. They inspired me.

A few years ago, I discovered for myself what true courage was really made of. I spent many hours in preparation before speaking at a teachers' seminar in New Zealand. I felt utterly weak and unqualified for the task. The only thing I was sure of was that God was asking me to do it, and that He wanted to speak through me. God was true to His Word. I discovered that God wanted me simply to step out in obedience. He would use that obedience as the key to bring the release of revelation, truth, and courage.

Long before that, I had heard someone say that courage is "acting on the knowledge that God will enable me to do what He asked me to do," no matter how big or small the task. I couldn't remember the speaker, only his words. Through that speaking assignment in New Zealand, God taught me that when He asks me to do something, He will enable me to do it.

Choose to be a man or woman of conviction, knowing that God is who He says He is! Then step out in obedience and act upon this knowledge, allowing the Holy Spirit to lead you.

Linda Cowie, an American, serves with her husband aboard YWAM's mercy ship, m/v *Pacific Ruby.*

Tuesday

Do not be afraid of what you are about to suffer. Be faithful, even to the point of death, and I will give you the crown of life.   Revelation 2:10

Ten years ago, Mark felt God call him to minister in China. At that time, it was very difficult for a Westerner to go to China, even as a tourist, let alone as a missionary. Nevertheless, Mark trusted God, and began looking for practical ways in which he could prepare himself. He went to the library, borrowed Mandarin language tapes, and began learning the language. He read all the books the library had on life in China.

About five or six years later, when the doors to China began to open, Mark was there, equipped and ready. He applied to the Chinese government for a job teaching English as a second language, and he was accepted and sent to a remote province.

Mark is still in China today. He has free access to the student dormitories where he holds evening Bible studies. As a result of his efforts, he has been able to lead many of his student friends to a relationship with Jesus Christ. Had Mark been unfaithful and failed to take the initiative when God spoke to him, he would not be doing what he is doing in China today.

Faithfulness is like the hinge on a door. It is only a small thing, yet without it, even the largest of doors will not open. By being faithful in everything God has presently spoken to us, we make a hinge on which He can swing the door wide open for us in the future.

Floyd McClung, an American, directs Leadership Development Programs for Youth With A Mission. He lives in California, USA.

From *Basic Discipleship* by Floyd McClung. Copyright © 1990 Floyd McClung. Published by InterVarsity Press, Downers Grove, Illinois. Used by permission [from page 44].

Wednesday

God said, "Let there be light," and there was light. God saw that the light was good, and he separated the light from the darkness. God called the light "day" and the darkness he called "night." And there was evening, and there was morning—the first day.   Genesis 1:3-5

When God created the heavens and the earth, He gave us a built-in time span to use as a guide. The phrase, "how time flies," means time tends to slip away from us without our realizing it. In His wisdom, God made a relatively short period of time: one day. He further divided that into two parts: light and dark. Though weeks slip into months and months into years, we consistently know when we go from one day to another. We always have a darkness followed by a period of light.

God made each day with a beginning and an end. In God's eyes, we are responsible only for today. Will we be obedient to Him today? Understanding that God views time in daily segments set me free from the not-enough-time syndrome.

Genesis 6:3 says, "his days will be a hundred and twenty years." In Genesis 25:7,8 (KJV) we read, "and these are the days of the years of Abraham." Job 42:17 reads, "[Job] died, old and full of years." Do you see the difference? Psalm 68:19 reads, "Praise be to the Lord, to God our Savior, who daily bears our burden."

His promise is not for this week or this month, but for today. If I disobey in what I do today, I can repent and be forgiven and begin tomorrow clean. If I obey today, I can lay my head on my pillow tonight and give praise to my Lord as an offering to Him.

Jack Hill, a Canadian, serves as Chaplain at the Mercy Ships Home Office in Lindale, Texas, USA.

Thursday

God is spirit, and his worshipers must worship in spirit and in truth.
John 4:24

We traveled for three weeks on the Trans-Siberian Railway across China, Mongolia, and the Soviet Union. Conversations with fellow travelers came easily. There were many opportunities to share the good news of Jesus using hand gestures and small copies of a Russian/English dictionary.

All along the way we prayed for these great nations which were so closed to the Gospel. We were sure others were praying, too.

In the cities of the eastern Soviet Union, we walked the streets, visited old churches (many now museums), and chatted with the local people.

In the city of Khabarovsk our tour guide scheduled a visit to a preschool/kindergarten complex, a model state-operated school catering to visitors. A huge portrait of "Grandfather Lenin" greeted us on the front wall of the main assembly hall.

In room after room the children eyed us, cautiously at first, then warmed up to our gestures of love and affection.

Our tour ended back in the assembly hall where we watched a song and dance performance by one of the classes of students.

When they learned that we would sing for them, they gave us rapt attention. While standing below the portrait of Lenin, we sang songs of worship to the one true God.

Now the Soviet Union is no more. Her people are openly hearing of Jesus, and are free to worship God. Churches are springing up throughout the land.

I know it wasn't our prayers alone that brought the change. Prayers of Christians around the world joined with the prayers of Christians within the USSR.

God was at work, though His work wasn't apparent.

Gail Maidment, an Australian, is director of the Small World Christian Kindergarten in Hong Kong.

Friday

Arise, shine, for your light has come, and the glory of the Lord rises upon you.
Isaiah 60:1

For two weeks, I agonized as I realized that the Lord was really calling us to the m/v *Anastasis*. Then, one morning in November, I sat at the kitchen table with my Bible before me, and began to reflect back over the last few years. I realized that many times, God had allowed wounding to come into my life in order to develop my character. Always, His comfort, His friendship, and His unconditional love had been there for me. In the midst of my deepest sorrows, He had never allowed me to be crushed. Why, then, couldn't I embrace this next step willingly?

Opening my Bible, I turned to Isaiah 60. It was the same chapter that God had first used to speak to Ben and me concerning a Christian ship 16 years earlier. I began meditating on what this verse meant. I could be part of a ship that someday would bring hope and love to a darkened world. She would be a shining light in the darkness; a vehicle to show God's love and mercy to thousands.

I closed my Bible and brushed a tear away. I knew what God was asking. Quietly, I bowed my head and gave Him my answer, *Yes, Lord, I'll go.*

Helen Applegate, a New Zealander, works with her husband, Ben, in Kiaora, a ministry of hospitality and prayer for the government of New Zealand.
From *Anchor in the Storm* by Helen Applegate with Renee Taft. Copyright © 1988 by Helen Applegate. Published by Frontline Communications, Seattle, Washington. Used by permission [from pages 120-121].

Saturday

For the eyes of the Lord range throughout the earth to strengthen those whose hearts are fully committed to him. II Chronicles 16:9

We sat by our broken-down van in the sweltering heat. How could we possibly get to the plane on time to leave for Jamaica? Even before the van broke down, I had felt nervous about finally going on outreach after weeks of praying and waiting.

When one of the other leaders said, "Let's pray and see what God will do," I began to relax. The situation seemed impossible, but we had been taught that the God we worship is a God of the impossible. We reminded one another that this was God's work. Surely he would get us there. We glanced at our watches as the precious minutes ticked away. We saw a van coming our way.

Would the driver help us? Our hearts were in our throats as it stopped. "I work at the airport. Jump in. I'll take you there," he offered. Our hearts leaped with joy.

As we drove through the gates our plane was taking off. The driver jumped out and said, "I'll do what I can." He raced to the terminal. Soon he came running back. "Hurry on in! I think you'll be fine."

Then the incredible happened! We watched as the commercial jetliner circled around, landed, and returned to the terminal. We grabbed our luggage and ran on board. How exciting to serve such an awesome God!

Glenn Martin, a Canadian, serves as the director of YWAM Belize.

Sunday

Meditation

I waited patiently for the Lord; he
turned to me and heard my cry. He
lifted me out of the slimy pit, out of
the mud and mire; he set my feet
on a rock and gave me a firm place
to stand. He put a new song in my
mouth, a hymn of praise to our
God. Many will see and fear and
put their trust in the Lord.

Psalm 40:1-3

Monday

My sheep listen to my voice; I know them and they follow me.

John 10:27

When I first joined YWAM, one of the most exciting things to me was the down-to-earth reality of not only relationship with God, but of communication with Him. Over the years, the still, small voice of God has become very real to me: challenging, convicting, or comforting. I grew in confidence, but confidence which is not born in humility does not long withstand the temptation to pride.

I was shattered if proved to have not heard correctly from God. I faced a dilemma: *If I'm wrong now, how can I ever trust myself to hear from God again? Is this relationship real?* I sought the help and counsel of loving friends. I began to look for balance in an area where pride and extremism could have broken and hurt my communion and communication with God.

I'm learning keys to walking in the fear of God, and I am seeking to discern and obey His voice. First, I need to remember that I'm human. I'm open to influences both from without and within. I'm prone to jump quickly to wrong conclusions when the Lord has only just begun to speak. Then there's the problem of interpreting "my opinion" as being from God.

Now I'm coming to a whole new freedom. When I'm wrong, instead of seeing it as a disaster, I see it as an opportunity to learn humility and to allow those wiser and closer to the Lord to teach and guide me. It's an opportunity to allow His Spirit to show me where I went wrong.

What about my confidence? It is not in my ability to hear from Him; it rests in His faithfulness to communicate with me.

Cheryl Robertson, from South Africa, works in administration and Discipleship Training Schools on YWAM's mercy ship, m/v *Anastasis.*

189

Tuesday

Seek first his kingdom and his righteousness, and all these things will be given to you as well. Therefore, do not worry about tomorrow, for tomorrow will worry about itself.   *Matthew 6:33-34*

The roar of the landing jet sent a wave of excitement through the waiting group of people on the tiny Pacific island of Niue. Excitement rose as the plane, their only link with the outside world, came to a halt.

Our family was among those waiting to leave. We felt sad to be leaving those of Niue to whom we had grown so close during our months of ministering among them. Yet we were excited. We were on our way to the Cook Islands, where we believed God now wanted us to minister.

The friends bidding us farewell were unaware that we had no funds to pay the $50 airport departure tax, and nothing with which to begin life in Rarotonga.

My husband and I moved away from the others and prayed again. With a quiet trust in God, we rested in Him.

A local family interrupted our prayers by pressing a farewell card into our hands. "A little something to get you started in Rarotonga," the mother said. Inside was $50. While I hugged them, my husband slipped away to pay the departure tax.

Flying over the high peaks of Rarotonga, we saw the white waves crashing on the reef below. Tomorrow would be another day. Our God would provide for those needs when the time came.

Faye Momoisea, a New Zealander, serves with YWAM in the Cook Islands.

Wednesday

"Test me in this," says the Lord Almighty, "and see if I will not throw open the floodgates of heaven and pour out so much blessing that you will not have room enough for it." Malachi 3:10

Loren Cunningham, YWAM's founder, came to Norway in 1972, challenging young Christians to witness during the Olympic Games in Munich. I took the challenge, and it changed my life.

It was wonderful to see people in the streets of Munich, longing for God's love, and receiving it right then and there. I experienced the Lord working through me with His love. I wanted to give my life completely to serving Him, so a few months after returning from Munich, I quit my regular job and joined YWAM in Oslo.

I sold my flat, and had the choice to buy a car or give the money to YWAM's School of Evangelism, recently founded in central Norway. I believed the Lord challenged me out of Malachi to bring the whole tithe to Him, and test His provision. So I gave the money, and trusted God to provide for me.

He was faithful! Within a few months, I received from others the entire amount! And money continued to come in: so much that I had to give some away. My family didn't understand what I was doing, nor did they agree with it. They were amazed. My brother and sister came to the Lord during that time. They saw that He renewed my life, and they wanted to get to know Him, too.

What about my need for a car? Early that autumn, I was given the opportunity to borrow a car. I found it much better than owning one.

Ingjerd Omdal, a Norwegian, is married to Sigurd Omdal, a YWAM base director in Norway.

Thursday

It is the Lord who goes before you; He will be with you, He will not fail you or forsake you; do not fear or be dismayed.   Deuteronomy 31:8 RSV

It was late afternoon in our office in Los Angeles, 36 hours before my husband, Jim, and I were to fly to Asia, when my phone rang.

It was a woman on the East Coast, who said, "I've never done this before with anyone, but the fear of God is on me, and I'm to ask you if you have your expenses paid for your trip to Asia?"

After asking her to wait, I asked Jim the same question. He did some quick reckoning and said we were short by $2,000.

The woman said that very amount would be sent to us immediately. After expressing our deep gratitude for her obvious obedience to the Lord on our behalf, we praised God for yet another manifestation of His faithfulness to us.

During the ten days we were in Korea, Jim discovered that he had miscalculated our expenses for the trip by $500. We simply committed the need to the Lord.

One day, a friend told us that several months previously, God had impressed upon her to give me a certain amount of money. She didn't have it to give at the time, but told the Lord she would certainly give it whenever it was released to her. Just as she was boarding the plane to go to Korea, our friend was handed that exact amount. She knew it was for me, and handed me a check for...you've guessed it, $500.

No one knew of these needs except God.

Joy Dawson, a former New Zealander but an American citizen for many years, is an international Bible teacher.

Friday

Always be prepared to give an answer to everyone who asks you to give the reason for the hope that you have. I Peter 3:15

It was strictly forbidden to bring Bibles into China, but after delivering my 80 pounds of the precious Scriptures to my contact from the local church, I was able to keep the ten copies of the gospels to distribute myself. We were now on the train leaving China, and I still had two copies left. I wondered who God might arrange to receive them.

Behind me sat two Communist Chinese soldiers. *I'd sure like to leave the gospels with them, Lord,* I prayed silently.

Personal cassette players were new during this trip in the early 1980s. Sometimes strangers would stop me, point to the headset, and want to examine mine. *Will it work again?* I wondered.

I slipped the headphones over my ears and started the music. I sensed the eyes of the soldiers on me. *They've probably never seen one of these before,* I thought. It didn't take long. The soldiers' heads were moving closer to mine. They were trying to learn what I was doing. Exactly what I wanted. *Just wait a little longer,* I told myself. Get their curiosity really hyped.

I turned and offered to let them listen. One of the soldiers slipped on the headphones. The sound of contemporary Christian music reached his ears. He smiled. Soon his partner wanted a turn. *If only they knew what they're listening to!* I thought. *Minister to their spirits, Lord. It's Your Word they're hearing.*

When the train reached the border, they returned the cassette player, and I reached into my pocket and pulled out the dog-eared gospels. I pointed out the English and Chinese on opposing pages, indicating these books could help them to learn English. Only after I got off the train and across the border would they discover the biblical texts.

David Caruso, an American, works in the mission field of the film industry in Hollywood, California, USA.

Saturday

As they were walking along the road, a man said to him, "I will follow you wherever you go." Jesus replied, "Foxes have holes and birds of the air have nests, but the Son of Man has no place to lay his head."   Luke 9:57-58

Ordinarily, when an outreach team arrives at their mission point, a local missionary is at the airport to greet them and has housing arranged for the group. But when our team from Belize landed in Kingston, Jamaica, no one was there to greet us or show us where to spend the night.

Upon calling the YWAM base, we found out that someone with a van would meet us in the morning to take us to the other side of the island. There was nothing that could be done that night. After hanging up the phone, we tried to decide what to do. We were on a very tight budget and had nowhere to sleep.

The team leader asked the airline agent if we could lay out our sleeping bags around the ticket counter. He said that would be fine. I remember sleeping fitfully, and being awakened occasionally by people walking around. Finally, dawn came.

As the morning sun shone in, we were struck by the words on the wall behind us. It was a catchy bit of advertising which read, "Challenge Airlines—Will You Accept the Challenge?"

We laughed at first, then I thought about how it could apply to the Great Commission. That slogan became God's Word to us regarding our work in Jamaica.

Glenn Martin, a Canadian, serves as the director of YWAM Belize.

Sunday

Meditation

Therefore, as God's chosen people, holy and dearly loved, clothe yourselves with compassion, kindness, humility, gentleness and patience. Bear with each other and forgive whatever grievances you may have against one another. Forgive as the Lord forgave you. And over all these virtues put on love, which binds them all together in perfect unity.

Colossians 3:12-14

Monday

Since you are my rock and my fortress, for the sake of Your name lead and guide me.   Psalm 31:3

On our outreach, we were helping a church finish their new building. They asked me to work on the roof—40 feet from the ground. I'm scared to death of heights. Anything over ten feet, and you can do it yourself! But I suppressed my fears and climbed onto the roof.

When I turned to go down the ladder, I noticed it had been moved. The only way down was to walk 50 feet along a 12-inch steel beam, 40 feet from the ground. I was paralyzed with fright.

The more I hesitated, the more my friends on the ground teased me. I was embarrassed, but still couldn't move. The job foreman came and kindly, gently led me down.

The next morning during my quiet time, I remembered the incident. I was still embarrassed, but God reminded me of the concern on the foreman's face. God said, "The foreman represented the exact way I was feeling. I wasn't laughing at you; I was concerned. I saw that you were scared, and I didn't think it was funny. Through that man, I came to help you."

I still cannot tell that story without crying. God proved to me that He will always be there when we need Him, because He cares.

Stan Richardson, an American, and his wife, Jane, are house parents for YWAM's Living Alternatives maternity home in Tyler, Texas, USA.

Tuesday

If you confess with your mouth, "Jesus is Lord," and believe in your heart that God raised him from the dead, you will be saved.   Romans 10:9

When our family of six served as missionaries in New Zealand, we hosted a Bible club in our home each Thursday at 6:15 p.m. Each week, Ranui, a wiry eight-year-old boy, ran to huddle in our doorway immediately after school. He always waited there—not so patiently—for the club to begin.

After Ranui came to his first Bible club meeting, he checked a Bible out of the school library and carried it everywhere he went. One Thursday, Ranui was sitting in our doorway, reading aloud from the book of Revelation. His expressionless words drifted into the kitchen where I was preparing dinner: "And then I saw a new heaven and a new earth...."

Ranui raced into the kitchen and blurted, "Sharon, there's gonna be a new heaven!" His enthusiasm was contagious, and I stopped cooking.

"Yes, Ranui," I said, "and do you know who gets to go there?"

We moved into the living room, which was filled with my four children plus about five neighborhood children, but Ranui and I barely noticed the noise as we explored God's plan of salvation in the Bible.

We finally came to Romans 10:9, and when Ranui read it, he broke into a grin. This was what he had been waiting for.

"I want to be saved!" he declared.

We knelt beside the couch, and Ranui put his finger on the verse in Romans, his little, brown face turned toward heaven. He said the Scripture aloud as his prayer, glancing at the Bible after each phrase, "because I'll forget the words if I don't read it."

And a new child entered the Kingdom of God.

Sharon Brookshire, an American, serves with her family on staff with YWAM Publishing in Lindale, Texas, USA.

Wednesday

For God, who said, "Let light shine out of darkness," made his light shine in our hearts to give us the light of the knowledge of the glory of God in the face of Christ.   *II Corinthians 4:6*

It was 7:30 a.m. on July 11, 1991, on the big island of Hawaii. Darkness reigned for almost five minutes during a total eclipse of the sun. The entire process took about two hours. It was probably one of the most spectacular natural wonders in our lifetime. The next total solar eclipse over this island will not be until the year 2106.

About 60,000 visitors, astronomers, and scientists swarmed to Hawaii. Five thousand new rental vehicles and fifty tour buses were imported to accommodate them. Our YWAM staff and students had a wonderful opportunity to share Christ on the streets or anywhere people waited to see this phenomenon.

As the silhouette of the moon moved slowly across the face of the sun, the Holy Spirit reminded me of how our sin blocks out the light of God. Sin brought darkness into the world. The good news is that Jesus is the Light of the world, and those who follow Him will not walk in darkness but will have the light of life.

As servants of the Lord, we are called to be light to the world, but when we make sinful choices, we are blocking the light of glory which shines through us. Until we are willing to repent, we will not be able to let that light shine in its fullness.

Bernie Tsao, an American, leads the AquaCulture Technology School at the University of the Nations, Kona, Hawaii, USA.

Thursday

My dove in the clefts of the rock, in the hiding places on the mountainside, show me your face, let me hear your voice; for your voice is sweet, and your face is lovely.   Song of Solomon 2:14

I was 18 years old, a new Christian, and was traveling alone halfway around the world to the island of Guam to do missionary work.

My plans were to start university immediately after this trip to Guam. *My plans* were to study psychology and social work so I could help people.

Now I was in an airplane over the Pacific Ocean en route to join an organization I had only heard of two months before. I was going to be doing something I'd never heard of—evangelism! In fact, I'd never even been on an airplane before.

While in Guam, I learned something that opened up a whole new life for me: God speaks to His people! He spoke to me! He wanted to be involved in my life. Up to this point, I thought God was far away and uninterested in my life. God showed me that He heard *my voice* and wanted a personal relationship with *me*. And amazingly, He wanted to use my life to be a blessing to the nations. Never in my wildest dreams did I imagine the plans that God would have for this 18-year-old midwestern girl.

After my training in Guam, I joined a team that went to Manila, Philippines, to help pioneer a ministry among the poor "squatter" people of the inner city. We brought the hope of Jesus to people who had no hope, love to children who had never been loved, food to the hungry, and clothing for those who were naked. That little "squatter" community now has a church. Young people we introduced to Jesus are now missionaries and evangelists.

I'm 29 now, and have been in full-time ministry ever since that time. God continues to speak to me and direct the details of my life. I am so glad I learned that He still speaks to His children, and that I followed His path and not my plans.

Michelle Drake, an American, served on staff with Youth With A Mission in the Philippines in the early 1980s. She is now on staff with YWAM in Seattle, Washington, USA.

Friday

I will bless her with abundant provisions.   *Psalm 132:15*

For two years, I had enjoyed working full-time at the national YWAM office in Norway, traveling with teams, working at the national office, and living in a house fellowship in Oslo. I longed to experience the reality of God in a setting outside YWAM. The Lord led me to a teacher training college far up north in Norway. The school would last three years.

It would be a tough place for a Christian to be; I would be surrounded by people involved in political activism and immorality. In a few months, the school would start, and I would need money for books, clothes, travel expenses, and an apartment.

It would not be difficult to get a loan from the state, but I felt that the Lord said I would miss a blessing if I did. I decided to trust Him as I had while I was with YWAM.

While I was waiting for God's provision, a friend decided to visit for the weekend. I was looking forward to seeing her again, but I had no money. I tried to figure out how to make her visit special. When I still hadn't received any money by Thursday, I made plans to bake bread for my friend—at least I had the ingredients for that. But I kept praying.

On Friday, two hours before the shops closed, I got a letter in the mail with 200 Norwegian Kroner. My friend and I had a great weekend. And I had the assurance that God would provide for my needs.

Ingjerd Omdal, a Norwegian, is married to Sigurd Omdal, a YWAM base director in Norway.

Saturday

I planted the seed, Apollos watered it, but God made it grow.

I Corinthians 3:6

Misha McClung was attending university in Amsterdam, and was praying for several of her friends to come to the Lord. Misha invited each one to her parents' home and witnessed to them. One of these friends was a young Romanian man we'll call Ivan. By the time Misha graduated, none of these friends had given their lives to God. She was deeply disappointed, but continued to pray that God would pursue them with His love.

A while later, I was with three other YWAMers on a train near Budapest, Hungary. A young man joined us in our compartment, and we soon started talking with him. Before long, we learned that he had been in the home of Floyd McClung in Amsterdam several times, but it was clear that he didn't know Jesus. His name was Ivan.

Though my friends were planting seeds of the Gospel in Ivan's heart, I felt an urgency to do more. Before Ivan got off the train, I had shared the entire message of the Gospel with him.

Several months later, I saw Floyd McClung at a conference, and shared about my conversation with Ivan. Floyd was excited, and shared what had happened years earlier.

When Misha heard about our meeting with Ivan, she was thrilled to have tangible evidence that God loved her friends enough to keep pursuing them, and that He loved her enough to let her know what He was doing.

Peter Caruso, an American, pastors in the USA, and travels often to preach and teach in churches and missions.

Sunday

Meditation

It was not by their sword that they won the land, nor did their arm bring them victory; it was your right hand, your arm, and the light of your face, for you loved them.
I do not trust in my bow, my sword does not bring me victory; but you give us victory over our enemies, you put our adversaries to shame.
In God we will make our boast all day long, and we will praise your name forever.

Psalm 44:3,6-8

Monday

Trust in the Lord with all your heart and lean not on your own understanding; in all your ways acknowledge him, and he will make your paths straight.

Proverbs 3:5-6

An important aspect of timing and the will of God is waiting for God's opportunity. In college, I played basketball. My team was especially eager one season to play against the University of Florida because one of their players was being considered as an All-American. We expected a tall and muscular player, but to our surprise, he wasn't. Indeed, from first appearances there seemed to be little that was remarkable about him.

As the game commenced, I noticed that he wasn't even fast on his feet. But he possessed an uncanny ability to be in the right place at the right time. If a team was moving one way and the ball bouncing another, he was right there where the ball was. His hands were up to catch the ball when they should be, and if it came bouncing to the floor, he was there to pick it up. It made him a great player.

God wants us to be like that basketball player. He wants us to have the spiritual alertness that puts us in the right place at the right time when the Spirit is wanting to do something.

As we seek His direction, we need to distinguish between the right thing to do and the right time to do it. God may put a plan or desire in our hearts, but we should not presume that means we do it immediately. God may be preparing our hearts, and we are to take plenty of time to think, discuss, and ponder what He is stirring in our hearts.

Floyd McClung, an American, directs Leadership Development Programs for YWAM. He lives in California, USA.

From *Basic Discipleship* by Floyd McClung. Copyright © 1990 by Floyd McClung. Published by InterVarsity Press, Downers Grove, Illinois. Used by permission [from page 68].

Tuesday

Will you not revive us again, that your people may rejoice in you?

Psalm 85:6

When my friend Floyd finished preaching and called for repentance, I was the first to my feet. During the message, I had seen myself clearly, and I was ashamed. I publicly confessed my sin that day, and asked the others at the conference for prayer.

What was my sin? Embezzlement? Adultery? No, the Holy Spirit was convicting me of the sin of unbelief. In that stark moment of honesty, I realized that I really had low expectations of what God would do in my city.

What do you expect God to do in your city? Or, to put it another way, who is your God? Is He the God of the Bible? Your God is only as big as what you expect of Him in space and time.

What do you expect God to do here on earth in this generation? Don't tell me about the God of your theology. It's easy to say that He's all-powerful, but do you expect Him to do powerful things here and now?

The God of the Bible is the God who sweeps in like a mighty, rushing wind. He answers by fire. He is the God of great awakenings and generation-wide revivals.

John Dawson, a New Zealander, is YWAM's International Director of Urban Missions.

From *Taking Our Cities for God* by John Dawson. Copyright © 1989 by John Dawson. Published by Creation House, Lake Mary, Florida. Used by permission [from pages 57-58].

Wednesday

So is my word that goes out...it will not return to me empty.

Isaiah 55:11

During a visit to a museum in Siberia, we asked Tanya, our tour guide, about the many paintings of churches.

"There is only one church here now," she said. "Only a few old people believe in God."

Our leader, Gary, told her we knew of thousands of young believers in Moscow and Leningrad. He explained that they meet in secret, in the forest.

"Young people? Believe in God?" she asked, amazed.

"Yes, and we're all believers, too," he confided. "God sent us here to tell a young tour guide named Tanya that He loves her very much."

"You're the first person who ever told me that," she said.

Gary began an impromptu interview, asking Barb (another team member) to tell about the character of God. Then he motioned to me and said, "Here's one who nearly jumped from a tall building because she didn't think there was meaning to life."

"It's true," I said, and shared my testimony. Egbert from Holland, and Dorothea from Germany, also shared about meeting Jesus and the changes that resulted in their lives.

Tanya told us she was an avid believer in Lenin, even worshiped him. She found it hard to believe that God could even exist, but claimed to be an honest seeker of truth.

Gary suggested she try a scientific experiment: to say, "God, if You are real, reveal Yourself to me."

She refused, explaining, "I can't make that statement with unbelief that God could exist."

Tanya accepted the Bible we offered, promising to read it "for literary reasons, not for the same purposes as you." But she didn't realize that God's Word never returns to Him void.

Dawn Gauslin, an American, is the International Coordinator for YWAM's field-based Leadership Training Schools. She is also an assistant to Darlene Cunningham.

Thursday

As a mother comforts her child, so will I comfort you; and you will be comforted over Jerusalem.   Isaiah 66:13

Only days before I was to leave Guatemala and return to the United States, my mail finally caught up with me. For the first time in three months, I got news from home. The letters from my family stunned me. My mother had suffered a heart attack on Christmas Day and had been hospitalized for about a week. But, according to my sister, Mom was doing fine.

Six weeks, I thought. *It's been six weeks since Mom had her heart attack, and I've only now found out.* A leaden weight seemed to settle down over my heart. Three months of wonderful ministry suddenly paled as I pictured Mom lying in a hospital bed with all the impersonal tubes, wires, and paraphernalia that accompanied a heart attack. Even though the letters assured me that it had been only a minor heart attack, I imagined the worst. *What if she had another? What if even now, she lay dying?* I felt helpless.

I kept to myself, reading and rereading the letters, trying to pray, and all the time, I wondered if being a missionary was worth being separated from my family. I knew the standard answers. I could quote Bible verses and I'd read books that testified of His intimate care. But nothing I prayed, nothing I read, could break through the burden of worry, fear, and grief.

Finally I asked some friends to pray with me. As I closed my eyes, I cried out to God, *Hear them!*

The change was immediate. Suddenly, I was free of the weight on my heart. Even later, as I reread the letters, the joy and peace remained. The circumstances, I realized, had not changed—I had. Through the prayers of my friends, God had entered into my situation and was assuring me that He was in control.

Now, I was able to pray, so I committed Mom into God's care. Even though it was two weeks before I was able to talk to Mom and hear her tell me she was fine, I never lost God's peace.

Jim Shaw, an American, is the editor of YWAM's *Personal Prayer Diary,* and is an editor with YWAM Publishing in Lindale, Texas, USA.

Friday

In addition to all this, take up the shield of faith, with which you can extinguish all the flaming arrows of the evil one.　　　　*Ephesians 6:16*

A good soldier never goes into battle unprepared. A man in the midst of strife who has been struck by an arrow does not reach for his shield to remove it. Once the arrow has struck, it is too late to use the shield.

Yet many of us react in this manner regarding our shield of faith. We wait until after the enemy's arrow has pierced our flesh to reinforce our faith. When we find ourselves in this position, we need to enlist the urgent help of those around us to pray and counsel together.

The shield of faith must be in position at all times; only then can it truly protect us. By knowing God's Word and trusting it, we can build our faith in God before we encounter adversity.

Paul Marsh, from England, serves as training director for YWAM in Lausanne, Switzerland.

Saturday

Carry each other's burdens, and in this way you will fulfill the law of Christ.
Galatians 6:2

I am thankful for the close, loyal friends I work with in Youth With A Mission. We have been encouraged to be accountable to each other over the years and share our struggles. This helps save us from many pitfalls.

Some believe that a spiritual person does not experience temptation. This isn't true. The truly mature man or woman of God readily confesses struggles with temptation. On the other hand, the devil loves to tell us individually how perverted and different we are. He tells us that we are the only person doing what we do. Others have found freedom from sin in Christ, but we are unique and hopeless. We will never be free. These, too, are lies from the enemy. The temptations we experience are common to Christians throughout the world, and their power over us can be diminished.

We all need a select group of friends where we can be honest with each other and share our burdens, our difficulties, and our temptations. Often victory comes only after we confess our struggles and our friends pray for us and accept us in love. This is a humbling experience, but one which allows us to walk free of the powerful drive behind our sin.

With God's grace, we are able to resist temptation to the point of victory. Jesus taught us to pray regularly: "Lead us not into temptation, but deliver us from evil...." As God leads our lives, He can help us escape heavy temptation.

Dean Sherman, an American, is an international Bible teacher, and lives in the USA.

From *Spiritual Warfare for Every Christian* by Dean Sherman. Copyright © 1990 by Dean Sherman. Published by YWAM Publishing, Seattle, Washington. Used by permission [from pages 144-146].

Sunday

Meditation

No, in all these things we are more than conquerors through him who loved us. For I am convinced that neither death nor life, neither angels nor demons, neither the present nor the future, nor any powers, neither height nor depth, nor anything else in all creation, will be able to separate us from the love of God that is in Christ Jesus our Lord.

Romans 8:37-39

Monday

When the crowds heard Philip and saw the miraculous signs he did, they all paid close attention to what he said.   Acts 8:6

There was a special expectation in my heart as we prayed before ministering that day: *Lord, send Your power upon these teenagers as we preach Your Word and share that You're alive.* We had been performing a pantomime drama in the Philippines. Now we had an opportunity to share at a large Catholic school.

Five boys gathered around me after the performance. Several days earlier, we had visited a nearby village. Many people were healed during that service. News about it had reached these boys who wanted to know more about the God who heals.

One boy asked me if God could heal his sprained wrist. It had an unusual bump on it. He said he'd been unable to write for a week.

"Let's ask God," I said. He was healed instantly. Holding up his hand, he twirled it in amazement. "It's all better!" he shouted. "It's all better!" The bump had vanished.

After witnessing this miracle, the boys were all the more receptive to the call to follow the God who heals the sick and frees the bound.

Nancy Vallese, an American, is the director of the Far East Evangelism teams in Hong Kong.

Tuesday

Even though I walk through the valley of the shadow of death, I will fear no evil, for you are with me.   *Psalm 23:4*

When walking in darkness, we cannot see what lies behind us; neither can we see the next step ahead. Our experiences and all that once was important seems far away. We do not know what is to come.

When the Father allows me to enter the valley of darkness, I don't always understand why. Sometimes I ask, "Lord, why do You allow situations in which I don't see, don't understand, and have nothing to which I can point?" Could Abraham understand why he should sacrifice Isaac? Could Job grasp why everything was being taken from him? These men knew the right thing to do—they worshiped God. They acknowledged that He was worthy, no matter what happened.

God doesn't change even when all of my circumstances change. He is with me even if I don't feel His presence. Therefore, I do not need to be afraid.

I can say, "Father, I do not understand, but I trust You." This helps bring my faith to a higher level. I must trust God, not for what He can do for me, but because my trust is rooted in His character.

Annemarie Lechner, an Austrian, is involved in the leadership of YWAM in Austria.

Wednesday

I will instruct you and teach you in the way you should go.   Psalm 32:8

We knew our long trip from California to Minnesota would be slowed by our large, new motor home. We also knew it would eliminate the need to pay hotel fees and restaurant bills.

We were only one state from our destination when the motor home refused to move. We soon discovered we were in the town where the vehicle had been manufactured. After having it towed to the repair garage, we registered for the repairs, then settled down to wait.

A young woman called our name and said quietly, "Pretend I have to show you something, and follow me." Once outside, she told us that she had seen our Bible. "I need help. Will you meet me in the parking lot at 4:30? We'll have to keep your vehicle overnight anyway." We agreed.

That afternoon, in the privacy of our motor home, we learned that this young woman had become a Christian only six weeks earlier. Her family members were harassing her. Her husband, an alcoholic, was threatening to harm her.

Our prayers were interrupted by the shouts and threats of her drunken husband. We hadn't realized that it was already 8:30 p.m. The gates were locked, but he had convinced the guard on duty to open the gate. After we got him calmed down, we shared Christ with him. In only an hour, he received Christ.

Three years have passed since that unexpected layover. We're still receiving letters from the young couple, letters that tell of them happily serving the Lord together.

Phyllis Coulombe, an American, works as a conference assistant at Richardson Springs, California, USA.

Thursday

God chose the foolish things of the world to shame the wise.

Carrying a large cross down a city street is not a conventional means of doing personal evangelism. It wasn't that my friend Chris and I wanted to be odd; we were simply obeying our hearts. We knew that, if nothing else, the cross could be a reminder of the way Jesus suffered for others.

We were about to go home when some teenage girls in a pickup truck across the street began yelling and making fun of us. We could have kept going, ignoring the mocking girls. Instead, we laid the cross down and crossed the street. I asked them what they were doing away from home so late at night.

"Just cruisin' for fun," one answered sarcastically.

I prayed a quick, silent prayer. Somehow, the conversation gradually turned toward Jesus. Before long, the girls poured out a tale of sorrow. Their father was in the hospital in a coma, dying with cancer.

We prayed with the girls that evening, and we watched their sad countenances change to joy. Then they asked us to visit their father in the hospital. A few days later, we did.

Despite the fact that he was in a coma, we felt that the Lord could cause him to hear. We shared Christ with him, and asked him to squeeze his hand if he wanted to pray to become a Christian. What a joy to lead this man to Jesus just a few days before he entered eternity.

Stephen Beiter, an American, works on maintenance staff at Richardson Springs, California, USA.

Friday

And the things you have heard me say in the presence of many witnesses entrust to reliable men who will also be qualified to teach others.

II Timothy 2:2

As Christians, we need to constantly examine ourselves. Are we living in such a relationship with our Lord and our fellow men that we can challenge others to follow our example?

There were "many witnesses" to Paul and Timothy's committed relationship to one another who saw the quality and depth of exchange in their lives. Sharing and openness of this nature requires an investment of time to work through problems, to share joys, and to discover the ways of God together. All of us are in need of this type of relationship.

We need a "Paul" in our lives who loves us enough to encourage us, exhort us, and to speak the truth in love. And we need to be humble enough to accept that strong kind of love gratefully.

How much time and how many mistakes could be spared if only we were open to receive help in this manner? As we receive, we can grow in the knowledge of God and His ways. We can learn to trust these things to others, and to challenge them to a life of holiness before the Lord.

We need the type of relationship Paul and Timothy had, then trust that those who learn from us will pass it on to other "faithful men."

Written by an American working in Asia.

Saturday

But Samuel replied: "Does the Lord delight in burnt offerings and sacrifices as much as in obeying the voice of the Lord? To obey is better than sacrifice, and to heed is better than the fat of rams."   I Samuel 15:22

At the YWAM base in Neah Bay, Washington, a group was preparing to travel to the western tip of Alaska for a special day of prayer. I was busy, didn't have the money to go, and didn't relish the extreme cold, so I never seriously considered being part of the team.

The prayer team needed a worship leader, so they asked me to go. I explained why it was impossible for me to be part of the team, but when they asked me to at least pray about it, I grudgingly agreed.

At 4:30 on the afternoon before the team left, I was kneeling in the bathroom, caulking the floor. I realized that I'd never really prayed about joining the team.

I lifted up a hurried prayer, "Lord, You know how I feel, but if You want me to go, I want to be willing to go. If I should go, please confirm it by providing the money this afternoon." I knew I hadn't given God much time to provide.

Thirty minutes later, a girl ran up to me and said, "One of the team members had to drop out, but he's made his ticket available. Has God spoken to you yet?"

My heart seemed to stop when she said that. I told her about my prayer, put away my tools, and packed my suitcase and guitar.

The trip wasn't easy, but as we looked across the Bering Strait into Russia, I realized that sometimes God asks me to do the very thing that is furthest from my mind. He just asks that I be available.

Ben Bradley, an American, was on staff in Neah Bay, Washington, USA.

Sunday

Meditation

Create in me a pure heart, O God, and renew a steadfast spirit within me.
You do not delight in sacrifice, or I would bring it; you do not take pleasure in burnt offerings. The sacrifices of God are a broken spirit; a broken and contrite heart, O God, you will not despise.

Psalm 51:10,16-17

Monday

Blessed [be] the God and Father of our Lord Jesus Christ, the Father of sympathy (pity and mercies) and the God [Who is the Source] of every consolation and comfort and encouragement. II Corinthians 1:3 Amp.

I had been married for 13 years, had four children, and was beginning my tenth year of ministry with YWAM when suddenly, with no previous symptoms, I woke up one day paralyzed on my left side. The doctor's diagnosis was a tumor in the center of my brain. Although it was benign, doctors predicted that I would have about six months to live before the mass burst. Surgery could mean either permanent paralysis or mental impairment.

Christians around the world prayed. After only a few days in the hospital, I felt two jolts go through my left leg. Within 15 minutes, I was able to stand—feebly. Within a short time, I was walking.

The threat of recurrence, however, shadowed this miracle. During months of uncertainty, I learned that my comfort is by God and from God. Comfort based on anything else is unstable.

I learned an important lesson from Joy Dawson's book, *Some of the Ways of God in Healing.* She wrote that God's grace is the divine ability to cope in difficult circumstances with praise on our lips, peace in our minds, and joy in our hearts. Joy says that grace is every bit as miraculous as the power of God in the most dramatic healings.

It is this grace that I discovered in the months following my crisis. My situation has not changed. But I have gained an overwhelming peace, knowing that I am completely and safely in God's hands.

Diana Gaines and her husband, Kip, both Americans, lead YWAM training programs in Tyler, Texas, USA.

Tuesday

And there is no God apart from me, a righteous God and a Savior....

Isaiah 45:21

When my wife, Diana, awoke paralyzed on her left side, I wasn't sure how to go on. The doctors finally found the cause—a brain tumor—and I cried out to God to heal her. Many people joined us in prayer and fasting, but no instantaneous healing occurred. In January, 1992, the doctors gave Diana six months to live.

I kept praying for Diana to be healed, refusing to believe that God would want anything else. After all, how could I do the things He had called me to do if I had to take care of our four children by myself?

God was merciful, and revealed my selfish attitude to me. I had to come to grips with the fact that God does not exist for the well-being of Kip. He is not obligated to do everything I need for my comfort. I repented of my selfishness, and asked God to work His character in me.

The six months came and went. Each day, I have awakened feeling like I have a rock in my stomach. I love Diana so much that I can't bear the thought of being without her. But God is faithful to give me grace day by day.

Why doesn't God bring perfect healing? I don't know about that, but I do know that He is just in all His ways and kind in all His doings. As I continue to love and serve Him, He is always with me.

I can truly say that I am not a victim of my circumstances—I am victorious, abiding in the shadow of the Almighty.

Kip Gaines and his wife, Diana, both Americans, lead YWAM training programs in Tyler, Texas, USA.

Wednesday

The peace of God, which transcends all understanding, will guard your hearts and your minds in Christ Jesus.　　　　　*Philippians 4:7*

The thatch-roofed bamboo house was built in a clearing cut out of a jungle in northern Thailand. Several iron and tin cooking utensils were piled on the floor nearby. Two faded advertising posters pinned to the wall, one in English, the other in Thai, provided the only visible color.

In this country of 300,000 Buddhist monks and 20,000 temples, fewer than 100,000 people claim to be Christians. To be a Christian results in the loss of one's nationality. Frequently it means the loss of all family ties.

A couple had brought me to this hut in this small village. I watched the wife, her back bent almost double from daily carrying heavy loads of bananas and vegetables up and down the steep mountain paths. Her teeth were brown from chewing beetle nuts. But her contagious smile confirmed the reality of her words: "I know there are ghosts [she was referring to evil spirits], but I'm not afraid of them because I have Jesus with me."

After I said goodbye and left the village, I thought of her smile. I recalled the peace in her eyes. I knew she faced daily danger, not only from national enemies but also from her non-Christian neighbors.

Yet the peace that reigned in her heart, the joy expressed in her smile, and the confidence of her words all conveyed freedom beyond political security and safety. The ancient Thai woman knew the Peacemaker.

June Coxhead Dooney, a New Zealander, is an author and a radio talk show host for Radio Rhema in Auckland, New Zealand.

Thursday

Ah, Sovereign Lord, you have made the heavens and the earth by your great power and outstretched arm. Nothing is too hard for you.

Jeremiah 32:17

It was a normal work day for me. I carefully reviewed the job: materials ordered, equipment in place. I used the earth-moving machine to prepare the ground for the new building's foundation.

To add strength to a building, long bars of steel are laid in place before the concrete is poured. Each steel bar must be tied in place. I took pride in doing my job well.

To my surprise, I was lacking a 4.25-inch piece of steel bar. As I glanced at my watch, I panicked. The concrete truck was scheduled to arrive in just minutes. *And they're always on time,* I thought.

I breathed prayer for help. "I only need a little piece, Lord."

My spirit heard a gentle, "It's all right, Dave, I'll fix it."

At the supplier's, I couldn't find any short pieces. In fact, the shortest was twenty feet long! I resigned myself to buying the twenty-foot length, and reached for my wallet. No wallet! It must be back on the job site.

I felt sick. My day and my job seemed to be falling apart.

I apologized to the salesman and turned to leave. "Wait, I'll see what I can do," he offered.

We went out back to the pile of steel bars. There on the ground was a small piece of steel. I was sure it hadn't been there before. I bent to pick it up, and said to the salesman, "Don't laugh, but this is all I need."

"Take it," he said.

I made it back to the job site before the cement truck arrived. I was actually afraid to measure the piece for fear it would seem disrespectful to the Lord. I did anyway.

Laughter sprang from my being. "It's right on, isn't it?" I sensed Him say.

Dave Clowser, an American, works as a campus service director at Richardson Springs, California, USA.

Friday

Always give yourselves fully to the work of the Lord, because you know that your labor in the Lord is not in vain.   *I Corinthians 15:58*

I had asked God to place me beside a person He wanted me to witness to during the flight. I took my assigned seat and fell into conversation with the young lady by the window. She was from Baguio, Philippines, where I'd lived for ten happy years. Juanita's parents had helped pay her trip to Hong Kong to find a job. Now she was fleeing from a cruel employer and wondering how her parents would react to her sudden reappearance.

Although she listened to the Gospel, she didn't give me the impression she wanted to give her life to God. Before we landed, I simply asked if I could pray a general prayer with her. It was the type I attempt to pray even with those who haven't responded to the Gospel—a simple prayer asking God to help them understand the message I have just shared.

Two years later I received a letter from Juanita. She wrote about my "leading her to Christ" on that Philippine Airlines flight. She now lived in the Middle East and was asking for tracts to distribute! I puzzled over that for several months until a friend shared the following: "We come to Christ when we say 'yes' to God, not when we pray the sinner's prayer."

Sometimes we can be doing good without realizing it—hence the encouragement of today's verse to always give ourselves fully to the work of the Lord.

Ross Tooley, a New Zealander, serves at large on the staff of the College of Christian Ministries of University of the Nations, Kona, Hawaii, USA.
Adapted from *We Cannot But Tell,* by Ross Tooley, revised edition. Copyright © 1993 by Ross Tooley. Published by YWAM Publishing, Seattle, Washington. Used by permission [from pages 127-128].

Saturday

You did not choose me, but I chose you to go and bear fruit—fruit that will last.
John 15:16

"There are no other places to look," I sighed. "It's hard to find a place to house and feed 60 people on such short notice." We were pioneering a new YWAM base in Montevideo, Uruguay, and were desperately trying to find housing for a group of Brazilians who would arrive for an outreach within eight weeks.

Every avenue we tried seemed to be a dead end. Public schools were prohibited from helping Christian organizations. Since YWAM was still unknown in Uruguay, pastors were unwilling to help. A Catholic retreat center seemed promising, but they would charge $10 per person per night, and our budget was for $2 per person. We had run out of options.

When our staff gathered for prayer, we felt that God wanted us to contact the retreat center director once again. This time, she was helpful and interested, but could only bring the price down to $5 per person.

"That's her best offer," I told the rest of our leadership group. "It means we would need $3,600 more for the twenty-day outreach." Without a fully supplied facility, we would still need to buy kitchen and sleeping supplies. Should we go for the retreat center and trust God to bring the funds in when needed?

We asked the Lord to let us know whether to reserve the retreat center by sending $20 for the reservation fee. That same day, we received that amount from a friend who knew nothing of the need.

The Brazilians arrived on the first day of the outreach, most without their outreach fees. This is common in Latin America, where Christian workers usually don't have much income and trust God daily to meet their needs. We prayed daily for the spiritual success of the outreach and for the funds to pay our bills.

By the last day of the outreach, we had been able to pay only $900 on our account with the retreat center. But two weeks later, a man from Brazil arrived with a check for $1,000. And 15 days after the outreach, we were able to pay off the entire debt.

Mara Dias de Oliveira, a Brazilian, leads the ministry in Montevideo, Uruguay.

Sunday

Meditation

Listen, I tell you a mystery: We will
not all sleep, but we will all be
changed—in a flash, in the twin-
kling of an eye, at the last trumpet.
For the trumpet will sound, the
dead will be raised imperishable,
and we will be changed. For the
perishable must clothe itself with
the imperishable, and the mortal
with immortality. When the perishable has been clothed with the imperishable, and the mortal with
immortality, then the saying that is
written will come true: "Death has
been swallowed up in victory."

I Corinthians 15:51-54

Monday

Encourage one another and build each other up.   *I Thessalonians 5:11*

In our marriage, I had to learn that I could not act as the Holy Spirit, bringing conviction to Sally when and where I thought necessary. That is God's job. God has charged me to love and cherish my wife, and to be a living example of His character for her (Ephesians 5:25). I am not called to be her judge. If there are areas of weakness in her life, then I am to pray for her and allow God to bring conviction to her heart—and she must do the same for me.

It is essential that love takes prime place in our relationships. Where there are differences, we must reach out in love to our brother and allow the Holy Spirit to do His convicting work in both our lives. He, after all, is the only One who is able to do this justly, since He knows the thoughts and intents of our heart.

As a father, I also need to seek unity with my two children. Just because they are my children, living in my home, does not permit me to dispense with the principles of love and unity. I cannot rant at them, belittle their feelings and ideas, or do anything that makes them feel less significant or worthwhile than I. Matthew and Misha may belong to a different generation than mine, but they are my brother and sister in Christ. One day we will stand as equals in Christ's presence. I am expected to live in unity with them as fellow believers. This is not always easy, but I have to release them from my expectations and allow them to be themselves—a principle that holds true for every relationship.

Floyd McClung, an American, directs Leadership Development Programs for YWAM. He lives in California, USA.

From *Learning to Love People You Don't Like* by Floyd McClung. Copyright © 1989 by Floyd McClung. Published by YWAM Publishing, Seattle, Washington. Used by permission [from pages 33-34].

Tuesday

Do not worry beforehand about what to say. Just say whatever is given you at the time, for it is not you speaking, but the Holy Spirit.   Mark 13:11

We were on one of our early trips into Russia in 1973. One of our purposes was to take Bibles to give to believers who couldn't get them otherwise.

My friend and I arrived at the Russian border for customs check. When it was my turn, the guard pointed at my suitcase.

"Open it," he ordered.

My heart sank. *How is God going to do this one?* I wondered.

"Bibles!" The guard spat out the word. Reaching into my suitcase, he pulled out one after another. Soon, guards surrounded me and took me off to the side. That first guard screamed at me, "We don't need this Christian garbage! We're going to take these Bibles and burn them."

I stood quietly listening. There was nothing I could say. I could only pray silently for God to bring something good out of this.

After some time, I looked into the guard's eyes and quietly asked, "Do you have a grandmother?"

"Of course I have a grandmother," he snapped.

"Is she a believer?"

His head dropped. He couldn't look me in the eye.

"Yes, she is," he mumbled.

Suddenly this Russian guard had changed from a lion to a lamb.

I said to him, "I imagine your grandmother would like to have one of these more than anything else in the world. How can you talk that way about something that is so precious to her?"

When we were allowed to leave, the guards left a few of our Bibles in our suitcases. Gesturing toward those we were leaving behind, I said quietly to the guard, "Give one of these to your grandmother."

Al Akimoff, an American, directs YWAM's Slavic Ministries.

Wednesday

The king's heart is in the hand of the Lord; he directs it like a watercourse wherever he pleases.   Proverbs 21:1

I was raised with the understanding that the only way to get things done was to "Plan what you do, and do what you've planned." My inflexibility at home and as director of a new YWAM school must have hurt many.

Flexibility was never my strength, but while on the mission field for three years, God had pushed, stretched, and extended my ability to cope. Most of His work in my life came through trials and changes of plans. Flexibility is not enough on its own, but if you stay "fluid," like a body of water, you won't break down under pressure.

I lead a University of the Nations school on aquatic culture, and one night, a power failure caused the death of all my fish. All my plans and hopes (and proud achievements) were gone at once. I had done the best I could, and it wasn't good enough. Circumstances outside my control had wrecked my plans.

The only thing we could do was to start over. If God had not laid the foundation of flexibility in my life during the previous three years, I would have been devastated.

Bernie Tsao, an American, leads the AquaCulture Technology School at the University of the Nations, Kona, Hawaii, USA.

Thursday

"Test me in this," says the Lord Almighty, "and see if I will not throw open the floodgates of heaven and pour out so much blessing that you will not have room enough for it."   Malachi 3:10

I had been with YWAM Brazil for over a year. Six months earlier, my mother had begun sending me regular offerings. They weren't much, but they covered my personal expenses, base fees, and tithe. I'd been praying for supporters and had, little by little, built relationships. In May, two friends began to send small offerings. This was the beginning of God's response to my prayers.

My mother also became involved with YWAM, and completed a Discipleship Training School in the evenings in Belo Horizonte. She got so excited about the Lord during this school that her outlook on the Christian life and on missions changed completely.

At the same time, I was involved in planning an evangelistic crusade in Bolivia. When I mentioned it to Mom, she wanted to participate in the crusade. However, she was directing all her finances to repairing the roof of her house before the summer rains arrived. She wouldn't have enough left to cover her costs for the crusade.

We determined that Mom would stop supporting me during those months and would use that money to go to Bolivia with us. When I returned to Brazil at the end of July, I would trust God to provide my needs. I left for Bolivia at the beginning of June to get things ready for the outreach, not knowing what I'd find in my bank account when I got back.

When we returned to Brazil, I checked my bank account. I was shocked by the total. It contained more money than I normally received. More friends had decided to send support; even my church had begun supporting me.

Mom and I have decided to bless other missionaries, because we have learned that it truly is more blessed to give than to receive.

Alberto Soares Tavares, a Brazilian, leads YWAM's work in Sao Paulo, Brazil.

Friday

When he has brought out all his own, he goes on ahead of them, and his sheep follow him because they know his voice. But they will never follow a stranger; in fact,...they do not recognize a stranger's voice.

John 10:4-5

Most of my life, I have worked with animals. The years I spent as a shepherd have proven valuable in helping me understand some of the farming illustrations in the Scriptures.

The above Scripture is very realistic. As the shepherd walks ahead of the sheep, he talks to them a lot. The sheep quickly learn to recognize their shepherd's voice, and they follow him. He represents security to them. They ignore other voices, responding only to their master. To them, his voice means they follow, and it also means they'll soon see green grass, cool water, and shady spots to rest.

The sheep connect the voice of the shepherd with the contentment of having their needs met. It never seems to occur to them that their shepherd would disappoint them.

It's the same with us as we follow the Good Shepherd. As we learn to recognize His voice and to walk with Him, He is everything we need. We only need to follow Him closely and listen to Him carefully.

Garry Tissingh, a Hollander who grew up in New Zealand, oversees teams in North Africa.

Saturday

For you are not sent to a people of unfamiliar speech and of hard language, but to the house of Israel.   *Ezekiel 3:5 NKJV*

In 1971 I left my home country of New Zealand to attend a Youth With a Mission training school in Lausanne, Switzerland. It was totally life changing. Speakers like Loren Cunningham, Brother Andrew, and Corrie ten Boom filled us with a desire to serve God as missionaries.

My most memorable experience was actually hearing God speak during a small-group prayer for the nations. God called whole prayer circles to pray for different countries. On the days following the end of classes, my fellow students left in teams for exotic places like Morocco, Germany, Spain, and Afghanistan, but I could get no clear direction from God.

I was nineteen years old, and I desperately wanted to be a missionary, preferably in a place like Brazil or New Guinea. Three days after classes finished, I decided to go to Germany because I had some knowledge of German and because I had friends on the pioneering German team, but my spirit was troubled.

"Dear God, just show me what country to go to, and I'll serve You there all my life," was the cry of my heart as I prayed through that day.

The next morning I awoke with the Scripture reference of Ezekiel 3:5 firmly implanted in my mind. I had never read the book of Ezekiel, so I had no idea of its content. As I read the Scripture, I knew it was God's word to me.

Throughout that morning, I listened to God. He spoke to me through portions of Scripture and spoke directly into my mind. To my surprise, He called me to the last place I would have considered for missionary service: the United States of America.

John Dawson, a New Zealander, is YWAM's International Director of Urban Missions.
From *Taking Our Cities for God* by John Dawson. Copyright © 1989 by John Dawson. Published by Creation House, Lake Mary, Florida. Used by permission [from pages 146-147].

Sunday

Meditation

Do not judge, and you will not be judged. Do not condemn, and you will not be condemned. Forgive, and you will be forgiven. Give, and it will be given to you. A good measure, pressed down, shaken together and running over, will be poured into your lap. For with the measure you use, it will be measured to you.

Luke 6:37-38

Monday

But whoever drinks the water I give him will never thirst. Indeed, the water I give him will become in him a spring of water welling up to eternal life.
                                                                    John 4:14

It was a balmy Hawaiian evening. My wife, Patti, and I took a walk through town to treat ourselves to ice cream. After window shopping and watching the last rays of an exquisite Hawaiian sunset, we headed for the bus stop. We boarded the double-decker bus and went to the second level.

Only one other person was there—a young man in his early twenties. Somehow I felt I should sit next to him, so Patti took a seat across the aisle. Within a few minutes, I learned that Sione had recently arrived from the Pacific island of Ponopei. He seemed open to the Gospel and in need of Christ. I sensed this must be a divine appointment.

I also realized we would be reaching our destination within 20 minutes. If Sione were to receive Christ in this time, I would need wisdom to communicate the Gospel clearly and bring him to a point of decision quickly.

While Patti prayed, I continued to tell Sione how God loved him and that He would give him a new life. Within minutes, our heads were bowed and Sione was inviting Christ into his heart. After prayer, I gave him some basic instruction on what to do in order to grow spiritually. I recommended a nearby evangelical church for him to attend.

As Patti and I said goodbye to our new brother in Christ and got off the bus, our hearts were filled with praise. In His sovereignty, God had again allowed us the joy of sharing hope and new life with another who "just happened" to pass our way.

Don Hall, an American, is an international Bible teacher and evangelist with YWAM.

Tuesday

Do not cast me away when I am old; do not forsake me when my strength is gone.
Psalm 71:9

I was packing our trailer after a long day of distributing clothing to refugees in a small town in El Salvador when someone asked, "How come that old man didn't get anything?" He pointed.

My tongue felt like lead from speaking all day in an unfamiliar language, and I just wished everyone would quit bothering me. Then I followed the pointing finger and saw Señor Duran.

That morning, I had seen him, looking confused and lost. I asked what he needed, and he replied that he needed clothes. Two buttons held his shirt together; a piece of rope held up patched gray trousers which were much too big in the waist, and too short in the leg. He wore no socks. I asked his name and age.

He straightened and said with dignity, "My name is Señor Miguel Duran. I am 80 years old." I wanted to spend more time talking with him but I had to keep working.

Now Señor Duran was on the verge of tears, disappointment evident on his face. "They didn't give me any clothes."

I ran to the trailer and salvaged the last few pairs of underwear, a T-shirt, and some socks. I also grabbed a gospel booklet and ran to catch Señor Duran as he shuffled out of the park, his old shoulders bent in despair.

"Señor, I'm very sorry you didn't get anything. This isn't much, but well...it's something." As I held out the clothes, his eyes opened wide, and he reached out his large, bony hands for them.

"Oh, thank you, thank you. God will repay you. God bless you." Tears flowed down his wrinkled cheeks as he looked up at me. I was suddenly embarrassed, and quickly said goodbye.

I had traveled 2,000 miles to give an old man some underwear. Was it worth it? Señor Duran was blessed, but I received something far greater—God had taught me a lesson in compassion.

Jim Shaw, an American, is the editor of YWAM's *Personal Prayer Diary,* and is an editor with YWAM Publishing in Lindale, Texas, USA.

Wednesday

...Your Father knows what you need before you ask him.   *Matthew 6:8*

As part of our YWAM school outreach, our team was doing construction work at another YWAM base. Because funds were low, we had eaten very little for three days. We were tired and weak; some even had diarrhea.

Edwardo, our leader from Ghana, West Africa, was leading our daily prayer time. When we asked the Lord what He wanted us to pray about, we each felt we should pray for provisions for the kitchen.

"Why don't we pray specifically?" I asked. So we asked the Lord to provide meat, crates of vegetables, sacks of rice, and so forth, being careful to mention the name of each item.

About two hours after we prayed, a van drove up, and I ran out to meet it. Peering into the windows, I called excitedly to my friends to help unload the van. What fun it was to carry tomatoes, cucumbers, green peppers, sugar, rice, and beans into the kitchen.

I looked around for the meat we had requested, but didn't see any. Just then, a pickup truck arrived with a huge package. Inside was half a pig, given to us by a neighbor.

How we thanked the Lord—while we carried the food into the kitchen, prepared it, and ate it.

Joao Bosco, a Brazilian, serves on staff in Belo Horizonte, Brazil.

Thursday

Look at the fields! They are ripe for harvest.   John 4:35

A highlight of our time in Gwang Ju, Korea, was on the campus of a university. Leaders of the local Campus Crusade for Christ ministry arranged for us to have outdoor gatherings.

After learning that only a year earlier, riots on this campus had caused the deaths of over 1,000 people, we wondered what kind of response we would see to the Gospel.

Just as we began singing, a nearby loudspeaker blared out another, disruptive message. The 300 people gathered around us strained to hear our message. We each focused our hearts in prayer on individuals. Before we finished our presentation, we realized the competing loudspeaker was now silent.

Breaking up for individual conversations, we were each practically pounced on by clusters of students with questions about God. It didn't take long to realize that the tragedy of the previous year had driven them to consider where their own lives were headed.

"How can Jesus be the same as God?" asked one. "Before Jesus was born on earth, where was He?" asked another. "How can I know God?" and "Tell me about your relationship with God," were heard here and there.

God's preparation in the hearts of the students was apparent in their eagerness. We were simply His instruments of carrying His message to them.

Celia Rawlins, an American, leads Far East Evangelism Teams in Hong Kong, Singapore, and Hawaii. She lives in Oregon, USA.

Friday

Never will I leave you; never will I forsake you.   *Hebrews 13:5*

The pounding rhythm of the van's tires worried me. Would the travel trailer hold up for the 3,000-mile trip from the United States to Guatemala City? My family and I were on our way to lead a short-term outreach.

The previous year, Rios Montt, then Guatemala's President, had called our YWAM base to request workers, Bibles, and survival supplies for his war-torn country. We responded by sending missionaries, Bibles, food, and clothing aboard the m/v *Anastasis*. During that outreach, many Guatemalans received Jesus as their Savior. Now we were to host follow-up teams.

A light rain fell as we wound down the narrow highway. Only three hours remained of our seven-day drive. Suddenly, our van lunged forward. I immediately applied the brakes, glanced in the side mirror, and saw that our trailer was demolished! The truck that hit us was a grotesque twist of metal.

I stepped from the van, praying silently, *Jesus, send help!* As I realized there was probably not one person in the gathering crowd who could speak English, the little Spanish I knew vanished from my memory. But a warmth covered me as words raced through my mind: "I'll be with you to the end of the age."

In just minutes, another truck stopped and an American stepped out. He offered his hand and said, "My name's Bill. Let me take care of the talking." Bill was the answer to my prayer. With his help, everything was settled in only five days.

Later, Bill told me he had not wanted to get involved in another American's accident. But when he started to pass us, "something" made his steering wheel turn to the side of the road.

Andy Huddleston, an American, is a leader in Elm Springs, Arkansas, USA

Saturday

Do you look at things according to the outward appearance?
II Corinthians 10:7 NKJV

The mammoth Olympic medal-winner stood in the crowded train station of an Eastern Siberian city. Two Eastern European athletes accompanying him seemed dwarfed beside him. I introduced myself and began a conversation that would resume many times over the next several days as we traveled on the same train and ship.

Despite Vladimir's intimidating size, he was a gentle man. He shared with us from an open heart. Each time we shared another aspect of the Gospel with him, his answer was, "I don't have enough faith to believe as you do!" Conviction and brokenness was apparent on his face as he considered God's love.

Vladimir seemed most affected by the joy and depth of relationship among our team members. He was amazed to learn that we came from several different countries and varied backgrounds; more so to discover the relative shortness of time we had known one another.

Because of his size, Vladimir was always hungry after finishing meals that would fill a normal-sized man. So at one of our last meals, we combined untouched slices of meat from our tables and took them to Vladimir. Accepting our plateful he said, "God must really be looking after me!"

The memory of Vladimir helps me remember not to judge someone by outward appearance. Those who seem the toughest may have the softest of hearts.

Gary Stephens, an American, is director of YWAM-Hong Kong.

Sunday

Meditation

My soul finds rest in God alone; my salvation comes from him. He alone is my rock and my salvation; he is my fortress, I will never be shaken.
Trust in him at all times, O people; pour out your hearts to him, for God is our refuge.

Psalm 62:1-2,8

Monday

*He has showed you, O man, what is good. And what does the Lord require of you?
To act justly and to love mercy and to walk humbly with your God.*

Micah 6:8

It says in the Bible that "Abraham walked with God...Noah walked with God...Enoch walked with God." When we walk with someone, we can talk to them all the time, even as we're busy with other things. We can talk to the Lord while we are washing dishes, ironing, driving, or taking the train to work. We often overlook times in our schedule when we can be with the Lord. Time management helps us learn to use all our time well and effectively.

When we walk with someone, we can also be silent. In fact, the better we know the person we're walking with, the more relaxed we are in their presence. We often just enjoy being with them. We also listen when we walk with them for whatever they might have to say. As we walk with God through our daily lives, we need to be careful not to miss the joy of being with Him and the opportunity of hearing Him speak to us. We do not have to be down on our knees for Him to speak. He loves to converse with us throughout the day.

Sally McClung, an American, has a ministry of hospitality and speaks internationally. She lives in California, USA.

From *Where Will I Find the Time?* by Sally McClung. Copyright © 1989 by Sally McClung. Published by Harvest House Publishers, Eugene, Oregon. Used by permission [from pages 30-31].

Tuesday

The angel of the Lord encamps around those who fear him, and he delivers them.
Psalm 34:7

Our family set out on a 36-hour train trip across India from Madras to New Delhi. We were excited at the adventure, but we had no idea how eventful our journey would be.

The train to Delhi passes through a jungle area which is notorious for bandits who frequently attack small villages and shopkeepers. We approached this area at midnight when we were all fast asleep.

Our eldest daughter, who was seven at the time, awoke and decided to use the bathroom at the end of our coach. As she walked back, two bandits riding in our car grabbed her and headed for the outside of the train. Still groggy, she didn't resist.

I awoke and instinctively ran toward the door where the bandits were. One man had an arm around my daughter and was perched on the ladder outside the train, ready to jump. The other was crouched beside him, waiting to follow. I grabbed my daughter and began pulling. But the harder I pulled, the harder her captor pulled back.

Finally, with one desperate surge of energy, I yanked her into the car, and the man fell backward off the train. The second man was immediately surrounded by a car full of sleepy, angry passengers. He was arrested at the next stop.

Safely back in our seats, my entire family knelt to thank God for His deliverance. My daughter, still visibly shaken, asked for forgiveness for the man who had tried to kidnap her. She has had no negative effects from the experience, and today, considers it evidence of God's protection.

Tim Svoboda, an American, is National Director of YWAM in India.

Wednesday

There is now no condemnation for those who are in Christ Jesus.

Romans 8:1

During an outreach in Hong Kong, our team had the privilege of staying at Mother's Choice, a maternity home for single women. One 28-year-old woman became our friend as she practiced English. We soon communicated quite well together.

She was full of shame and guilt, feeling she had disgraced herself and her family through her pregnancy. She felt she could never be forgiven.

What a joy it was to be able to share the love and forgiveness of God with her. Jesus died for our sins so we could be reconciled to God, our Father.

We watched as God forgave her and took away her tears and despair. He put a smile on her face, and a testimony of forgiveness on her lips. Our God is an awesome God!

Dee Ross, a Canadian, works with her husband as Mission Builder Coordinators in Richardson Springs, California, USA.

Thursday

Because Thy lovingkindness is better than life, my lips will praise Thee.
Psalm 63:3 NASB

During my Quiet Time, I often sing hymns. I was not raised in an evangelical environment, but became a Christian during the "Jesus Movement" of the early 1970s. I had little exposure to the rich heritage of hymns we have in the Church. One day, however, I purchased several old hymnals and began reading the words to the hymns.

As I read, I was astounded at the depth of understanding and insight about God, His ways, and His character that these hymn writers displayed. I often sing those hymns I know to the Lord during my Quiet Time. Even though my singing does not rival Michael W. Smith or Sandi Patti, God is blessed! I read aloud the hymns I don't know to the Lord, lifting up the words of such great hymn writers as Fanny Crosby, Charles Wesley, and Isaac Watts as praise to the Lord.

There are other times when I sing spiritual songs (Colossians 3:16). A spiritual song is a song that wells up from deep inside my heart, and I spontaneously make up the melody and words. To someone listening, such a song may sound disjointed and childish. Be that as it may, it remains a glorious way to express worship from the depths of my spirit.

Danny Lehmann, an American, directs the YWAM base in Honolulu, Hawaii, USA, and travels extensively in a teaching ministry.
From *Before You Hit the Wall* by Danny Lehmann. Copyright © 1991 by Danny Lehmann. Published by YWAM Publishing, Seattle, Washington. Used by permission [from page 43].

Friday

So I will restore to you the years that the swarming locust has eaten....
Joel 2:25 NKJV

When I recommitted my life to the Lord in November, 1982, I felt like I had wasted so much time being away from the Lord. A cousin told me, "Watch it, Wanda. Satan will be on your back like a blanket!" And he was.

In March, 1983, my lung collapsed, and I began the first of nine years of cortisone treatments—I felt like I was married to a machine! I asked my church leaders to pray for me, but I slowly realized that mine would be a gradual healing.

It was hard not to be discouraged as year after year passed without any hope of breathing easily once again. But something else was happening: the years I had lost while away from the Lord were being restored as I sat studying God's Word and praying.

Finally, I gained enough strength to work six months each year as a volunteer with YWAM in Hawaii. Being home in Alberta, Canada, during the warm season, then in Hawaii the rest of the year helped my lungs heal.

In 1991, I was released from the medication and the treatments on the machine.

Wanda Carter, a Canadian, serves as receptionist and bookkeeper for the International Office in Kailua-Kona, Hawaii, USA.

Saturday

Though the fig tree does not bud and there are no grapes on the vines, though the olive crop fails and the fields produce no food, though there are no sheep in the pen and no cattle in the stalls, yet I will rejoice in the Lord, I will be joyful in God my Savior.
Habakkuk 3:17-18

I grew up on the Pacific island of Palau. I had never traveled outside our island group by myself. But now I was on my way to New Zealand to work on staff with a Discipleship Training School.

When I bought my ticket, the airline employee told me I could get a New Zealand visa upon arrival there. I believed her. But when I arrived in Nauru at midnight to change planes, they told me I couldn't get on the plane to New Zealand without a valid visa. I would have to go back to Guam and work it out with the embassy there.

There was only one problem. The next flight back to Guam didn't leave for seven days, and I had hardly any money. I was stranded. I stayed in the airport all night, my anger rising by the moment.

Then I sensed God asking me, "David, do you still love Me even when everything has fallen through?" I was too angry to even answer.

But when He asked the question again, I said, "Lord, I love You, but right now I don't know what to do."

A few minutes later, a man approached me and asked if he could drive me to a nearby motel. I took the ride, and had just enough money to get a motel room for the week. Since that emptied my pockets, I spent the week fasting...not exactly by choice.

When the day came for the flight to Guam, I returned to the airport and checked my luggage. I still had several hours before departure, so I went outside to get some fresh air.

A stranger came up and started talking to me. When he heard my situation, he offered to take me to his house to wait for the flight. I discovered he was a Christian. What a blessing from the Lord! He treated me to a big dinner—my first meal in a week—then returned me to the airport in time for my flight.

David Beches, from Palau, serves on staff with the School of Biblical Studies in Singapore.

Sunday

Meditation

And I pray that you, being rooted and established in love, may have power, together with all the saints, to grasp how wide and long and high and deep is the love of Christ, and to know this love that surpasses knowledge—that you may be filled to the measure of all the fullness of God.

Now to him who is able to do immeasurably more than all we ask or imagine, according to his power that is at work within us, to him be glory in the church and in Christ Jesus throughout all generations, for ever and ever! Amen.

Ephesians 3:17-21

Monday

Obey your earthly masters in everything; and do it,...with sincerity of heart and reverence for the Lord.
Colossians 3:22

Nothing more clearly reveals the motives of the heart than how we react when asked to serve others. Do we consider some tasks below our dignity? Do we feel we're too mature in the Lord to mow the pastor's lawn or work in the nursery? Are we too busy to help with the lowliest jobs?

A large inner-city convent had a nun who always sang hymns while hanging out the laundry. There was an infectious quality of joy about her. A young novice, after several weeks at the convent, was intrigued by this older nun and asked why she was always so joyful.

The older nun replied, "The Lord called me to serve here many years ago, and I find it a privilege to hang out the laundry for others." The novice was impressed with this attitude, but was even more blessed when she heard the full story.

For many years, this nun had been the Mother Superior of the convent until she grew too old to carry the load of responsibility. She had been offered a position with less responsibility in a smaller convent, but felt God had specifically called her to the convent she was in. The only other position at that time was for a laundry person. So she gladly took the position.

Floyd McClung, an American, directs Leadership Development Programs for YWAM. He lives in California, USA.

From *Basic Discipleship* by Floyd McClung. Copyright © 1990 Floyd McClung. Published by InterVarsity Press, Downers Grove, Illinois. Used by permission [from page 146].

Tuesday

These three remain: faith, hope, and love.   I Corinthians 13:13

Thousands of crippled survivors of the guerrilla war along the Thai-Cambodian border have little hope for the future. Bun Nath was a captain in the non-Communist Cambodian army. When his truck overturned, he was paralyzed from the neck down.

With no social welfare for Cambodia's war victims, Bun Nath, his wife, and their three children had no means of income. Bun Nath didn't want to be a burden to his family. He asked his young son to buy poison and put it in his food.

When he awoke in a hospital and realized that his suicide attempt had been unsuccessful, he tried committing suicide several more times. Each time he failed. Fellow refugees and friends tried to encourage Bun Nath, but each time, he turned them away with anger.

I worked at one of the refugee camps on the Thai-Cambodian border. I learned of Bun Nath's plight from Barnabas, a Cambodian pastor working at Site II Refugee Camp. We prayed for Bun Nath and went to visit him.

As we entered his small bamboo hut, we were astounded by his warm greeting. I realized that God had heard our prayers and had prepared Bun Nath's heart.

I told Bun Nath about a refugee I knew who also was paralyzed from the neck down; that he had accepted Christ Jesus and looked forward to the future with joy and hope. I related a dream the man had where a snake came to kill him. But Jesus entered the room, and the snake fled. Then Jesus took him to heaven and showed him the glory of His Kingdom and the wonderful home Jesus had prepared for him.

Bun Nath's heart opened that day to the love of Jesus. Though he and his family still live in a refugee camp on the Thai-Cambodian border, they have God's love, a hope for the future, and the joy of sharing the love of Christ with other refugees.

Mark Erickson, an American, worked with Cambodian refugees in Thailand, and now lives in Finland.

Wednesday

If you forgive men when they sin against you, your heavenly Father will also forgive you.
Matthew 6:14

Five of us were visiting the infamous Manila dump where thousands of squatters eke out a meager existence from the garbage of the city's eight million residents.

Marty, an American medical worker, was showing us where he labored as the sole "doctor" for the people of the dump. Suddenly, he stopped his explanation mid-sentence and turned to watch the approach of four men carrying an elderly man.

"The old man is named Lorenzo," Marty said. "Last week he was stabbed six times."

Marty explained that the stabbing was revenge for a knifing Lorenzo had done years before in rage. Lorenzo knew that someday, according to custom, the man would seek to avenge himself. Ironically, shortly before he was knifed, Lorenzo and his entire family had become Christians.

Lorenzo vowed that as soon as he was able to leave the hospital, he would go to the jail to assure his assailant that he had forgiven him. He also wanted to share Christ's forgiveness with him.

Now Lorenzo was returning from the jail where his assailant was being held. As the procession drew nearer, I could see ugly red scars with large suture marks crisscrossing Lorenzo's chest. He was drawing deep, laborious breaths, but smiled and motioned for us to follow him.

We fell in line behind the others, trudging over the trash and grime that had been pounded down by hundreds of bare feet between makeshift dwellings.

People were clustered in Lorenzo's doorway to hear once more the now-familiar story that had spread throughout the dump. I leaned back and watched with joy as his audience listened, enraptured by the strong, clear message of this living sermon.

Stacy Sells, an American, is a nonresidential missionary living in Singapore and working to reach a tribal group in India.

Thursday

If anyone is in Christ, he is a new creation.   *II Corinthians 5:17*

For several years, I've worked in Mexico in an orphanage sponsored by the Richardson Springs, California, YWAM base. My main responsibility was to develop and lead a King's Kids group. We combine singing and choreography for Christian and secular music. Between songs, and afterward, the children and teenagers talk one-on-one with their audience about God's love.

When I learned we would be taking nine children from our King's Kids group to the Barcelona Olympic Outreach, I was overjoyed. But how would I select nine children from over 40?

After prayer, I felt God gave me certain guidelines concerning the selection of the nine. At least I felt confident until I came to the name of Marcos, a rebellious 14-year-old boy. Yet his name kept coming to my mind when I prayed.

Against my rational judgment, I chose Marcos as part of the team. When I shared this fact with other leaders, I received such reactions as, "Are you sure? He's not even a Christian. How can you send him on an evangelistic outreach?" Their questions made me reevaluate. Yet I felt I'd made the right decision.

Throughout our training time, Marcos remained rebellious and disruptive. Extra exercises, extra work details, and other disciplinary activities didn't help. There was even discussion of sending Marcos home to Mexico.

At the dress rehearsal, there was a sense that God's Spirit was present in a special way. Afterward, I could not find Marcos. After an extensive search, I found him backstage, crying. I sat down on the floor beside him. After we talked together, Marcos surrendered his life to Jesus Christ.

It was a changed Marcos who traveled with us to Barcelona. We had many fun and satisfying experiences. Yet I consider Marcos' commitment to Christ as the greatest event I witnessed during the summer of 1992.

Keith Durkin, an American, works with King's Kids at an orphanage in Mexico.

Friday

A wife of noble character who can find? She is worth far more than rubies....She can laugh at the days to come.   Proverbs 31:10,25

As part of the staff leading an evangelism outreach in Mexico, I had heard that visitors often became sick after eating locally prepared food, so I was glad that our housing arrangements included a kitchen where we prepared our own meals.

One day some ladies from the church offered to prepare our evening meal to help us out. I wasn't feeling well, so when I heard about this, all my fears of illness came to the surface.

While I was waiting for the meal to be prepared, I sat in a room with some others from our team. The darkened room did nothing to ease my fears, even though the other team members were playing games and enjoying the break.

In the past few months, I had been asking God to make me a virtuous woman like the one described in Proverbs 31. Now, as I sat in the gloom with my fears, I remembered what the Bible had said about how a virtuous woman can laugh at the future because her trust is in God, not in herself. I felt that God was challenging me to trust Him with my health and that of my husband and our two children.

By the time I joined the others in the food line, I was so fearful that I was close to tears. But I decided to take God's challenge and to "laugh at the future." I looked at the food and laughed aloud. My husband looked puzzled, but I just laughed again. Something changed in my heart. As I determined to obey God, He gave me peace. By the time I had my food and sat down at the table, I was able to enter into the conversation and enjoy my fellowship with the others. I even enjoyed the food.

None of us got sick. More importantly, I learned that God can work a change in my heart and in my perspective when I choose to trust Him. I was learning to become like the virtuous woman.

Kim Dale, an American, serves on Discipleship Training School staff and with the Living Alternatives Crisis Pregnancy Center in Tyler, Texas, USA.

Saturday

We do not know what we ought to pray, but the Spirit himself intercedes for us.
Romans 8:26

The classroom was full of students, many of whom were Asians. We were in the midst of a three-month School of Intercession, Worship, and Spiritual Warfare in Singapore.

One of the emphases in the course is the need to seek God for His topic and methods for prayer. On this particular day, we felt God urging us to make a large map of the Soviet Union. We took time to do this, taking care to include all the individual republics making up that huge nation. We returned to prayer with the map on the floor before us. We weren't in a hurry.

Over the course of two hours, we prayed earnestly for each republic by name. Often we waited some time to discern what God wanted us to pray for, and what He wanted us to do. During periodic silent times together, specific needs came to someone's mind. We then prayed together about them, one by one.

Each time a republic had been covered in prayer, we felt we were to tear its portion of the map from the whole: Uzbekistan, Estonia, etc. As we prayed, we each experienced a deep concern for the land we were praying for. When we sensed a release of the prayer burden, we realized that every republic had been removed from the map. Only Russia itself remained in place.

This took place on the first day of the coup which resulted in the dismantling of the Soviet Union. In two days, the coup was over. We had no way of knowing that in the following months, we would see those republics separate from Russia.

Paul Hawkins, an American, teaches on intercession, worship, and spiritual warfare.

Sunday

Meditation

Your word, O Lord, is eternal; it stands firm in the heavens. Your faithfulness continues through all generations; you established the earth, and it endures. Your laws endure to this day, for all things serve you. If your law had not been my delight, I would have perished in my affliction. I will never forget your precepts, for by them you have renewed my life.

Psalm 119:89-93

Monday

You intended to harm me, but God intended it for good to accomplish what is now being done.   Genesis 50:20

When my sister Karen and I were teenagers, Mom felt God was saying that she shouldn't be away from us more than 12 days out of each six weeks. She was careful to keep within those limits. One week, Mom and Dad were both in Europe, and had a free weekend they could spend together. But this was Mom's twelfth day away. She came home on Thursday.

The next morning, I ditched school and left for Hilo with my friend. Unknown to any of us, Dad was just then on a train in Europe, and had a strong impression from the Lord that the enemy would try to take his son's life. He began interceding for me.

I had an accident, and I wanted to postpone having to admit to Mom that I not only ditched school, but also had lied to her. So instead of having the police call Mom, I had them call YWAM's radio station in Hilo. I didn't know that the staff called Mom immediately. She heard only that I had been in an accident, that it happened on Saddleback Road, and that I was not injured.

We later learned that at that same time in Germany, Dad got off at a train station, intending to call home to see if I was okay. He put his hand on the phone, then stopped. He decided to call later, and jumped back on the train. This gave Mom some much-needed time to sort out the facts, to settle her own spirit, and to be ready to tell Dad what happened.

God used this experience as a turning point for me in my commitment to Him. I learned two lessons: that it is important to walk consistently with the Lord, and that the enemy tries to take advantage when we're not walking with Christ.

David L. Cunningham, an American, runs a film and television production company in California, USA.

Tuesday

The peace of God, which transcends all understanding, will guard your hearts and your minds in Christ Jesus.　　　　　　　*Philippians 4:7*

Our family was sleeping peacefully, being gently rocked on our 48-foot houseboat on the Purus River of Brazil's Amazon basin. My sleep was interrupted by the voices of men calling out from a small boat. My husband, Kent, went to the rail to talk with them. I silently prayed, asking God to meet whatever need they had. I also secretly hoped that their need didn't involve my nursing skills. I dread middle-of-the-night house calls, but I understand the need and go when asked.

Kent returned, and I learned that a woman had been in labor for five days. I dressed and boarded the small canoe. Only after we were on our way did I think about my circumstances. I was riding in a small canoe down a dark river with two total strangers. Once again, I focused my thoughts on my heavenly Father. *Lord, I'm doing Your work in Your name. Protect me tonight. Give the woman a safe delivery, and let the baby be healthy.*

Hours later, I tried to doze as the canoe made its way back upriver. I thought of Kent and his ministry to these 700 river people living nearby. I thought of our four young children, and remembered the laundry needing to be done at the river's edge after sunrise. I whispered a prayer for strength to do the day's work with a body lacking normal sleep. I offered thanks for the healthy child born during the night. And I thanked God for protecting me during my nighttime journey and for His peace that accompanied me the whole way.

Josephine Truehl, an Australian, does church planting and health care work in Brazil.

Wednesday

Whether you turn to the right or to the left, your ears will hear a voice behind you, saying, "This is the way; walk in it."   Isaiah 30:21

We were in China, traveling from city to city, praying and sharing one-on-one about Christ. We had prayed specifically that we would contact people ready to make a commitment to Christ.

After I settled into the hotel, I started reading my Bible. God said, "Go ride the Number Two bus."

I thought, *No, I'm reading my Bible.*

As I read more, I was impressed, "Go ride the Number Two bus." I didn't even know whether there *was* a Number Two bus.

When I went outside, I found the Number Two bus about a block away from the hotel. I got on and rode it through the city. I asked God again and again, *When should I get off?* I reached the end of the line, paid the fare again, and asked the Lord one more time, *Where do I get off?*

In the center of the city, I felt it was time. I stepped off and asked God, *Now where should I go?* I felt that I should walk into a store across the street, so I did. As I stood in the lobby, a Chinese man approached me and asked if he could help me.

I told him that the One True God had told me to come to this building to tell him about Jesus Christ. He looked interested, and we made an appointment for an hour later—after he finished teaching an English class.

At the end of our discussion, the man told me he wanted to believe in Jesus.

Joe Rystrom, an American, is a member of a Far East Evangelism Team in Hong Kong.

Thursday

My grace is sufficient for you, for my power is made perfect in weakness.
II Corinthians 12:9

Paul is known for the wonders and guidance of God in his life. Through Paul, we see the richness of God's goodness, His power, and His wisdom. Paul learned that absolutely nothing is impossible for Him.

Although Paul was a great man, he did not rely on his natural abilities. Instead, he emphasized the importance and necessity of his unconditional dependence on God. He had a secure and trusting relationship with God.

God is not in any way limited by our incapabilities. Sometimes fear and pride hold us back from giving God freedom to do what He wants in us. When we admit our weaknesses to God, we are demonstrating submission of self, and honoring God in the situations and circumstances He allows. When we are honest with ourselves about our insufficiencies, God can reveal Himself in us and through us. He wants to work with us to fulfill His plan for the whole body of Christ.

Roswitha Teuber, a German, serves as secretary at YWAM Germany.

Friday

I have seen you in the sanctuary and beheld your power and your glory.

Psalm 63:2

I have found that it helps me greatly to have a physical place (closet, desk, room, etc.) that I can call "my sanctuary"—the place where God and I meet together. I have fixed up a closet in my apartment with a bookshelf, pillow, prayer reminders, and maps on the wall. However, since nearly a third of my time is spent traveling, I have learned to make do with airports, planes, trains, buses, and cars as my sanctuary.

Even so, when I get to the place where I will be staying, I find a sanctuary where I can spend time with the Lord. Sometimes it's on a rooftop or under a tree; other times it's the corner of a library or a chair on a balcony. Occasionally I take a prayer walk, but mostly, I like a physical place where I can go and commune with the Lord.

Other Quiet Time accessories I like to have on hand in my sanctuary are a hymnal, a Bible dictionary, and a concordance, as well as several different translations of the Bible. I also like to have a few standard devotional books on hand. These are helpful, but I would add one caution: don't let revelation from someone else's Quiet Time be a substitute for what you can get directly from the Lord.

A regular Quiet Time is one of the greatest joys we as Christians can enter into with the Lord. However, it takes time and determination to develop. Our natural inclination at 6:00 a.m., when it is dark and cold, is to reach over and switch the alarm off and go back to sleep. It takes a deliberate act to crawl out of bed and spend time with the Lord.

Danny Lehmann, an American, directs the YWAM base in Honolulu, Hawaii, USA, and travels extensively in a teaching ministry.

From *Before You Hit the Wall* by Danny Lehmann. Copyright © 1991 by Danny Lehmann. Published by YWAM Publishing, Seattle, Washington. Used by permission [from pages 49-50].

Saturday

Can a mother forget the baby at her breast and have no compassion on the child she has borne? Though she may forget, I will not forget you! See, I have engraved you on the palms of my hands.   Isaiah 49:15-16

We prayed that morning for God to use us specifically in someone's life who spoke English. For five days, we had walked the busy streets, enjoying the sights, sounds, and smells of the Chinese city, but without a contact.

We were startled by a man's voice, "Hello, you speak English?" We scanned the crowd for a Western-looking face, but saw none. Again we heard his voice, "English! You speak English?"

We saw a man grinning at us. He was taller than most Chinese men, and had a distinctive look about him. He pushed through the crowds toward us, and we saw excitement on his face. We, too, were thrilled with our answer to prayer. He eagerly questioned us as to where we were from, what we did, and why we were in China.

We learned he was from a city in the far northern part of China and had come to this city to study English. He was delighted to be able to practice it on us.

We recognized his name as being an Asian version of a Bible name. We showed the man his name in our English/Chinese Gospel. His eyes jumped across to the Chinese writing on the opposing page, and he nodded in acknowledgment.

He laughed with delight when we told him he would find his name in other places in the book, also. We took his picture, exchanged addresses, and gave invitations to visit in one another's homes.

In the years since that encounter, God has often brought the man's face before me. I pray that God will continue to bring Christians across his path. Perhaps, even now, he is leading others to the One who led him to us.

Beverly Caruso, an American, is a Bible teacher and author who leads YWAM Writer's Seminars. She lives in California, USA.

Sunday

Meditation

We believe that Jesus died and rose again and so we believe that God will bring with Jesus those who have fallen asleep in him. According to the Lord's own word, we tell you that we who are still alive, who are left till the coming of the Lord, will certainly not precede those who have fallen asleep. For the Lord himself will come down from heaven, with a loud command, with the voice of the archangel and with the trumpet call of God, and the dead in Christ will rise first. After that, we who are still alive and are left will be caught up with them in the clouds to meet the Lord in the air. And so we will be with the Lord forever. Therefore encourage each other with these words.

I Thessalonians 4:14-18

Monday

During that long period...God heard their groaning and he remembered his covenant with Abraham, with Isaac and with Jacob. So God looked on the Israelites and was concerned about them.   Exodus 2:23-25

As we began a new thrust among Polish refugees, my daily Scripture reading led me to these verses. It was like I was being provided a wide-angle shot after a long series of telephoto shots. From this, I gained a new perspective of God's calling to individuals. Often we distort our vision by focusing on a fixed point in time and location; we see only a person receiving a "calling." By the time we are finished, the reason for the call is lost, and the means has become an end.

These verses show us a God who, over a long period of time, heard the groaning of His people. He looked on them and was concerned. He was not removed from the situation. When God later called Moses at the burning bush, we can see the work of the calling. It was an act of God in history, based on His heart of love.

So, too, our calling needs to be seen from this larger perspective. It is a God-initiated response of concern to the human dilemma. We are significant, but not indispensable. We are then able to humbly accept our limitations, and allow God to carry what only He can carry. On the other hand, we must be awed by the privilege of the call in order to be constantly obedient.

John Hess, an American, led a work among Polish refugees in Austria and now leads the work of YWAM Poland.

Tuesday

Let us then approach the throne of grace with confidence, so that we may receive mercy and find grace to help us in our time of need.

Hebrews 4:16

We are told to be persistent, forceful, and specific in prayer. In Mark 10:46-52, we have the story of blind Bartimaeus. Jesus was heading out of Jericho when blind Bartimaeus heard He was coming. Bartimaeus yelled out at the top of his voice, "Jesus, Son of David, have mercy on me!" Everyone around him tried to hush him. He was disturbing the dignity of the occasion. But Bartimaeus "began crying out all the more." Not only did he not quiet down, he yelled louder and more often, "Son of David, have mercy on me!" Jesus finally walked over to this man and asked him, "What do you want Me to do for you?"

Jesus loves it when we are persistent and refuse to let Him go, even when we don't receive an immediate answer. He wants us to press in and keep praying. And He wants us to be specific. Jesus is still asking us today, "What do you want Me to do for you?" We need to pray specifically, in detail—not vague, religious prayers that don't really tell God what we want. We must be specific in order for God to bring about specific answers. We don't always know details, but we should pray as specifically as we can.

Every Christian should pray with boldness, expecting God's response to every prayer. We need to give God no rest until our prayers have been answered. If we become totally convinced that God moves in the affairs of men, then we will pray like this. And when we pray, we will see the hand of God move. Prayer will become one of the most exciting parts of our life. We will begin to shake our world. We will become effective prayer warriors.

Dean Sherman, an American, is an international Bible teacher, and lives in the USA.

From *Spiritual Warfare for Every Christian* by Dean Sherman. Copyright © 1990 by Dean Sherman. Published by YWAM Publishing, Seattle, Washington. Used by permission [from page 166-167].

Wednesday

Whatever you did for one of the least of these brothers of mine, you did for me.
Matthew 25:40

In a leper colony on an island in the tiny country of Macau, my commitment to do whatever God asked of me was fully tested.

Most of the 40 lepers had lived there for decades. The Chinese believe leprosy is caused by evil spirits, so they don't visit their loved ones. Despite the difficulties, these joyous people created their own family among the patients.

The clinic where I worked had almost a party atmosphere. Patients came early and stayed long after I scrubbed and bandaged their open sores. One tiny man, Lei Ming, had a toothless grin, and chattered constantly in Chinese, answering questions we must have asked with our eyes. By our last day, Lei Ming was constantly at my side.

Lei Ming rattled off something in Chinese, and the patients erupted in giggles and guffaws. The nurse laughed, too, as she translated, "He wants to adopt you as his goddaughter."

What a perfect godfather, I thought. I knew he spent two hours praying in the Catholic church building each morning. I could use a few extra prayers.

The room silenced when the nurse translated my, "I'd be delighted." Lei Ming's chest puffed up. He tilted his chin proudly and showed off his charming gums.

As a memento, I gave him a ring, but it wouldn't fit onto his gnarled fingers. His family went into action. One fetched a tool to hang it on his neck chain. Lei Ming's tears ran all the way to his grin. Suddenly his eyes lit up, and he reached for his wallet, then handed me the prized Japanese coin a visitor had given him after the war. Soon a woman shuffled over and handed me a banana. Another came with an orange. Another, a pear. Soon, someone brought a basket to hold my armload of fruit.

I had given them only a few weeks. These wonderful people had nothing, yet they gave me all they had.

Shirley Walston, an American, is a freelance writer for YWAM, living in Washington State, USA.

Thursday

The Lord is my shepherd, I shall lack nothing. Psalm 23:1

How often have we read that verse and not fully been aware of its meaning? When I was a child, it was one of the first Scriptures my parents had me memorize. I repeated it hundreds of times, yet it wasn't until I left home and became a full-time missionary that I understood what it said. Now it is no longer only in my head, but it is in my heart, as well.

A shepherd knows each one of his sheep by name. When a sheep falls on its back and can't get up, the shepherd comes and sets it up right. When the sheep's wool is thick and beautiful, the shepherd shears it off. He gives the wool to those who might be cold or needy, so that others can also benefit from it.

The shepherd is always watchful, and takes his sheep to the best areas for food and drink. He never lets his flock go away thirsty. Sometimes he takes his sheep where the trail is difficult and the terrain is hard. But he knows what is best, and he will never lead his followers astray.

The shepherd tries to keep his sheep together. When one wanders away, the shepherd goes off and searches for the lost sheep. When he finds him, he returns him to the fold for strength, comfort, and companionship.

In the lives of missionaries, there are times when we aren't in the finest fields, and the weather is unpleasant. Sometimes we don't get the best food or have a soft place to lay our heads. Many times we are surrounded by spiritual wolves. But in all those times, our Shepherd is right there with us, and we can honestly say that we lack for nothing.

Brian Burgoyne, an American, directs YWAM's Language School in Helsinki, Finland.

Friday

A man's pride brings him low, but a man of lowly spirit gains honor.

Proverbs 29:23

A teachable spirit and a willingness to learn quickly from others is the greatest protection we have from the consequences of other people's sins against us. As strange as it may seem, the greatest release from hurt, rejection, and emotional damage other people force upon us is to walk in humility. It protects us from problems that we otherwise have no control over.

Many times in my life, I have had to rely on others for help in recognizing my own pride. If you pray for God to reveal pride to you, don't be surprised if others start exhorting you about weaknesses in your life. When confronted, we don't always find it easy to admit that we are wrong. But if we are to enjoy the blessing of humility, it is imperative.

My wife, Sally, and I have sometimes disagreed about how we should discipline our children. When disagreements arose, we would immediately take sides and argue. Attitudes would harden, and before long, all sorts of other issues were dragged into the disagreement. When this happened, my objective shifted from what was best for the children to proving, at any cost, that I was right. After one such encounter, Sally told me she felt I was allowing this to make me judgmental and proud. My focus was no longer on what was best for the family, but on getting my own way. It was hard to admit at first, but she was right.

God's intention in revealing pride in our lives is always for our benefit. He longs for us to be freed of it by taking the crucial step of asking Him to reveal the pride lurking in our hearts.

Floyd McClung, an American, directs Leadership Development Programs for YWAM. He lives in California, USA.
From *Basic Discipleship* by Floyd McClung. Copyright © 1990 Floyd McClung. Published by InterVarsity Press, Downers Grove, Illinois. Used by permission [from pages 114-115].

Saturday

Don't be deceived, my dear brothers. Every good and perfect gift is from above, coming down from the Father of the heavenly lights.   James 1:16-17

I was single until I was 27 years old, traveling from country to country as a missionary-evangelist. I longed for a wife, and hated being alone. I remember standing on top of the Eiffel Tower, looking out over Paris. The view was stunning, and in my excitement, I turned to remark on the beautiful panorama—but no one was there. I felt truly alone.

While I was still in Bible school, I had discovered the passage in I Corinthians 7 where Paul said it was a gift to be single. I sincerely hoped that God wasn't planning to give this gift to me! Time went by. Then I came to understand that this Scripture in I Corinthians was not to be skipped over and left for someone else.

I responded by placing my right to be married on the altar. That was a phrase I learned from my parents—"putting something on the altar" was another way of saying, "I give up my right." I told God, "Okay. I'm willing to never get married, if that is Your will."

An amazing thing happened. There was a new freedom. No longer was I preoccupied with what I jokingly referred to as "the search." I was able to concentrate on what God wanted me to do next. A few months later, as I continued pursuing God's call on my life, my path crossed with that of a vivacious blond in Redwood City, California. She had also just laid her desire to be married "on the altar." God brought us together.

In God's right time, if He sees you can be more fulfilled and effective for Him with a life partner than without, He'll bring the very one that is right for you and for His Kingdom.

Loren Cunningham, an American, is founder and president of YWAM. He lives in Hawaii, USA.

From *Winning, God's Way* by Loren Cunningham with Janice Rogers. Copyright © 1988 by Loren Cunningham. Published by YWAM Publishing, Seattle, Washington. Used by permission [from pages 30-31].

Sunday

Meditation

The way of a fool seems right to him, but a wise man listens to advice. A fool shows his annoyance at once, but a prudent man overlooks an insult.
Reckless words pierce like a sword, but the tongue of the wise brings healing.

Proverbs 12:15-16,18

Monday

See that you do not look down on one of these little ones....Your Father in heaven is not willing that any of these little ones should be lost.

Matthew 18:10,14

Skip had AIDS. When I first met him, I mentioned in passing that I was a Christian missionary. He responded, "Never, *ever,* say anything to me about God, Jesus, or the Church. If you do, our relationship will be terminated at that point."

I thought, *Why bother with someone so bitter toward God?* I was about to walk away from him when God gave me a sense of His unconditional love for Skip. He wanted to work in Skip's life. So began a journey of serving Skip for seven long months without talking about Jesus. I knew that it would not be my words, but my life, that would make the impact.

One day during my quiet time, I sensed that God wanted me to make chicken soup for Skip. Not my wife, but me. I didn't understand, but I obeyed, stumbling through the process.

When I took the soup to Skip, I simply said that I had made it for him. He knew I was married, and that my wife could have made it.

The next time I saw Skip, he asked why I brought the soup. I told him about my prayer time, the impression from God, and the result of making the soup. Only then did he tell me that before I arrived with the soup, he had a craving for homemade chicken soup. AIDS victims often lose their appetite. This opened the door for me to share more with Skip about God and about his need for Jesus.

After seven months of showing God's love to Skip, I was called to the hospice to be with him in those final hours. This would be my last opportunity to talk with him about eternity.

Also in his room were his lover, the director of the hospice, the nurse, and someone from a New Age group. I prayed silently. Within eight minutes, the room was cleared. I bent close to Skip and spoke softly. Skip repented. The others soon returned. Thirty minutes later, Skip passed into the arms of Jesus.

John Bills, an American, serves as U.S. Southwest Director for YWAM.

Tuesday

O Jerusalem, Jerusalem, you who kill the prophets and stone those sent to you, how often I have longed to gather your children together, as a hen gathers her chicks under her wings, but you were not willing. Matthew 23:37

I had worked for seven months serving Skip, who was dying of AIDS. The afternoon he died, I was able to lead him to Christ. I returned to my home late that afternoon, having gone through one of the most emotional days I have ever had.

I got as far as my living room and began to weep over the agonizing experience of those months. I heard myself telling God that I couldn't handle all this pain. If ministry to people with AIDS was going to be like this, I wasn't sure I wanted it.

In the next few moments, I heard the following words that I believe every Christian longs to hear. I sensed the heart of God saying, *Now you know a little of how I feel!*

I had prayed for years to know how God feels over those who don't know Him. God answered that prayer in a way I could never have imagined. It took serving a young man dying of AIDS to understand, in a greater way, God's heart of unconditional love that is deeply broken over lost souls. Now I am more determined and more committed to see people dying of AIDS, and the lost at large, ushered into the Kingdom of God.

John Bills, an American, works as U.S. Southwest Director for YWAM.

Wednesday

The devil said to him, "If you are the Son of God, tell this stone to become bread." Jesus answered, "It is written: 'Man does not live on bread alone.' "

Luke 4:3-4

It's not surprising that Jesus was hungry after 40 days without food, and the devil was out to tempt Him at this vulnerable point. For Jesus, the temptation was to take advantage of His power and provide food to satisfy his very natural hunger.

At first glance, it is difficult to see how something as commonplace as eating could possibly be wrong. The human reaction would be to go ahead and eat. We are usually most tempted by things that seem quite ordinary. Old habits die hard.

God has called us all to abstinence in one form or another. We have all had to say "no" to things that hinder our walk with God. Perhaps we have stopped smoking or have refrained from watching too much television to allow us more time with our family and with the Lord.

Jesus' answer is wise. He doesn't condemn eating. He simply states God's Word, that a man should make his relationship with God the most central thing in his life: "Man does not live on bread alone but on every word that comes from the mouth of the Lord" (Deuteronomy 8:3).

Paul Marsh, from England, serves as training director for YWAM in Lausanne, Switzerland.

Thursday

Be careful to do what is right in the eyes of everybody. If it is possible, as far as it depends on you, live at peace with everyone.　　Romans 12:17-18

Any planning we do for spending time together working on the vital ingredients of a good marriage should include an honest discussion of our individual expectations. We often misunderstand one another because we don't know what our partner is expecting. Of course, we must also be willing to make adjustments along the way. Frequently our expectations are totally unrealistic.

When Floyd and I were newly married, I had my own clear idea of what a perfect marriage should be. It included constant harmony and no disagreeing. Unfortunately, Floyd and I were too human to live up to that ideal. We had to have a very open discussion of our expectations and whether or not they were realistic. Mine weren't! I had to make very strategic adjustments.

I once saw an article on marriage called "Marriage License—a Learner's Permit." Just as we have to learn to drive a car, so we have to learn to guide our marriages. We may have to turn a little to the right or left to avoid some bumps, and we may need to slow down to keep us from crashing. Divorce courts are filled with couples who haven't learned to make the necessary adjustments.

We must plan for time together to grow in our relationship and understanding of one another. Time spent together is an investment—there are rich dividends from it.

Sally McClung, an American, has a ministry of hospitality and speaks internationally. She lives in California, USA.
From *Where Will I Find the Time?* by Sally McClung. Copyright © 1989 by Sally McClung. Published by Harvest House Publishers, Eugene, Oregon. Used by permission [from pages 41-42].

Friday

Jesus said, "Let the little children come to me, and do not hinder them, for the kingdom of heaven belongs to such as these." Matthew 19:14

I was alone early in the morning on my first day with the street children in Rio de Janeiro, Brazil. I met nine filthy, smelly kids. Most wore no shoes or shirts. I knew the love I felt was God's love for them. I thought, *I'd love to take them to that park. I just want them to be children.* I'd been told they weren't allowed to enter the park, but I asked God to make it possible.

We just walked in, and no one stopped us! We sang and danced. The children ran and chased the ducks.

Suddenly five wardens arrived. The chief demanded, "Get out!" The children started crying. One little boy in particular stood there looking up at the man. I guessed he was saying in Portuguese, "Please, leave us alone. For the first time in a long time we are really happy and having a nice time." The man only barked, "Get out!" I could see hatred in his eyes, and I understood that the enemy was using the authorities against the children. Dejected, we started to leave.

Then I heard in my mind Jesus' voice say, *Sarah, they are only children.* I walked up to the chief guard, the children in tow, and repeated the words Jesus had spoken.

"They are only children."

He called one of the guards and said, "Go with them as they go around the park." The totally bemused guard escorted us in the park. It was all I could do not to burst out laughing!

Sarah de Carvalho, from England, works with street children in Brazil.

Saturday

Did I not tell you that if you believed, you would see the glory of God?
                                                             John 11:40

Christ didn't resurrect Lazarus at the exact moment that Mary and Martha wanted Him to. After Jesus heard that Lazarus was sick, Jesus stayed where He was for two more days. He loved Lazarus, but He did not rush to help him.

God has a purpose and a time for everything He does. Sometimes, it seems like He's too late. But He may be waiting so we will gain a greater revelation of His power and His glory.

God only asks that we not lose faith. It's easy to have faith for a day, a month, or maybe even a year. But our faith shouldn't be subject either to time or to circumstances. It needs to be grounded in the sound knowledge of who God is.

When God seems to delay, it's not designed to make us doubtful or discouraged. God's motives are based on His love for us. He always wants the best for us and for His Kingdom. God sometimes waits to respond to us because He wants to give us His best in His time.

Margarita Piña, a Spaniard, works with children, drama, and accounting with YWAM Spain.

Sunday

Meditation

The Lord upholds all those who fall
and lifts up all who are bowed
down. The eyes of all look to you,
and you give them their food at the
proper time. You open your hand
and satisfy the desires of every living
thing. The Lord is righteous in all
his ways and loving toward all he
has made.

Psalm 145:14-18

Monday

Those who know your name will trust in you, for you, Lord, have never forsaken those who seek you.   Psalm 9:10

It was the middle of the night, and I was flying over the Middle East. Most of the plane's passengers were sleeping. I had just finished writing in a letter that our knowledge of God's character will always determine our reactions to difficult circumstances.

Unexpectedly, the captain told us we would soon make an unscheduled stop at Bahrain in the Persian Gulf. I had flown enough to know that something was wrong. I asked the flight steward for an explanation. He responded rather tensely, "It's all right, lady. Everything's going to be okay."

I persisted by assuring him that I had absolutely no fear and would appreciate knowing the cause of the change of plans. His response was the same. Despite his effort, his eyes betrayed fear. Aware of recent hijacking incidents and bomb threats on international flights, I asked outright, "Is there a bomb scare?" When I assured him I would not tell any of the other passengers, he nodded in affirmation. I returned to my seat.

I knew I was in the center of God's will—the safest place at any time. A peace settled on me as I thought about God's character. I committed everyone on the plane into God's hands, and trusted Him completely. Then I resisted all satanic forces in the name of the Lord Jesus and resumed writing my letter, totally relaxed.

As we were landing, we were instructed not to leave the plane under any circumstances. Five minutes later, the order was reversed: we were told to take all our belongings and leave the plane.

After 45 minutes at this small, remote airport, we all reboarded and resumed our journey through the night—without incident.

The crew knew of potential danger and were fearful. The passengers were ignorant of it and were perplexed. Many were disgruntled at being "needlessly" disturbed. I was fascinated by the whole situation, knowing that God had given me a unique opportunity to prove the truth of His Word.

Joy Dawson, a former New Zealander but an American citizen for many years, is an International Bible teacher.

Tuesday

Your Father knows what you need before you ask him.   Matthew 6:8

Just that morning, my husband and I had been looking through the classified ads for a place to live. We knew a place might be difficult to find because we needed it for only a short time.

As we walked toward the YWAM office, we saw a man parked by the side of the road in his camper. We were intrigued, and stopped to talk with him.

In the course of our conversation, he mentioned that he was looking for someone to live for a short time in a house he was restoring. We told him we were looking for a place.

He said that we would need to pay only $200 to move in, then $100 per month. I couldn't believe my ears as I listened to his description of the house: a stone fireplace, newly polished wood floors, and a large backyard with fruit trees.

We prayed that night, and asked God to show us His will. The very next night, we received a totally unexpected check for $200. We knew in our hearts that God was leading us.

We moved into the house the next week, and began looking for summer employment. Nothing came through until we returned from a short trip. Both of us were hired to work for the U.S. Census Bureau. Not until they asked for our home address did we learn that we would be working directly across the street from our new home.

We often had opportunity to tell our co-workers about God's provision for us, when they learned where we were living. God certainly had a plan that day when we talked to a stranger parked at the curb.

Sandy Falor, an American, teaches at YWAM's Christian Heritage School in Tyler, Texas, USA.

Wednesday

And now these three remain: faith, hope and love. But the greatest of these is love.
I Corinthians 13:13

When we think about this verse, we think of love: God's love for us and His commandment to love our neighbors as ourselves. Or we think of the type of faith that Abraham and Moses had, or other heroes of the Bible. Too often we forget about hope. But hope has its place among these three things that remain.

In Romans, we read: "We also rejoice in our sufferings, because we know that suffering produces perseverance; perseverance, character; and character, hope. And hope does not disappoint us, because God has poured out his love into our hearts by the Holy Spirit, whom he has given us" (Romans 5:3-5).

The hope of the world lies in things which perish—a better job, a higher income, a bigger car, a larger house. In contrast, the hope that God offers us is divine and eternal. He shows us a glimpse of heaven, with us as people of His household, citizens of His Kingdom. This hope is a gift from God to His children.

If we are not experiencing this hope in our lives, we can ask the Lord to reveal what He longs to give us so we can experience Ephesians 1:18, "The eyes of your heart may be enlightened in order that you may know the hope to which he has called you, the riches of his glorious inheritance in the saints."

Paul admonished us to be joyful in hope. Jesus said that He came to give us peace. The two go together. Without hope, we can never fully know peace. So let us place our hope in God's promise of eternal life.

Philippe Mermod, a Swiss, works in the video ministry in Lausanne, Switzerland

Thursday

I have hidden your word in my heart that I might not sin against you.

Psalm 119:11

Our capacity to experience true freedom is increased as we make more truth available to our hearts. Hence, we need to memorize Scripture.

Scientists tell us that the human mind is capable of storing 100 trillion bits of information. Surely we should be making a little effort to fill up at least some of those bits with God's Word.

I have discovered some principles and practices which have helped me greatly. The most important is this: You must love the Word. Remember English Literature in high school? The teachers could recite line after line of Shakespeare, or verse after verse of Milton. We wondered, "How on earth do they remember all that stuff?" They remembered all those lines because they loved them. For them, nothing was of greater pleasure than to sit for hours and read Shakespeare and the poets, absorbing not only what was said, but how it was said.

The same is true for the Christian. It is highly unlikely that we will ever develop a consistent discipline of Bible memorization if we do not love God's Word. The Bible writers spoke often and passionately about their love affair with the Holy Scriptures. David set aside 176 verses of Psalm 119 to express his regard and love for the Scriptures.

If we don't have this kind of love for the Word of God, then we need to humbly ask the Lord to give us such a love for His Word. It is a prayer God is delighted to answer. By His grace, He will create in our hearts a hunger and thirst for righteousness and truth that can only be satisfied by spending time reading, studying, hearing, meditating upon, and memorizing His Word.

Danny Lehmann, an American, directs the YWAM base in Honolulu, Hawaii, USA, and travels extensively in a teaching ministry.

From *Before You Hit the Wall* by Danny Lehmann. Copyright © 1991 by Danny Lehmann. Published by YWAM Publishing, Seattle, Washington. Used by permission [from pages 70-71].

Friday

You will see neither wind nor rain, yet this valley will be filled with water, and you, your cattle and your other animals will drink. This is an easy thing in the eyes of the Lord. II Kings 3:17-18

In YWAM, each worker trusts the Lord for his or her support. This usually comes through individuals or congregations who believe in the worker and make a commitment to pray and financially support the worker.

On one occasion, my wife, Irma, and I needed to do laundry, but didn't have the 70 cents needed for the washing machine. In faith, she signed up for two time slots for the next day.

The following morning, we found an envelope under our door containing $11. I said, "There may be others who are in similar situations to ours. Why don't we keep one dollar for our immediate need, and see if others have an urgent need?"

The Lord reminded me of a church in Argentina that not only passed the offering plate for the tithes and offerings, but they instructed the members of the congregation who had specific financial needs to take from the offering plate the amount that would meet their needs.

With Irma's agreement, I told the class that afternoon of the Lord's provision for us. I said that God wanted us to put $10 on the floor in the center of the circle of students. We would pray, and any who had special needs could seek the Lord and take what was needed. We all prayed. While my eyes were still closed, I could hear quite a bit of movement.

Finally, a student said, "I think it's time for us to finish, and I believe that Irma and Rix should have what is left." Though some had taken money, others must also have been adding more. When we counted what remained there was $70.

Rix Warren, an Australian, works with Hispanics in the United States.

Saturday

Give, and it will be given to you. A good measure, pressed down, shaken together and running over, will be poured into your lap. For with the measure you use, it will be measured to you.   Luke 6:38

I was about seven years old when YWAM first learned of the property in Kona, Hawaii, that has become the main campus of the University of the Nations. We all believed God wanted us to have the property, and prayed for God to provide the funds.

It seemed that everyone had given about all they could, yet still more money was needed for the purchase. My sister Karen and I had long saved for bicycles. We'd studied the Sears catalog and carefully selected just the models we wanted. Every nickel and dime we got (after paying our tithe, of course) went into those piggy banks.

Karen and I wanted to do our part to help buy the property, so we decided to give all we had—our bike money. We carefully emptied the money onto a towel. Taking hold of two corners each, we carried the towel out to our parents. We knew this meant we would have no bikes. We truly gave them up in our hearts. But God had other plans.

The very next day, family friends came to our island for a visit. They gave Karen and me each a new wallet. Tucked inside each was enough money for our bikes. We were ecstatic! Through a check from our grandfather, God even provided enough money to pay our tithes and still buy the bikes.

I remember telling my friends on the school bus the next day, "My folks don't have ten cents, but I have money to get a bike." We went down the next day to the Sears catalog store and ordered our bikes. Each time I jumped on my bike for a ride, I was reminded once again of God's provision for us. I saw Him as a loving Father who cared for us. I knew that even though we didn't expect to have the bike money replaced when we gave it away, God did it anyway.

David L. Cunningham, an American, runs a film and television production company in California, USA.

Sunday

Meditation

For the grace of God that brings salvation has appeared to all men. It teaches us to say "No" to ungodliness and worldly passions, and to live self-controlled, upright and godly lives in this present age, while we wait for the blessed hope—the glorious appearing of our great God and Savior, Jesus Christ, who gave himself for us to redeem us from all wickedness and to purify for himself a people that are his very own, eager to do what is good

Titus 2:11-14

Monday

When the Lord saw her, his heart went out to her and he said, "Don't cry." The dead man sat up and began to talk, and Jesus gave him back to his mother. They were all filled with awe and...said, "God has come to help his people." This news about Jesus spread throughout Judea and the surrounding country. Luke 7:13,15-17

A very real demonstration of God's character comes through miracles. A few years ago I attended a city-wide evangelistic meeting in India. With me were students from our School of Evangelism in Kona, Hawaii.

After the meeting I heard my name. I turned to see one of the coordinators of the event, a young Indian brother. With him was a fearful looking, sari-clad Indian girl named Lila. My friend explained that just four days earlier Lila had been accosted by someone who put a Hindu curse on her tongue. She could no longer speak. Could we help?

The students and I began to pray one by one. After about ten minutes we asked Lila to remove a fetish from around her neck and she complied. She couldn't pray aloud so I asked her to move her head in agreement as I led her in forsaking the deity the fetish represented. As we began to praise the Lord after that, Lila's speaking ability was restored!

Lila was so thrilled that she came back to the meetings several times, bringing friends and neighbors with her. The miracle demonstrated God's character to her, and she wanted to share that with others.

Ross Tooley, a New Zealander, serves at large on the staff of the College of Christian Ministries of University of the Nations, Kona, Hawaii, USA.

Adapted from *We Cannot But Tell,* by Ross Tooley, revised edition. Copyright © 1993 by Ross Tooley. Published by YWAM Publishing, Seattle, Washington. Used by permission [from page 74].

Tuesday

You intended to harm me, but God intended it for good.   Genesis 50:20

With great anticipation, my wife and I arrived in Singapore to serve on YWAM staff and to minister in local churches and surrounding nations. Our work permits had not yet been approved, so we were given 30-day visitor's passes. We were unaware of that island nation's strict laws regarding the necessity of a special permit each time a visitor speaks in a public place. When we learned about it later, we were told that the policy is usually overlooked for guest speakers in churches.

At the end of 30 days, we got a phone call from the Immigration Department. We were to appear for a review to extend our passes. In answer to their questions regarding our activities, we were reprimanded and were required to sign a statement assuring them we would not engage in additional public speaking without a permit or work visa.

We left the office shocked and disappointed, yet knowing that the Lord was in control and would continue to direct us. We postponed all scheduled speaking engagements.

We had planned to attend the International Staff Conference of YWAM in Manila a few days later. After prayer, we contacted missionaries and pastors in the Philippines for possible speaking engagements. As a result, during an additional month of ministry following the conference, several hundred students received Christ in public schools. Others were reached in jails, churches, and open-air crusades.

Upon our return to Singapore, we learned that our work permits had been approved, and we could resume our public ministry.

Don Hall, an American, is an international Bible teacher and evangelist.

Wednesday

There is...a time to be born and a time to die, a time to plant and a time to uproot.   *Ecclesiastes 3:1-2*

There seems in life to be an unmistakable, but timed, succession of extremes. Joy replaces tears as winter replaces fall. Sometimes, the sadness that comes after rejoicing causes us to question past blessings. That is because we have failed to pay attention to the lessons of the Bible.

Perhaps we are being nourished by the Word in a Bible college situation, a sabbatical, or even a quiet time. We would do well to remember that whatever God gives us is not just for the present. It is also to prepare us for whatever lies ahead. When an hour of insufficiency strikes, how will we respond? Will we have stored spiritual reserves, or will we be destitute because we failed to gather in time of plenty?

It is worth noticing that the first famines in the Bible occurred in an unexpected place, the Promised Land. Of all those mentioned, one of the best-known famines is probably the one foretold by Joseph in Genesis 41. It immediately followed a period of blessing. In Egypt, Joseph was prepared. He had stored up during the years of abundance against the years of famine.

We are given both a warning and a valuable lesson here. Times of plenty seem to go by much more quickly than the same period of deprivation. Let us be careful how we live when we have much. It will determine how we survive when we have little. By storing God's provisions in times of abundance, we will not want in times of trial.

Albert Joly, a Swiss, is the administrator for YWAM in Harpenden, England.

Thursday

Be kind to one another, tenderhearted, forgiving one another.

A number of years ago, when we had our own business, one of our stores was broken into in the night. About $1,500 was stolen, mostly in cash.

My wife and I were saddened by the burglary, but decided to pray daily for the person who had broken in. About three weeks later, I received a postage due notice in the mail. Thinking it was probably an advertisement, I didn't want to pay the postage. Instead, I left it at the post office, unclaimed.

A week later, I got another notice that I owed postage on the letter. Again I ignored it. When I received a third notice, this time stating it was the final notice, I decided to claim it and pay the postage due.

It was a plain brown envelope with only my store's name on the outside. When I opened it, I was astounded to discover $1,500 in cash. Somehow the local newspaper picked up the story, then it was printed across the country. The headline given was: The Power of Prayer.

Ian Ross, a Canadian, works with his wife as Mission Builder Coordinators at Richardson Springs, California, USA.

Friday

Jesus wept.   *John 11:35*

When Michael applied to attend a Discipleship Training School, he voluntarily told us that he was HIV positive. After prayerful consideration and consultation with the staff and other students, we welcomed him.

When Michael was one of the few that didn't get ill during our outreach to the Amazon in Brazil, I sensed that God was honoring him for his commitment to use for God whatever time remained on this earth. After the outreach, Michael joined our staff in ministering to street kids in Hollywood.

While I sat in a hospital waiting room during one of Michael's weekly blood tests, God called me to minister to AIDS patients—such as taking them to doctor's appointments and even cleaning toilets.

During Michael's last year, he developed full-blown AIDS. Stomach cancer prevented intake of food by mouth. He needed nightly injections of food through a tube in his chest. He had no family nearby, so my wife, our children, and I prayed together about taking Michael into our home. When I discussed this with a doctor, her eyes filled with tears. She knew better than we the risk we were taking. She knew, too, the loneliness of many AIDS patients.

For the next few months, we worked around the clock caring for Michael. Toward the end, I had to bathe and diaper him—humiliating for both of us. Michael and I spent hours talking and praying together. On December 2, Michael went to be with Jesus while Jill and I sat at his bedside.

Through this personal involvement, as painful as it was, we gained an understanding and identification with those dying of AIDS. We learned that the compassion of Jesus is more than having an attitude of "that's too bad." Jesus became involved in the needs of humanity.

John Bills, an American, works as U.S. Southwest Director for YWAM.

Saturday

And he made known to us the mystery of his will according to his good pleasure, which he purposed in Christ. Ephesians 1:9

After our Discipleship Training School (DTS) on board YWAM's emergency relief ship, the m/v *Anastasis,* my wife and I felt a strong calling to join the Mercy Ships office in Lausanne, Switzerland. However, we struggled with what we felt was God's direction.

We wanted to work with people in developing nations—to do what we had seen in Mexico during our DTS outreach. Why were we going to Switzerland?

To make matters worse, we had to raise financial support by telling people we were going to be "missionaries" in Switzerland. Needless to say, it was difficult. We found it hard to stand decisively on what we believed God had told us.

It has been four years since that decision. We now direct the Mercy Ships Office in Lausanne. The m/v *Anastasis* is leaving for its third outreach to West Africa, and has, in the past few years, served six of the poorest nations in the world.

Through our office, the ship is supported by seven European nations. It is a fantastic thing for us to be involved in the support structure that serves the nations of West Africa from Europe. Only God could have foreseen this work four years ago when He placed us here.

Robert Ole Berg, an American, directs the Mercy Ship Support Office in Lausanne, Switzerland.

Sunday

Meditation

Praise the Lord, O my soul; all my inmost being, praise his holy name. He does not treat us as our sins deserve or repay us according to our iniquities. For as high as the heavens are above the earth, so great is his love for those who fear him; as far as the east is from the west, so far has he removed our transgressions from us.

Psalm 103:1,10-12

Monday

The steps of a man are established by the Lord; and He delights in his way.
Psalm 37:23 NASB

Our outreach team was in southern Albania to help start a church. We had no address or telephone number for our friend who was living there. He had assured us that because he was the only foreigner living in the town, anyone would be able to tell us where he lived.

Now we were two days late, and it was after midnight. The streets were deserted except for a few nervous-looking policemen. We prayed for someone who spoke English to help us.

Soon, a young man walked by who understood a few words of English. He motioned for us to follow him. He led us to the post office where two American women were at the telephone. We never found out how the man knew they were there.

One of the women wrote a note in Albanian, listing our friend's name and his village. While some local men unsuccessfully tried to locate our friend, three policemen approached our van.

We were relieved to hear they weren't going to arrest us. They were simply nervous about our safety, and wanted us to move closer to the police station so they could protect us. After reading our Albanian note, the police chief and an officer who spoke some English drove us to find our friend.

Awakened out of a sound sleep by two policemen, our friend listened intently to the tale of how God led us to him. Even when we had no idea where we were going, we were never out of God's care.

Sandy Oestreich, an American, works with Slavic Ministries.

Tuesday

As a prisoner for the Lord, then, I urge you to live a life worthy of the calling you have received. Be completely humble and gentle; be patient, bearing with one another in love.

Ephesians 4:1-2

In Ephesians 4, the Word of God tells us we need to be diligent to preserve the unity of the Spirit until someday we all attain to the unity of the faith.

Did Jesus say, "By this shall all men know that you are my disciples, because you have the same statement of doctrine"? No, He said they would know we belonged to Him because of our love for one another.

I once heard a Baptist minister speaking about this. He told how God had called him to minister among Catholics in South America. He protested, "But God, how can I work with them? I don't agree with all they do and believe!" He said that God replied to him, "I work with you, and I don't agree with all you do and believe, either!"

Dr. D.G. Barnhouse was a respected Presbyterian theologian and the editor of *Revelation,* the precursor to *Eternity* magazine. Even though he had taught that Pentecostals were in error, he accepted an invitation late in his life to spend a week ministering among Pentecostals. Later he said, "I found that 95 percent of what they believe, I believe. Two percent was totally contradictory, and three percent was in a hazy area. I decided that I could set aside my differences of five percent for any brother or sister in the Lord."

The Body of Christ is a fellowship of those who have found true liberty in Jesus Christ. As we walk in that liberty, we will find that He calls us to leave behind even the good things He has given us in order to find something greater—servanthood to His Great Commission and unity with others who are different, but love Him as we do.

Loren Cunningham, an American, is founder and president of YWAM. He lives in Hawaii, USA.

From *Winning, God's Way* by Loren Cunningham with Janice Rogers. Copyright © 1988 by Loren Cunningham. Published by YWAM Publishing, Seattle, Washington. Used by permission [from pages 60-62].

Wednesday

Is anything too hard for me?   *Jeremiah 32:27*

There was absolutely no way to get home! I had been teaching in Indonesia and Singapore, and had repeatedly tried to get a confirmed seat for the flight from Taiwan to Hawaii.

Shirley, the booking agent in Singapore, told me she had been awakened early to pray for my situation. But even with all those prayers, nothing changed. I asked the Lord if I should go ahead and fly the first half of my flight, trusting Him to confirm the Taiwan/Hawaii portion while I was in the air. This was quite risky, because each passenger must have a confirmed flight to receive hotel and food accommodations in Taiwan.

I received a Scripture clearly confirming that I was to go ahead. In Taiwan, I fully expected my name to be on the list! When I told the agent that my name should be on record, he graciously offered me a free ride to the hotel so I could check on it.

While waiting for the bus, I explained my situation to a friendly Chinese man. He said that his sister was meeting him at the hotel, and that he would be glad to give me the hotel and meal vouchers that he would no longer need.

When we met the man's sister, she shared that she had just received his letter that afternoon, and would not have known of his arrival without it. My new friend checked me into the hotel, and handed me his vouchers.

I then felt God directing me to go to the office of the president of China Airlines to see about my flight. I didn't get to see the president, but it turned out that I didn't have to. After telling the president's secretary about my situation, he called the person in charge at the airport and gave them clear orders that I was to have "first priority" standby, and special attention.

David Gustaveson, an American, leads YWAM's Global Opportunity Network, mobilizing local churches into missions. He lives in California, USA.

Thursday

Whatever you ask for in prayer, believe that you have received it, and it will be yours..
Mark 11:24

I moved and dusted this notebook many times. Part of my student work duty was to clean the prayer room in Building 2 at the University of the Nations campus in Hawaii. The notebook lay on a corner table by a lamp and a Bible. The room was small, but from the window, I could see the sparkling blue ocean. The walls were lined with soft cushions, and a worn carpet completed the furnishings.

My curiosity got the best of me, and I picked up the notebook to glance through it. Fascinated, I sat on one of the cushions and began reading. It was a prayer journal, and the entries appeared in many different languages and handwriting.

Some entries were dated back many months; others were more recent. The prayers were both general and global: for a country, a people group, or a nation's government. Others were specific and personal: for the safety of an outreach team heading for a difficult field; for a sick staff member; for needed funds to pay school fees; for the family of a leader away on a trip.

I felt that I was holding something almost sacred. In the weeks and months since these requests had been written, many had been answered. I had heard firsthand stories of God's intervention, His provision, and His enabling.

Reverently, I returned the notebook to the table. I continued cleaning, but with a new awareness. This was the most important little room on base, because this was where God and His children loved and shared what was on their hearts.

Beverly Caruso, an American, is a Bible teacher and author who leads YWAM Writer's Seminars. She lives in California, USA.

Friday

Now faith is being sure of what we hope for and certain of what we do not see.
Hebrews 11:1

Grandma went to a camp retreat in the redwoods of Northern California. At the end of one of the meetings, a lady walked up, placed a piece of paper in Grandma's hand, and said, "The Lord told me to give this to you."

Grandma had never seen the woman before. She took the paper, put it in her pocket, and thanked the woman. When she looked at it later, she found that the paper was a check for $55. Grandma prayed about what she was to do with the money, and felt she should send it to me.

I had been in Alaska for some months, and longed to spend the Christmas holidays with my family. I had made reservations to fly to California, even though I didn't have enough money to buy a ticket. Then the check from Grandma came in the mail. It covered the balance of my airline ticket exactly.

Immediately, I went to the travel agent to buy my ticket. She told me the fare had gone up $50—the deadline had passed for the lower price.

Later, I went to a prayer meeting and shared about Grandma's check and the higher fare. In light of all that had happened, I was looking forward to seeing how God would provide the $50. After the meeting, a couple asked me to visit with them. They wrote out a check for the remaining $50.

Off I went to spend a joyous holiday with my family. And it turned out that this would be my last Christmas with Grandma—she died the following year.

Lori Durham, an American, is secretary of the School of Worship and Intercession in Kailua-Kona, Hawaii, USA.

Saturday

He who has compassion on them will guide them.   *Isaiah 49:10*

A YWAM team from Arkansas was on outreach in Central America. They gave out vegetable seeds to families in the run-down part of Managua, Nicaragua, to help them grow food, and used the gifts as an opportunity to share their faith.

The packets were accepted enthusiastically by one young mother in her cardboard and nylon dwelling. She responded to the gift with groans and gestures.

"She wanted so badly to understand us and to talk to us, but she couldn't," said Lisa King, who recognized the movements as similar to the deaf sign language she'd learned at home.

Lisa was the only member of the 25-person team visiting the area who was able to use sign language. She used her hands to describe the Gospel to the woman. Then she and her friends performed a short, wordless drama. The team had prepared this presentation to explain the Gospel across the English-Spanish language barrier. They prayed with the woman, and helped her plant the first seeds in her small garden.

Later that day, they returned and met the woman's husband. He was delighted to meet someone who could help him better communicate with his wife. Lisa taught him several basic signs and made a simple set of hand-drawn deaf sign cards for further lessons after the group left.

God had answered the team's earlier prayer for guidance to just the right house.

Robert Itzin, an American, works with primary health care in El Salvador.

Sunday

Meditation

For it is by grace you have been saved, through faith—and this not from yourselves, it is the gift of God—not by works, so that no one can boast. For we are God's workmanship, created in Christ Jesus to do good works, which God prepared in advance for us to do.

Ephesians 2:8-10

Monday

Jesus took bread, gave thanks and broke it, and gave it to his disciples.
Matthew 26:26

The wish of every true disciple of Jesus is clear. He wants to serve Jesus. However, he often asks himself, "Who am I that I could do something to alleviate so much suffering and need in the world? What can I do?"

Jesus simply says to us, "Give Me what you have; give Me yourself."

I must answer, "Here I am, Lord. Take me as I am."

Jesus took what was given to Him and gave thanks. He didn't say it was too little. He didn't say it was worthless. He simply took it. Jesus takes what I give to Him. He takes my temper, my old character, my sin, my failure, my pride, and my abilities. He thankfully takes everything.

Then He breaks it.

He breaks the power of sin. He breaks my pride; He breaks my selfish character; He erases the stain of the past and the harmful effects of my temper.

Jesus then took what He had broken and gave it back to His disciples. "Use this to feed others," He said. This is how He makes me into an active co-worker with Him.

After He has broken me, I become the answer to the needs around me. I discover that I have enough to give because what I give comes from His hand. Therefore, He alone deserves the credit.

Hans Fritz, a German, is a leader with YWAM-Austria.

Tuesday

The Lord is close to the brokenhearted and saves those who are crushed in spirit.
Psalm 34:18

It's easy to confuse brokenness with aloneness. I recently went through a period of time where it seemed that everything around me was crumbling. In such times, I usually tended to become deeply depressed and to complain about my problems to everyone around. I would become frustrated and discouraged at being unable to understand what was happening to me or why.

But this time, I decided to apply what I knew as a Christian to my problems. I began searching for the Lord's hand in my situation, and as I did, I could recognize the ways He was working in me. As I gained new insights, I learned to be thankful in all things.

The worse my circumstances became, the more I leaned on the Lord and felt Him beside me. I still shed tears, but they were tears of joy. I was secure in the knowledge that the One in control never abandons us.

Vincente Forner, a Spaniard, works in the areas of music and publishing in Spain.

Wednesday

I will lie down and sleep in peace, for you alone, O Lord, make me dwell in safety.
                                                                    Psalm 4:8

I lay in my sleeping bag on the concrete, listening to rats scurrying across the floor. Our two babies slept nearby, also on the floor. This cement schoolhouse was also used for food storage. The rats indulged themselves freely.

"Oh, God, what are we doing in this remote tribal village with two babies?"

I was unable to relax and sleep again for fear that the rats would decide to munch on our ears. I didn't dare light a candle—I might actually see the rats. *What do I do in this dilemma, Lord?*

As I prayed this, I remembered my friends at home and began to pray for them. In order to concentrate on my friends, and not think of the rats, I whispered my friends' names out loud. It awakened my husband.

He listened as I told him my seemingly impossible situation, and my temporary solution. He suggested that I listen to praise music on our portable tape player. I hadn't realized that the tape player was lying right beside me. I took it, thanked my husband, and as I listened to the music, I began to cry. Only moments before, I was experiencing fear, restless confusion, and claustrophobia. Now, because I had interceded for my friends and inadvertently awakened my husband, I had set in motion the solution. I was blessed by beautiful music and fell asleep in peace.

Sharon Egert, a Canadian, serves on staff in Hawaii, USA.

Thursday

Never will I leave you; never will I forsake you.   Hebrews 13:5

It was one of those crazy weekday nights. I rushed to the Parent-Teacher Fellowship (PTF) at the Christian school where my two girls go. On PTF nights, the children often do a small program in their classroom to demonstrate what they've been learning. It's a great way to keep up with what's happening.

Except for one thing. These programs happen simultaneously in the different classrooms. Understandably, each of my girls wants me to be at *her* program. This causes me great concern since I want to be with each of them, too.

This particular night, I really tried. First I checked with Rebekah's teacher, who said Rebekah would be on at the beginning. Then I ran down to Rachel's class. Her teacher told me Rachel would be doing her part toward the middle. Perfect!

I returned to Rebekah's class for the program, but as I entered the classroom, Rebekah was just sitting down. I'd missed her! I then literally ran down the hall to Rachel's class, hoping I hadn't missed her, too. Gladly, I made it to her class with time left over to sit and reflect.

I felt miserable! I'd done my best to juggle my time, but blew it...and failed Rebekah. I just couldn't be in two places at once.

Then God reminded me that *He* is never at a loss with His children. He is not limited like we are. God's not in a panic, running up and down hallways trying to be in two places at the same time. On the contrary, God is totally relaxed while He's in every place at the same time!

Do you sometimes feel like God isn't with you? Well, maybe you can't feel Him, but rest assured, He's there! He is the perfect parent. Always with you. Never late. Filled with perfect love.

Melody Green-Sievright, an American, directs Last Days Ministries in Lindale, Texas, USA.

Friday

I have hidden your word in my heart that I might not sin against you.
Psalm 119:11

How do you start memorizing Scripture? Let me demonstrate. I memorized I Peter. I started at the beginning: "Peter, an apostle of Jesus Christ, To God's elect, strangers in the world, scattered throughout Pontus, Galatia, Cappadocia, Asia and Bithynia." I repeated this phrase until I could say it without looking at the page. Then I moved on to the next phrase: "Who have been chosen according to the foreknowledge of God the Father, through the sanctifying work of the Spirit...." Again, I repeated this phrase until I could quote it without looking at the page.

Then I strung all the phrases I had learned together, and recited verses, paragraphs, and chapters until I was able to recite the whole book. This may seem tedious, but it's really not. It's like a snowball tumbling down a snow-covered hill; once you start, your collection of memorized Scripture, and your love for the process of memorizing it, will keep growing.

I would suggest you start in the following way. Start by learning your favorite Bible chapter (Psalm 23; I Corinthians 13; John 3; Romans 8). The fact that it is your favorite chapter gives you a head start in memorizing it. I would suggest avoiding Psalm 119 or anything in Leviticus as your favorite chapter (for obvious reasons), at least until you get started!

At your most alert time of the day, set aside 30 minutes to recite your favorite chapter from the translation of the Bible you like the best. You'll be amazed at how much of the chapter you've already committed to memory. Build on what you already know, and if need be, fill in any memory gaps. Continue to repeat the half hour each day until you have the whole chapter memorized. You'll be amazed at what memorizing your first chapter does for your confidence.

Danny Lehmann, an American, directs the YWAM base in Honolulu, Hawaii, USA, and travels extensively in a teaching ministry.
From *Before You Hit the Wall* by Danny Lehmann. Copyright © 1991 by Danny Lehmann. Published by YWAM Publishing, Seattle, Washington. Used by permission [from pages 73-74].

Saturday

God is not a man, that he should lie....Does he speak and then not act?
Numbers 23:19

Midway through my outreach in Seoul, Korea, I found myself ensconced in an impossible situation. The airline had accidentally canceled my return charter airline ticket to Europe. They reimbursed the $350, but said it was impossible to reinstate the ticket. God directed me to apply to escort Korean orphans being flown to Europe, and even instructed me to give my $350 to someone else who needed it.

The next day, I applied with the adoption agency, but they had no flights available for Europe. As the weeks passed, I started getting anxious. My nonrenewable Korean visa would expire on October 31.

The people at the Holt Adoption Agency were understanding, but others kept saying the word *impossible*. God buoyed my spirit with the verse in Psalms, "I will send you with the fatherless and orphans."

One day, God gave me a specific directive: "Phone the president of Holt." At the moment I phoned, Mr. Tice was passing by the receptionist's desk in the six-story orphanage. I knew he was a Christian, so I told him my story. "It sounds like you've done all that's possible—but keep praying," he said kindly.

Within minutes, the phone rang. Mr. Tice's secretary offered me a flight to Denmark on October 22—the exact date I felt God had told me to go.

When I met Mr. Tice on October 22, he excitedly told me the details. While we were talking together on the phone, one of the three escorts scheduled for that flight had called and canceled. This was the only flight going to Europe before my visa expired. It was also the last moment the airline would allow my name to be exchanged for hers.

Dawn Gauslin, an American, is the International Coordinator for YWAM's field-based Leadership Training Schools. She is also an assistant to Darlene Cunningham.

Sunday

Meditation

Sing to the Lord a new song; sing to the Lord, all the earth. Sing to the Lord, praise his name; proclaim his salvation day after day. Declare his glory among the nations, his marvelous deeds among all peoples. For great is the Lord and most worthy of praise.

Psalm 96:1-4

Monday

Flee from sexual immorality,...he who sins sexually sins against his own body.   *I Corinthians 6:18*

Anyone who gets sexually involved outside of marriage is going to get hurt. God created us to give ourselves sexually in marriage to a life partner of the opposite sex. Violation of the way God intended us to live does not bring freedom, but bondage, and not to tell others about this is unloving.

Through many years of working with young people in Afghanistan and Amsterdam, I have had a number of opportunities to become friends with people who were ignorant of, or disobedient to, God's laws regarding sexual purity. I remember confronting one young couple about why it was wrong to live together outside of marriage. We talked about trust, and how that can only come with public commitment to an exclusive, lifelong relationship. We discussed God's plan for secure, happy families and how this can never be achieved without such commitment. The bond between them gradually dissolved as they honestly faced up to the selfish and superficial nature of their relationship.

Today both of them are Christians, happily married to other people, and actively serving the Lord. They often thank me for helping them face the sin in their lives. Hitting them over the head with the Bible wouldn't have worked, but sharing openly with them why God asks us to be totally committed to another person in marriage did. With God's help, I achieved a balance of tenderness and directness that let them know I was deeply committed to them while challenging them about inconsistency in their lives. It is possible to uphold a biblical standard and be loving at the same time.

Floyd McClung, an American, directs Leadership Development Programs for YWAM. He lives in California, USA.
From *Learning to Love People You Don't Like* by Floyd McClung. Copyright © by Floyd McClung. Published by YWAM Publishing, Seattle, Washington. Used by permission [from pages 26-27].

Tuesday

Let us run with perseverance the race marked out for us.   Hebrews 12:1

On television, I watched the finals of the men's 4-by-100-meter relay at the 1992 Summer Olympics in Barcelona. Within seconds, the leading runners were pounding down the track toward the finish line. In just a few fleeting moments, it was over. Each runner dashed one hundred meters. Three times the baton had been faultlessly passed. When it was all over, the American team had done it better and faster than anyone had done it before. They had made it look so simple. They were the Olympic and World champions and took their places atop the podium to receive their gold medals.

The mission field is like that race. God calls us to run a leg of the race. In running our leg, we join the ranks of a long and illustrious line of people God has called to carry the baton in reaching the lost of the world with the Gospel. There are those for whom running a leg of the relay has meant a lifetime of faithful service on the mission field. For others, it has been several years, while some were called only for the short term. The length of time for which God calls us to serve is not important. What is important is that we serve diligently to the best of our abilities. When that period comes to a close, it is time to pass the baton on to the next person God has called.

Peter Jordan, a Canadian, leads YWAM Associates International, a ministry to YWAM alumni. He lives in Vancouver, B.C., Canada.
Adapted from *Re-Entry...Making the Transition from Missions to Life at Home* by Peter Jordan. Copyright © 1992 by Peter Jordan. Published by YWAM Publishing, Seattle, Washington. Used by permission [from pages 66-67].

Wednesday

I love the Lord, for he heard my voice; he heard my cry for mercy. Because he turned his ear to me, I will call on him as long as I live.   Psalm 116:1-2

I didn't tell anyone about my need. I was just wishing I had a little bit of money to spend on my days off. It didn't seem all that important. I didn't even have much faith that the Lord would think it was important. So I just prayed one simple prayer: "Do You think I could just have $20?"

About a week later, my friend Kay and I were chatting in my room. The topic of money had never even come up. After a while, Kay left, then showed up again a few minutes later.

"I was asking God what to do with some money I'd received for my birthday," she said, "and He said I should give it to you."

Kay handed me some money, and my mouth fell open when I saw—it was a $20 bill! It was exactly the amount I had asked God for. Only then did I tell her about my need and my prayer.

Diane Belanger, a Canadian, is a staff member in Kailua-Kona, Hawaii, USA.

Thursday

I am my beloved's, and my beloved is mine.　　　*Song of Solomon 6:3 NASB*

My fiancé seemed far more concerned than I that he couldn't afford an engagement ring. The night before he left for his Discipleship Training School outreach, he held my hand and said, "I believe the Lord is a romantic God. I'm going to keep praying and looking for a ring for you."

When he returned, he told me that he'd spent hours looking for the right ring, checking prices, and getting depressed. A teammate even offered to charge it to his credit card, but it just didn't feel right. He returned empty-handed.

He was discouraged, but I nearly forgot about my naked finger. We got busy helping lead a Musicians' Summer of Service outreach to Europe, so I pushed the lack of a ring out of my mind.

The day after we returned, my friend Joan approached us with the answer. Her husband had died seven years earlier in a car accident, leaving her alone to raise their two sons.

Joan said she had been praying about the money for a ring for us. She was still wearing her own wedding ring when God spoke to her to give it to us. She cried, then took it off, knowing she would be in disobedience not to give it to us. She had thought that one day she would give it to one of her sons, so she discussed it with them first, and they were in agreement. While she was telling this to us, one of the boys said, "You need to do what God is telling you, Mom!"

Today, I wear the ring proudly. It has more significance than any we could have paid for.

Barb Foye, an American, works on YWAM staff in the Czech Republic.

Friday

If I had cherished sin in my heart, the Lord would not have listened.

Psalm 66:18

I stood in the dark in my own backyard. The black sky matched my mood. I had been struggling with resentment. Now I couldn't sleep because guilt gnawed at my soul. "God, forgive me," I said one more time, but my own best efforts at repentance brought only the ashes of further failure. I knew what I should be feeling. I should be feeling love, and I should be extending forgiveness. But I had to admit the bitter truth: In spite of all my knowledge of right principle, I was failing at the simplest level of my Christian walk. I'd been hurt and disappointed by a friend, and I could not forgive.

I suddenly saw the awesome truth. John Dawson had not become one bit better after all these years of Christian life. Staring at me from the grave was the same vain, selfish person who had come to the Cross so many years before. It's no use putting cosmetics on a corpse, teaching it a new behavior and a new vocabulary. No one knows how wicked he or she is until that person truly has tried to be righteous.

"God, rescue me," I prayed. "Rescue me from myself." A familiar theme invaded my understanding: the Cross of Jesus, His life for mine, the indwelling Christ. Yes, I have always believed that Jesus lives within a believer. But that night in my despair, I saw my total need for His life to be the only explanation for any victory of mine. That night I came back to the Cross. I experienced again His cleansing and forgiveness. The consequences of my sin had fallen upon the Lamb that was slain. The blood was again sprinkled on the doorposts of my heart. Instead of perfecting righteousness in me, He who is righteous was standing up within me and beginning to live His life.

John Dawson, a New Zealander, is YWAM's International Director of Urban Missions.
From *Taking Our Cities for God* by John Dawson. Copyright © 1989 by John Dawson. Published by Creation House, Lake Mary, Florida. Used by permission [from page 188].

Saturday

Some faced jeers and flogging, while still others were chained and put in prison....the world was not worthy of them. Hebrews 11:36,38

In 1985, the nation of Nepal had stringent laws against preaching the Gospel, converting someone to Christianity, and water baptism. The nine outreach team members from five different nations used great care as they shared Christ with the Nepali people.

As the team walked into a village to witness, policemen arrested them and took them and their porters to jail. They were there for seven days, not knowing whether anyone outside the village knew of their arrest. The police gave them only small amounts of food. In order to go to the bathroom, they were chained together in pairs.

During their trial, they learned that if they were convicted, they would serve three years in jail. They faced their biggest discouragement when false witnesses testified against them.

Before the trial ended, one of the Nepali porters escaped with instructions to go to Kathmandu and tell of the team's captivity. Not knowing where to look for help, he approached a stranger. The man was an official with the United States Embassy, and had just eaten lunch that day with some other YWAMers.

Within hours, a group from Kathmandu was on its way to West Nepal. They were able to arrange for the release of the team members and their porters.

The team members had to report back to the village nearly every month for the next three years. At last, a verdict of "not guilty" was declared for all.

Steve Cochrane, an American, is Regional Director for YWAM in South Asia

Sunday

Meditation

Therefore, since we have a great high priest who has gone through the heavens, Jesus the Son of God, let us hold firmly to the faith we profess. For we do not have a high priest who is unable to sympathize with our weaknesses, but we have one who has been tempted in every way, just as we are—yet was without sin. Let us then approach the throne of grace with confidence, so that we may receive mercy and find grace to help us in our time of need.

Hebrews 4:14-16

Monday

Imitate those who through faith and patience inherit what has been promised.
Hebrews 6:12

Much has been said about the necessity of faith. Without it, God is not pleased. Little is said about perseverance, patience, endurance, and waiting. Scriptural examples of men and women of faith exhibit this important, additional element. God's formula for those who would inherit what He has promised is:

Faith + Patience = Fulfillment of God's Word to us.

It is one thing to have faith at a particular moment in time. But faith is usually tested as time passes, without instant fulfillment of God's promise. Of Abraham it is written, "Without becoming weak in faith...with respect to the promise of God, he did not waver in unbelief, but grew strong in faith, giving glory to God, and being fully assured that what He had promised, He was able also to perform" (Romans 4:19-21 NASB).

As we look at God's character and His Word, faith can grow in the face of disappointment, hurts, personal failure, change, satanic opposition, and the testings of God. Endurance that pleases God is not just gritting our teeth and holding out, but rather a joyful expectancy that God's goodness will yet be realized, even while there is no firm evidence. Faith is the "assurance of things hoped for, the conviction of things not seen." If, like Moses, we endure, as seeing Him who is unseen, God is pleased, and is able to fulfill His Word to us.

"Having patiently waited, [Abraham] obtained the promise" (Hebrews 6:15 NASB). May we be counted among those who inherit God's promises. Most of all, may God's desires and plans not be left unfulfilled because we did not endure in faith.

Jim Orred, an American, directs YWAM's ministry in the Balkan area.

Tuesday

For by the grace given me I say to every one of you: Do not think of yourself more highly than you ought, but rather think of yourself with sober judgment, in accordance with the measure of faith God has given you. Romans 12:3

My first awareness of the deception of status and partiality occurred when I was 19 years old. I accompanied my father to an annual pastor's conference. I felt very comfortable at the first meeting. I knew most of the pastors present. A number of them had stayed in our home over the years.

After one of the evening services, we headed for a nearby restaurant which had become the unofficial place to congregate during the conference. As we sat together in the restaurant, my teenaged mind was confronted with a startling revelation.

Pastors who had been so friendly when they were guests in our home now seemed barely civil toward my father. It took no genius to quickly recognize that the unfriendly pastors were generally those who pastored churches larger than the one my father pastored. These pastors, unconsciously I'm sure, clustered together in cliques away from the others. The pastors of medium-sized churches also sat together in groups. I looked around the restaurant and could not see any pastors from the denomination's smaller churches.

Status is such a blind spot for us of the evangelical church in the western world. We castigate, and rightfully so, the inescapable caste systems of India. Yet our own culture wraps its capitulation to status around us in such subtle ways that we deny its reality and its hold on our thinking.

Denny Gunderson, an American, serves as North American Director for YWAM, and lives in Seattle, Washington, USA.
From Through the Dust...Breaking Leadership Stereotypes by Denny Gunderson. Published by YWAM Publishing, Seattle, Washington. Used by permission [from pages 62-63].

Wednesday

Enlarge the place of your tent, stretch your tent curtains wide, do not hold back; lengthen your cords, strengthen your stakes.   Isaiah 54:2

Often we imagine the Lord stretching us for His purposes, but I have seen in my life that He asks for our cooperation. I realized this when I was praying about making a commitment to teach at International Christian Schools in Hawaii. I felt ready to do anything but teach.

Eventually, I decided to ask the Lord why this decision was such a struggle. He showed me that inside my "tent," my ability to love was already exhausted. I had no more room in my heart.

God showed me that if I were willing to have my tent enlarged, my capacity to love could be increased. This increase would not come in a mystical way, but He would provide the grace.

I agreed to cooperate, and for years after that, He sent the right people to accomplish His work in me. It was not always easy. Sometimes I fought to pull back the ropes and move the tent pegs in closer to make my space smaller. But by His grace and persistence, my tent enlarged, and the glory is all His.

Do you feel stretched? Maybe you need to consider asking the Lord to open your heart to the people and situations that will stretch you.

Corinne Templeton, from Scotland, teaches English as a Second Language in Whitby, England.

Thursday

For the earth will be filled with the knowledge of the glory of the Lord, as the waters cover the sea.   *Habakkuk 2:14*

This verse speaks of the ultimate, final realization of God's glory covering the whole earth in the time of the millennial reign of Christ. It shines like the wonderful promise of sunshine after a storm or a bitter cruel winter's night. It speaks to us of peace and security after a life of strife and conflict; the difference between heaven and earth.

Jesus said, "the kingdom of God is within you." Because this is true, we do not have to wait; we only need to understand.

For many years I retained this verse from Habakkuk incorrectly in my mind, leaving out the words *knowledge of.* One day I thought of God's wonderful promise after the flood: "As long as the earth endures, seedtime and harvest, cold and heat, summer and winter, day and night will never cease" (Genesis 8:22). I realized that the knowledge of God's glory is here around us all the time. Only He could fulfill such a promise. Only He could maintain the seasons, the days and nights, seedtime and harvest. He reveals Himself in the sunrise, the snowdrop, the ripening grain, the roar of surf on the seashore.

Ben Applegate, from New Zealand, leads Kiaora, a ministry of hospitality and prayer for the government of New Zealand.

Friday

"You will seek me and find me when you seek me with all your heart. I will be found by you," declares the Lord, "and will bring you back from captivity. I will gather you from all the nations and places where I have banished you," declares the Lord, "and will bring you back to the place from which I carried you into exile."   Jeremiah 29:13-14

God has commanded us throughout His Word to seek Him diligently, earnestly, and with a whole heart. Yet we easily fall into a nonchalant relationship with the Lord: loving Him, worshiping Him, and serving Him, but developing a reserve whereby our fervor is diminished. It's usually nothing noticeable, and yet we feel an emptiness inside, knowing that things are not "just right." We can even begin to tolerate sin: wanting revival in others, yet preventing it in ourselves.

I believe the dealings of God are closely linked in the Kingdom of God. God often uses suffering to expose areas of our hearts that He wants to develop and transform into the character of Christ. If we respond to God in the midst of difficulties, He gives us security and confidence. If we fear His dealings because our hearts have grown cold, we pull back in our hearts, shutting out the Lord.

Are you seeking God with humility and an open heart? Are you willing to do anything He asks you to do today? Do you view repentance as a joy-filled experience, or one to be feared and dreaded? Richard Shelly Taylor said, "Holiness is inwrought by the Holy Spirit, not because we have suffered, but because we have surrendered."

Debra Buenting, an American, served with YWAM in Switzerland and on the m/v Anastasis for eight years, and now works as a television producer in Texas, USA.

Saturday

How is it that each of us hears them in his own native language?

I was with a team in Ecuador, 12,000 feet above sea level, in a city surrounded by snow-capped volcanoes. After a quick dinner, the pastor opened the heavy door of a modest building which was soon filled with more than 100 people. Children sat on the floor; adults leaned against walls and stood in the doorway.

After singing, personal testimonies, more singing, and a sermon, our leader asked for anyone wanting prayer to come forward. I wondered how many people would respond. I quickly found out.

Immediately after the benediction, men, women, and children rushed to the front. I panicked. I knew our leader was the only member of our team with enough knowledge of Spanish to be effective. I looked helplessly at him.

"You and Tom be one prayer team, and Russ and I will be the other," he calmly said. "Try to get them to form two lines."

Tom and I exchanged desperate glances as we were surrounded. A frail lady tugged my arm, pulled my head down, and said something into my ear.

"What did she say?" Tom asked.

"She said she has recurring headaches," I responded.

He was wide-eyed, but I was too busy to explain. For over an hour, we prayed with each person in line. They stated their need, and together we prayed. Not until the last person left did I have time to think about what had happened.

Lord, I asked quietly, *how did I understand those people? I don't speak Spanish.*

Then I realized that God cared so much for them He had used me as an intercessor to state their needs, which, of course, He already knew.

Stacy Sells, an American, is a nonresidential missionary living in Singapore and working to reach a tribal group in India.

Sunday

Meditation

I lift up my eyes to the hills—where does my help come from? My help comes from the Lord, the Maker of heaven and earth. He will not let your foot slip—he who watches over you will not slumber....The Lord will watch over your coming and going both now and forevermore.

Psalm 121:1-3,8

Monday

Do not worry about tomorrow. *Matthew 6:34*

When my wife and I joined the Alberta, Canada, YWAM staff, we believed God would provide for our family. I was surprised by an unexpected provision.

The office was empty that morning as I worried about our financial struggles. As "home missionaries" working in our own country, we relied on the gifts of a small faithful support team. We were falling behind on our rent, and bills were piling up.

All was quiet as I knelt and cried out to the Lord. "Father, what should I do?" I asked. A peculiar thought popped into my mind: *Call the minibus company.*

For some reason, I hadn't considered that God might want me to take a part-time job. I was supposed to be in full-time Christian service. But I had noticed the minibus driving around town, usually full of either boisterous kids or seniors.

With rising hope, I phoned the minibus company. "Will you be hiring any part-time drivers in the near future?" I asked.

"Yes," the man answered. "We'll be placing an ad in the newspaper in a few days."

After hearing about my five years of professional driving experience, he encouraged me to apply for the job. I talked the idea over with my base director, and applied. Two days later, before the want ad was published, I was driving the minibus.

The job was ideal, giving me the flexibility to work on alternating weekends and fill in when regular drivers were ill or on vacations. The income eased our financial pressures, and I was able to meet many people in the community.

God's provision came in an unexpected way, but He was faithful to meet our needs as He'd promised.

Doug Lockhart, a Canadian, is Director of Corporate Communications at the University of the Nations in Kailua-Kona, Hawaii, USA.

Tuesday

I rejoice in your promise like one who finds great spoil.   Psalm 119:162

Warren, Linda, and David drove up to the border between Austria and Communist-controlled Hungary. Their specially equipped van concealed their precious cargo in well-hidden compartments. They were risking their freedom to deliver the Gospel to Hungarian believers.

Their silent prayers intensified as they saw guards armed with assault rifles. Linda, strategically positioned in the back seat, continued knitting a scarf. The stitches became tighter and smaller. The three tried to look like carefree vacationers.

After asking if they had any bombs or guns, the guard motioned the van toward an open gate. As the gate slammed behind them, they saw another gate ahead. As they approached the second checkpoint, they felt the terror of an animal caught in a trap.

Armed guards pushed Linda aside and searched the entire van. After a thorough inspection, the guards waved them into the office. There, they were faced with endless paperwork and the clerk's ever-changing demands. They had to fill out three identical sets of the forms—by hand. They wondered, *Can the guards read our minds? Is our behavior betraying our secret?*

At last they were waved on. Night was falling, and they headed for the home of a couple in a small town outside Budapest. The husband worked for the railroad, and would have ample time to distribute the books and Bibles on his frequent travels.

Approaching the small town, they praised God for His faithfulness and sustaining grace.

As told to Diane Orozco, an American who works in food services at Last Days Ministries in Lindale, Texas, USA.

Wednesday

Taking the five loaves and the two fish...he gave thanks....They all ate and were satisfied.   Matthew 14:19-20

The base in Samoa already had 13 regulars for meals. To feed that many, I had doubled the meatball recipe, the rice, and the vegetables. Tonight, there was enough dessert for everyone.

We were just ready to serve dinner when a car pulled up. I went downstairs to greet the five friends who had come to see our bookstore. Only then did I learn that my husband, the base leader, had invited all five visitors to join us for dinner.

After sending everyone upstairs to eat, I returned to the bookstore. I wanted to talk to my heavenly Father about the food, and to ask Him to multiply it to cover all the extra mouths.

After about 30 minutes, I went upstairs. To my amazement— though I shouldn't have been amazed—there was plenty of food left. I learned that some people had even taken second helpings.

After everyone left for either a church service or other responsibilities, I enjoyed my meal, then washed the dishes. I savored the quiet kitchen. My heart was full of praise and thanks to the Lord. I still don't know whether He increased the food or decreased everyone's appetite. However He wants to feed His children is up to Him.

Lydia Hall, a Hollander, leads Women's Ministries in Kona, Hawaii, USA.

Thursday

"Not by might nor by power, but by my Spirit," says the Lord Almighty.
Zechariah 4:6

Shortly after my conversion, God gave me a promise that He would cleanse my mind from the effects of psychedelic drugs. Drugs had taken such a toll on my mind that I couldn't hold down a job which required a memory span of longer than a few minutes.

But as I made God's Word a priority in my life, He began stretching and restoring my memory span, and gave me the capacity to remember hundreds of Bible verses. Not only this, but I was able to work at jobs other than washing dishes, washing cars, or other assembly line work.

I recount my experience because it confirms what the Scripture says. My I.Q. had nothing to do with what God did in my mind. It was a work of His Spirit.

Ask the Holy Spirit to make this true in your life. Ask Him to fill your spirit with His Word. As you believe, He will store up His Word in your spirit.

Danny Lehmann, an American, directs the YWAM base in Honolulu, Hawaii, USA, and travels extensively in a teaching ministry.
From Before You Hit the Wall by Danny Lehmann. Copyright © 1991 by Danny Lehmann. Published by YWAM Publishing, Seattle, Washington. Used by permission [from page 72].

Friday

Who shall separate us from the love of Christ? Shall trouble or hardship or persecution or famine or nakedness or danger or sword?   Romans 8:35

A pastor had been put in prison for preaching the Gospel. When he arrived, he decided this prison was his mission field. He began looking around for the worst criminal he could find. (Soviet prisons combine political and religious offenders with common criminals.) He focused his prayer and witnessing efforts on a murderer, a man who was so vicious the prison guards feared him.

Every prisoner was required to work twelve hours a day. The Christian decided that he could only reach this murderer if he fasted and prayed, so he gave up the meager prison food but continued his hard labor. When others sank into exhausted sleep, the pastor climbed out of his bunk onto the bare floor to pray.

One night, while he was on his knees, he sensed someone behind him. He turned.

The murderer was staring him in the face. "What are you doing?" he asked.

"I'm praying," he replied.

"What are you praying for?" he asked gruffly.

"I'm praying for you," the pastor answered, wiping away tears.

Soon, that man gave his heart to the Lord. The change in him was so drastic that news of what had happened spread through the prison. A real change took place in the overall atmosphere of the prison. This so impressed the prison boss that he transferred the pastor to the worst prison in Russia, with the promise that if he could bring a change there, they would give him an early release.

A move of God started at the second prison, leading the pastor to write his wife a painful letter. He begged for her to understand his decision. He was turning down his parole in order to continue his ministry in that prison.

Loren Cunningham, an American, is founder and president of YWAM. He lives in Hawaii, USA.

From Winning, God's Way by Loren Cunningham with Janice Rogers. Copyright © 1988 by Loren Cunningham. Published by YWAM Publishing, Seattle, Washington. Used by permission [from pages 70-71].

Saturday

He is the Rock, his works are perfect, and all his ways are just. A faithful God who does no wrong, upright and just is he.   Deuteronomy 32:4

There was a time when that verse in Deuteronomy took on a new meaning for me. I began to wonder if God knew what was going on in my life, or if He even cared. I wondered if He were in control. I wondered if He were truly just.

At one point, I even questioned God's love and righteousness. Realizing that it would be impossible for me to be obedient to the Lord without knowing Him and His character, I prayed to know who Jesus really was. I disciplined myself to read the Word every day, and as I did, a clear picture of Christ began to emerge. I needed to confess that the Lord was the One I placed my trust in and that He was still as faithful to me as He had always been.

The Lord can help us in every situation. He walks beside us every day. He knows us and what is best for us. If you have given your life to God in the past, renew your commitment today. Make Him Lord over your future. Give thanks to the Lord. The only true happiness is in knowing Him.

Anja Miemela, of Finland, is base interpreter and works with leaders of small groups in Finland.

Sunday

Meditation

How great is the love the Father has lavished on us, that we should be called children of God! And that is what we are! The reason the world does not know us is that it did not know him. Dear friends, now we are children of God, and what we will be has not yet been made known. But we know that when he appears, we shall be like him, for we shall see him as he is.

I John 3:1-3

Monday

And these signs will accompany those who believe:...they will place their hands on sick people, and they will get well.   Mark 16:17-18

In the heart of India is a people group called the Kolamis. They are considered a tribal people. Their religion is animism—worshipers of spirits believed to dwell in inanimate objects such as rocks and trees.

A young Kolami girl wasted away with a debilitating illness. Her heartbroken father sent for the village shaman (witch doctor) to use incantations in order to bring the girl back to life. He failed. The father sent him away.

Then he remembered hearing of a community of Kolami Christians who embraced a powerful God called Jesus Christ. The father traveled the long distance to find the community. Several Kolami elders returned with the father. After earnest prayer in the name of Jesus, the girl opened her eyes—to the utter shock of everyone. The conversions of the girl's parents to Christ were the first of many conversions in the Kolami village.

Steve Cochrane, an American, is Regional Director for YWAM in South Asia.

Tuesday

I pray that you, being rooted and established in love, may have power...to grasp how wide and long and high and deep is the love of Christ.

Ephesians 3:17-18

In this passage to the Ephesians, the apostle Paul described four aspects of the love of God. In the first verse of chapter five, he exhorted us to be imitators of our heavenly Father as dearly loved children. Paul found the completeness of God's love strong enough to stagger his understanding, and compelling enough to inspire him to strive to evangelize the world.

Following his example, Paul issues this challenge to us:

...To have a love wide enough to encompass the world. In the same way that God loved the world, we are instructed to love other nations by interceding for them, praying fervently that they might come to know the Lord.

...To have a love which is long lasting. With an awareness that everyone will face eternity someday—with or without the knowledge of God—we are admonished to work tirelessly to share the Gospel with the rest of the world.

...To have a love which is high. In God's infinite wisdom, He has made love His highest priority, and He implores us to do the same. The greatest aim of our Christian walk should be love; not a second-rate love, but the love of God poured into our hearts by the Holy Spirit.

...To have a love which is deep. Christ's love for us is not just a superficial acceptance. He knows us perfectly and accepts us with all our faults and weaknesses. Our goal is to love others with that same depth of love. The more we get to know one another, the deeper our love for each other should grow.

The thirteenth chapter of Romans tells us that each day we have a continuing debt to pay off—the debt of loving one another.

Carlo Brugnoli, a Swiss, served as leader of YWAM in Lausanne, Switzerland for three years, and is now an evangelist and writer.

Wednesday

The King's daughter is all glorious within; her clothing is interwoven with gold. She will be led to the King in embroidered work.

Psalm 45:13-14 NASB

In this passage, God beautifully describes His bride—you and me—as being prepared for the King. How do we view the preparation? God's dealing in our lives is like embroidery. It takes time, and requires a master plan to produce a valuable design. At times, it is uncomfortable for us. But precious gold thread, God's character, is being worked into our lives.

The biblical bride also wears jewels and pearls. Jewels are formed in dark, underground places through the application of great pressure. Pearls are formed when foreign matter enters a mollusk and the irritating material is covered with layers of pearl. In the same way, God's design is to transform the irritants and pressure in our lives into something precious.

Myrna Hill, a Canadian, serves on the mercy ship, m/v Anastasis.

Thursday

Humble yourselves, therefore, under God's mighty hand, that he may lift you up in due time. I Peter 5:6

Californian Celeste Yohai is soft-spoken and petite. She loves to recall the time she had to travel to a concert in a small canoe, her guitar balanced precariously. Her prizewinning song, "I Will Go," which espouses the theme of compassion and availability, was chosen as the anthem for a Love Europe Missions Conference.

Although the song was chosen to be part of a missions-worship album from Kingsway, Celeste isn't looking for fame and glory.

"I'm not what the market wants, but that suits me, because I want to be able to go to the tiny places and encourage the little flame. I don't want the pressure of having to sell a lot of records and T-shirts," she says.

As a member of YWAM's Musicians for Missions team based in the Netherlands, Celeste played in many small, out-of-the-way places: schools, orphanages, and churches among some of the less-populated Philippine islands, and took part in an impromptu candlelight concert in a South African home.

Yet the news of her success came at an important moment. As part of a group for several years, she felt uncertain about moving out as a solo artist.

"It encouraged me to keep going. My choice would be to be part of a group, but the Lord had been talking to me about stepping out on my own. Having the song chosen helped me to see that all we have to do is give Him the little we have, and He will multiply the rest—just like the little boy with the loaves and fishes."

All of Celeste's music is initiated by prayer, "because I want to be able to communicate God's heart to touch people." Through the song and her life, Celeste has touched the lives of millions.

Andy Butcher, from Great Britain, directs the Press & Media Services Department of YWAM's International Operations Office, and lives in Colorado Springs, Colorado, USA.

Friday

You are a chosen people, a royal priesthood, a holy nation, a people belonging to God, that you may declare the praises of him who called you out of darkness into his wonderful light.
I Peter 2:9

In Old Testament times, one could be either king or priest, but not both. In Christ, royalty and priesthood are blended together, and we as His followers have the privilege of functioning in both capacities. Each is complementary to the other.

As royalty, we are called upon to "do" certain things. Being royal carries with it both opportunity and obligation. We are to make God's laws known. These are His rules and regulations, established for our highest good.

As members of the priesthood, we are to "be" a certain way. We are to show our love for the Lord through praise, worship, adoration, thanksgiving, and intercessory prayer.

A godly nation will have national days of celebration and mourning. It will boast unity, peace, loyalty, a flow of communication, exchanges of ideas, freedom of expression, and freedom of movement.

As citizens of God's Kingdom, we need to be sure that we ourselves promote unity and act as peacemakers. We need to demonstrate loyalty, not just to our local community or national project, but interdenominationally and internationally. We are responsible for personal witnessing, teaching, and distribution of Christian literature. We are accountable to provide for the needy in practical ways. We are to aid in making possibilities for service open to others by our encouragement and financial support.

Malachi 3:16 tells us that those who feared the Lord talked with each other, and the Lord listened and heard. Today let Him hear us all proclaiming His Word to a waiting world.

Rudy Lack, a Swiss, is director of the YWAM base in Einigen, Switzerland.

Saturday

My grace is sufficient for you, for my power is made perfect in weakness.
II Corinthians 12:9

One day, my husband and I went to visit a friend. We met his lovely daughter, who was with a young man, his legs totally paralyzed from a football accident. He was in a wheelchair.

The first thing I noticed were his dark brown eyes. They were so soft. His face was radiant, and although I knew nothing about him and was just introduced to him, I walked right over to him, looked into his eyes intently, and said, "I love you. I'll tell you one of the reasons I love you. I don't have to ask you one single thing. I see the wheelchair. I see your legs hanging limp, and I see there's not a particle of resentment in your eyes toward God. I don't need to hear your story to know that you have come to terms with God in total rest."

Then I heard the story that proved the truth of what I had said. The Holy Spirit had given me that instantaneous witness through the shining countenance of that young man.

He told me he had been bitter; he had had questions. But he had come to understand, as he had pored over the Word of God, and as he looked into the face of Jesus, that God was "...just in all his ways, and kind in all his doings," just as the Bible says in Psalm 145:17 (RSV).

He shared with enthusiasm some of the dynamic purposes that God had started to reveal for his life since he accepted God's sovereignty and received God's miraculous grace. God had shown him that he was to write a book about his life, and this lovely Christian girlfriend was helping him do it.

Physical healing? No. Spiritual, mental and emotional healing? Yes. A manifestation of miraculous grace and powerful purpose.

Joy Dawson, a former New Zealander but an American citizen for many years, is an International Bible teacher.

From Some of the Ways of God in Healing by Joy Dawson. Copyright © 1991 by Joy Dawson. Published by YWAM Publishing, Seattle, Washington. Used by permission [from pages 85-86].

Sunday

Meditation

Trust in the Lord with all your heart and lean not on your own understanding; in all your ways acknowledge him, and he will make your paths straight.

Proverbs 3:5-6

Monday

For he will command his angels concerning you to guard you in all your ways; they will lift you up in their hands, so that you will not strike your foot against a stone.   *Psalm 91:11-12*

As my friend Nanci and I stood waiting to board the subway in Hong Kong, my body was pushed about by the whim of the crowd. Fortunately, Nanci was taller than most of those around me, so I was able to keep sight of her.

We agreed to meet at a certain subway entrance should we lose one another. Just then I heard a rumble of an approaching car and felt the platform shake beneath my feet. When the car stopped, in the crush of the crowd, I felt like a swimmer caught in a wave. I completely lost sight of Nanci.

When at last I was positioned in front of a car door, I raised my foot and aimed it inside. It slipped off the edge of the step and continued sliding until it was lodged between the train and platform. I fell to my other knee, dodging and deflecting the feet that hurtled my body. I could feel the heat of the tracks against my pinned leg. The train was about to take off, and I was unable to move.

Panicked, I screamed, but my voice was drowned out in the din. Suddenly a hand emerged from the mass of legs on the train and stretched out, beckoning me. Instinctively, I took hold of it. As I did so, I was gently lifted up and inside the car. Just as I struggled to my feet, the train raced away from the station.

My heart was still pounding when I swiveled around to offer an emotional thanks. There was no one there to receive it. From the looks on the faces of my fellow passengers, it was obvious none had played a part in my little drama.

I'll never know for sure where that hand came from. It disappeared just as quickly as it appeared. But no one will ever convince me that there are no guardian angels. I met one there that day.

Stacy Sells, an American, is a nonresidential missionary living in Singapore and working to reach a tribal group in India.

Tuesday

He gently leads those that have young.　　　　　　*Isaiah 40:11*

"You mean you're actually moving to the inner city? That's no place to bring up your kids. Working with street kids is one thing, but taking your kids into that kind of environment is another."

My friend showed genuine concern, and I could understand. Belo Horizonte, a megacity of four million people, would be drastically different from the pleasant rural setting where we now worked. However, we knew the Lord had called us to work with street kids, and believed the best way to start was to live in their midst and open our home to them.

We found an ideal location. True, the house needed lots of work, but it had a separate apartment for our family. Money was miraculously provided to cover the first month's rent.

In my mind's eye, I reviewed the apartment: two small rooms, a tiny kitchen, and an outdoor bathroom. I tried to imagine our four lively kids, ages one to six, playing in the postage stamp-sized yard.

Silently I began praying, "Lord, please help us make this move. It's hard leaving this nice home and going to that tiny apartment. I'm concerned about our little ones. They've enjoyed playing outside freely with their friends, and there they'll be confined to the small yard. What can we do to make it easier for them? They need to know You care for them. Thank You, Lord."

We had moved 15 times in seven years of marriage, and had seen God's loving care every time. We knew His faithfulness—only this time, the move seemed more difficult. Within a few days, a letter arrived from a friend.

"I believe the Lord impressed me to send you money to buy a plastic pool for your children."

When we told the children, they couldn't wait to move.

That pool was God's perfect gift to all of us. The children played in it for hours at a time.

Jeannette Lukasse and her husband, Johan, both from the Netherlands, are the leaders of YWAM's urban ministry base in Belo Horizonte, Brazil.

Wednesday

My God will meet all your needs.   Philippians 4:19

My wife and I were directing a Discipleship Training School about ten miles from the main YWAM base in Kona, Hawaii. Our car broke down, and we had no funds to repair or replace it. There was no way to buy groceries, get to church, or take care of ministry affairs. We needed a car.

My wife and I spoke to the Lord about our need. We knew He could work this out somehow.

"But Lord," we prayed, "we are more interested in serving You, and if it means begging for rides, we will."

One Sunday, a friend called to invite us over to watch the Super Bowl on television. "We'd love to," I responded, "but we have no transportation."

"No problem," he said. "I'll come and pick you up." I knew it was not a problem for him, but I was humiliated to have to ask.

On the street where they picked us up, another friend drove by, spotted us, and stopped. I knew this friend was moving away soon, so I asked what he planned to do with his van.

"Why, do you want it?"

"Yes, how much are you asking?"

"Wait a minute," he said, going to his car and returning with a piece of paper.

"Here's the title; it's yours. I asked God to send the right person for my van, and you're it."

To our amazement, our friend hitched rides himself for the rest of the month he was there, and we enjoyed his van.

Randy Thomas, an American, leads the King's Mansion Discipleship Training School in Kailua-Kona, Hawaii, USA.

Thursday

Jesus replied,... "The Son of Man has no place to lay his head."

Matthew 8:20

In the summer of 1969, five of us (a married couple, their child, and two singles) arrived in Port Moresby, Papua New Guinea, with only $11. In those early days of YWAM, $11 was a lot of money. We usually had no money, but strong faith, a firm commitment to God, and prayer sustained us.

An organization in town provided rooms and car rentals for missionaries, so we spent $10 there on one night's lodging for the women. Kalafi and I expected to sleep in a park. With the other dollar, we rented a car for the day. We hoped to find a relative of Kalafi's who was attending medical school. We thought perhaps he would offer us help.

We hopped into the car and discovered the fuel gauge was on empty. We drove off, praying as we went. The relative could not help, but as we left, Kalafi felt impressed to talk to a group of girls standing outside the school to ask whether they knew of accommodations.

One of the girls introduced herself as Rosemary, and said, "If you want, all of you can share my apartment. I have an extra bedroom and a lounge."

After we accepted, she gave us directions. We went to the car, wondering whether we had enough fuel to get there. This time, however, Kalafi noticed that the gauge showed a full tank. He checked, and fuel was even overflowing from the tank!

But God wasn't finished! Rosemary's boyfriend introduced us to a man who offered us the use of his house, rent free.

Although we arrived in town with $11 and only one contact, within 24 hours we saw God's great power work out the impossible. That final house eventually became the YWAM base in Port Moresby.

Tom Hallas, an Australian, is director of YWAM in the Pacific and Asia.

Friday

God chose the foolish things of the world to shame the wise.

I Corinthians 1:27

The U.S. Marines had invited our YWAM school to lead a retreat for them on the island of Hawaii. As we prayed, the Lord showed us that the enemy wanted to destroy the outreach. He gave us clear directions to send a handpicked "Gideon's army," and to have the rest stay behind to pray.

After three hours of traveling, our team arrived, only to learn they had been directed to the wrong location. Realizing it was too far away to make the original retreat, our leader asked if they could minister to the hundreds of noisy marines in the nearby Quonset Hut Theater. The officer laughed and described how dangerous it would be to allow our girls to go into this rowdy crowd.

The officer finally agreed. When their movie ended, a marine made what must be the most ungodly invitation to a church service ever given, mixing in a few swear words. It worked! Everyone remained seated.

The little army of untalented YWAMers marched in singing, smiling, and setting up the sound system. While one girl gave her testimony, a few marines got angry, but no one moved. They laughed as she continued, but were quickly captivated by her obvious sincerity.

In response to an invitation to follow Jesus, over 100 marines rushed to the front. Each team member met with a group of about ten guys.

One stunned marine kept pointing to a place on the stage while exclaiming, "The guy with the beard knows everything I have ever done." We realized he must have seen a powerful manifestation of Jesus—no one on the team had a beard.

When the team returned home, they learned that the prayer team had taken detailed notes of their prayers; almost everything that had happened was described in their prayer notes.

David Gustaveson, an American, leads YWAM's Global Opportunity Network, mobilizing local churches into missions. He lives in California, USA.

Saturday

Every good and perfect gift is from above. James 1:17

I was working with YWAM in Heidebeek, Holland, and lived in a village two miles away. Each day, I either had to borrow a bike or find a ride to work. When I did have the use of a bike, I enjoyed riding in the forests around Heidebeek.

"Father God, I'd like a bike. Is it okay to ask You for one?" I prayed.

After the prayer, I sensed that God wanted to give me a bike. It would be an expression of His love for me. I felt impressed that I was to tell no one, not even my boyfriend.

Two days after my prayer, we had a base meeting. Our leader, Jeff Fountain, put up a large board and said we were to call out our specific requests. Jeff would write them on the board.

People called out various items. Often, someone else would say that they had the item to share. I wrestled within myself about whether or not I should mention my need for a bike.

God, did I really hear from You? I asked silently. *Should I tell them?*

In my mind, I heard Him say, *I love you. You can tell the group, and you will get the bike. Or you can remain silent. Then when the bike comes, you will know it is a special gift from Me.* I chose to say nothing.

A few days later, some of the guys were cleaning out a shed at the base. It had several old bikes left behind by students or staff. One of the guys asked my boyfriend if he needed one, or if he knew of someone who did. He passed along the word to me, and soon I was the proud owner of a "new" bicycle.

Terrie Koller, an American, serves in discipleship and as a homemaker in Hong Kong.

Sunday

Meditation

Therefore, since we are surrounded by such a great cloud of witnesses, let us throw off everything that hinders and the sin that so easily entangles, and let us run with perseverance the race marked out for us. Let us fix our eyes on Jesus, the author and perfecter of our faith, who for the joy set before him endured the cross, scorning its shame, and sat down at the right hand of the throne of God. Consider him who endured such opposition from sinful men, so that you will not grow weary and lose heart.

Hebrews 12:1-3

Monday

Always be prepared to give an answer to everyone who asks you to give the reason for the hope that you have. I Peter 3:15

When I was a teenager, sports were more interesting to me than prayer and Bible reading. But over time, I began to sense the importance of being a Christian influence to my classmates, and began praying to that end.

One day a fellow student loudly aired his anti-religious sentiments to a few of us as we walked down the corridor. Here was an opportunity. Should I say something?

I decided to give it a go. I said what I could, which wasn't much, then felt impeded. Soon a thought popped into my head. *Why not take him to another Christian who would know what to say?* So I put the proposal to him, and to my surprise, he accepted.

The agreed Sunday afternoon arrived, and I introduced my classmate to some young men from our church. One of them took my friend aside to speak with him. To my amazement, my classmate ended up coming to Christ!

The result of all this? Thirty years later I can say that my prayer and Bible reading have never been the same since. Immediately after my friend's conversion, I was fired up and arose early each morning to seek the Lord. I felt responsible to disciple my classmate and see others come to know the Lord, as well. Prayer and Bible reading become far more meaningful when we are involved in the real world of people, their needs, and wanting to win them for Christ.

Ross Tooley, a New Zealander, serves at large on the staff of the College of Christian Ministries of University of the Nations, Kona, Hawaii, USA.

Adapted from We Cannot But Tell, by Ross Tooley, revised edition. Copyright © 1993 by Ross Tooley. Published by YWAM Publishing, Seattle, Washington. Used by permission [from page 23].

Tuesday

The angel of the Lord encamps around those who fear him, and he delivers them.
Psalm 34:7

It was winter 1978, and a friend and I were traveling around Norway with Christian literature. We filled our van with books and drove from north to south, conducting services and distributing literature. We taught young people to use the books in evangelism, and trained them in door-to-door witnessing.

In the far north of the country, our 7,000-kilo van was full of books. It was cold, and the icy roads were very slippery.

Suddenly, as we were driving along the sea, we lost control of the van. To the right was a steep hillside ending in a rugged beach with big rocks. We both saw what was about to happen, and cried out, "Jesus!"

The van went over a road marker, and we could hear the stones scratching under the van. It passed a curve, and somehow it landed on the road again. When the van stopped, we walked to the place where we could see the wheel tracks. The tracks showed that, according to the law of gravity, the van should have rolled down the hillside and smashed against the rocks.

We drove on, thanking God for our lives.

Sigurd Omdal, a Norwegian, is a YWAM base director in Norway.

Wednesday

For I was hungry and you gave me something to eat...I was a stranger and you invited me in....I tell you the truth, whatever you did for one of the least of these...you did it to me.   *Matthew 25:35,40 NASB*

My first night in Hong Kong, I followed the team leader in and out of Kowloon's alleys. One moment we passed fancy bars and restaurants, the next moment we entered alleys of human misery, where pieces of cardboard made up the meager homes. I was accompanying the "Street Sleeper Team" as they delivered meals to those living in the alleys. We carried boxes containing simple meals of rice and meat for each person.

Our leader, a former drug addict, was now leading others to rescue those in distress. He knew every bag lady, cripple, and needy person on the route, and gave attentive care to each. The team members sat and visited in Chinese with those they fed.

I'll never forget one old woman we visited. She was clothed in layers of dirty rags. Tears stung my eyes as I thought of my own grandmother, so well cared for. Here was someone else's grandmother, alone in such a filthy place.

Our leader greeted her with a warm smile, and handed her a box. When she opened it, her eyes lit up like a child with a new toy. Her toothless grin radiated appreciation. My heart was touched by her delight over a simple meal given with care. I realized that I was the needy one.

"Oh God," I cried, "Forgive me. Forgive me for my arrogant pride and ingratitude."

Now, years later, I sometimes complain. Then I remember her eyes and that toothless grin, and thank the Lord for the reminder.

I saw Jesus that night in the giver—a reclaimed drug addict— and two receivers, a toothless old woman and a humbled American.

David Kyle Foster, an American, served with YWAM in Hawaii, USA.

Thursday

So neither he who plants nor he who waters is anything, but only God, who makes things grow.   *I Corinthians 3:7*

Sometimes we feel that we have to plant, water, and reap, all in a half hour. I've found it's not usually that way. God has many workers. They may be in another church or in another mission group. We are all fellow laborers. We just don't usually know each other.

We're to be content to work together with one another. Some work with children, some with literature. Others hold crusades. We all have our place as a part of God's process.

One night, I was driving back from speaking in a church in the United States. I saw a car parked along the side of the road. A young man and woman were sitting on the embankment. I pulled over to see if I could help.

"Thank you for stopping; our jack doesn't work," said the man. "No one would stop to help."

While I used my jack, he asked where I was coming from.

"I just finished speaking at a church," I replied.

"Oh, you're a man of God."

"What do you mean?"

"You're a man of God. I should have known it."

He told me that the young woman he was with had been telling him about Jesus all evening. He'd been mocking her. Just before I arrived, she had prayed that God would send someone to help them.

"Who should come along but a man of God?" he concluded.

While we finished tightening the lugs on the spare tire, I told him that everything she was telling him was true, and that he should listen to her. I drove away, wishing I could listen in on their conversation.

What a thrill to know that we are fellow laborers. God sends others along to help with the process of leading others to Christ.

Al Akimoff, an American, directs YWAM's Slavic Ministries.

Friday

"Bring the whole tithe into the storehouse, that there may be food in my house. Test me in this," says the Lord Almighty, "and see if I will not throw open the floodgates of heaven and pour out so much blessing that you will not have room enough for it." Malachi 3:10

I write anonymously to preserve the identity of my very cool 12-year-old son. I'll call him Fred. He's had spiritual input from lots of sources, but the Lord Himself taught Fred about tithing.

"Mom," he said one night, "remind me to tithe on my car wash money."

This was a test. If I showed any enthusiasm, I knew I'd get "Mommmm!" and the rolling eyes. I'd been practicing the art of "poker face." I suppressed the urge to shout, "Hallelujah!"

Our church members were asked to choose the name of a needy child to help at Christmas. Fred chose a 12-year-old boy.

The next night, Fred said out of the blue, "How much is ten percent of $500?"

"Fifty dollars," I casually replied. "Why?"

"I never tithed on my savings account. I was thinking of buying that boy a gift out of it."

I said, "That's a nice idea. I'm sure he'd appreciate it."

Over the next few days, Fred argued against his plan. I reminded him of the Lord's promise to bless our obedience. Since it wasn't my idea, I didn't have to defend it. The choice was his.

Fred bought the gift he would have loved—a $40 gift certificate at a sporting goods store. I added a sweatshirt so the boy had a package to open. We delivered it, and left the rest to God.

A week later, our church's missions committee chairman delivered Christmas presents for us. Mine contained a gift certificate to my favorite store.

But both our mouths fell open when Fred opened his gift. A $40 gift certificate—to a sporting goods store.

Poker face? Impossible.

This YWAM mother remains anonymous for the sake of her son.

Saturday

"Who are you, Lord?" Saul asked. "I am Jesus, whom you are persecuting,"
he replied. Acts 9:5

Ahmad Khusro was the eldest son of a religious leader living in the predominantly Islamic area of Northern India. While on a business trip, Ahmad was handed a gospel tract which he tore up immediately.

The next day, he was again given a tract by a group of Christians who convinced him to take their address, as well. Ahmad planned to tear up the second tract but decided to give it a quick reading first. His curiosity deepened, and he decided to visit the young people who gave it to him.

During several visits, Ahmad was impressed by the love he saw. One night, he had a strange experience. Jesus Christ stood in his room, saying, "I am the Way, the Truth, and the Life."

Ahmad's whole body shook. Though it was early morning, he went immediately to the Christians' house, where he readily gave his life to Christ.

When his family was unable to dissuade him from following Jesus, they declared him dead. For the next seven years, he had no contact with his family. Ahmad continued to pray for them and trusted that someday God would bring reconciliation.

During those years, Ahmad studied with Youth With A Mission, and eventually joined the mission. He planted a church for Muslims, and God gave him a wife and son. Ahmad knew that God was blessing him, but he longed for his family to know Christ.

After seven years, his family came to visit him. They were reconciled. Later, Ahmad and his wife returned to his place of birth. His family gave him a welcoming party attended by more than 500 people. As a result, he has enjoyed many opportunities to witness for Christ.

Ahmad's father recently told him, "You have chosen the right path."

Steve Cochrane, an American, is Regional Director for YWAM in South Asia.

Sunday

Meditation

The Lord is gracious and righteous;
our God is full of compassion. The
Lord protects the simplehearted;
when I was in great need, he saved
me. Be at rest once more, O my
soul, for the Lord has been good to
you.

Psalm 116:5-7

Monday

I pray that you, being rooted and established in love, may...grasp how wide and long and high and deep is the love of Christ. Ephesians 3:17-18

At the spacious campus of the International Christian University in Japan, we learned that the majority of these students from many nations make no claim to be Christians. We knew that only God could reach their hearts.

I approached two girls who spoke English quite well. Keiko immediately told me she was a Christian and had been baptized in water. Turning to Sansido, I asked, "What does Jesus mean to you?"

She had not given Him much thought, she told me. I told her my story: I gave my heart to Jesus as a young girl. But as I grew up, I withheld my heart from Him through compromise. I was empty, insecure, and often plagued by feelings of guilt. Finally I turned my life completely over to Jesus and found peace.

"That sounds like me," Keiko interrupted. "I feel such an emptiness way down deep, though from the outside, people think I have it all together. I find it so hard to accept myself."

I was surprised that she was being so honest, especially in front of her friend.

With tears streaming down her face, Keiko admitted the difficulty she had of giving God her whole heart; of letting Him direct the course of her life.

I shared the goodness of a loving Father who wants only the very best for her. Her fears gave way to a desire to let Him have more control of her life and to get to know Him better.

Before we parted, Keiko prayed in Japanese, then both girls allowed me to pray for them in English. Perhaps Keiko will now be the catalyst to lead Sansido to the Lord.

Barb Nizza, an American, serves on staff of the College of Early Childhood Education, University of the Nations, Kailua-Kona, Hawaii, USA.

Tuesday

Jesus looked at them and said, "With man this is impossible, but with God all things are possible."
                                                              Matthew 19:26

After two weeks of seeing children either dead, sleeping out in the open, fighting, or so drugged that they were knocked down by cars as they crossed the road, I wondered, *What am I doing here? I want to go home.* I thought it was hopeless. The problem was enormous, and I saw nothing I could do to change it.

I had answered God's calling, and had left my home, job, family, and friends to come to Brazil to share His love with these children living on the streets. But the situation seemed so awful and so huge. Eight million children made the streets their home; they had nowhere else to go.

Then, one day, I met a handsome, young black man about 18 years old. He was sweet and kind. He told me he had been a street kid for 14 years. This amazed me, because I'd heard that one third of them die before they reach the age of 18! He told me that he had become a Christian through the love of some missionaries. For the first time in 14 years, he had turned from stealing, fighting, and taking drugs. Now he was studying so he could get work. He spent his free time on the streets, helping his old friends to know Jesus.

As I looked into his gentle and peaceful eyes, I thought, *That's why I'm here.* I knew I would stay in Brazil.

Sarah de Carvalho, from England, works with street children in Brazil.

Wednesday

Look at the birds of the air; they do not sow or reap or store away in barns, and yet your heavenly Father feeds them. Are you not much more valuable than they?   Matthew 6:26

During one ministry trip, a storm had covered everything around our home with ice and snow. Many small birds were trying to find something to eat in our snow-covered back yard.

Our supply of birdseed was gone, so my wife, Jewell, had put out some rice, then some pearl barley. That was almost gone, and Jewell was worried they might go hungry. We got more birdseed, and watched as the birds hungrily fed on the dinner we had provided for them.

Then I remembered something my son, Loren (YWAM's founder and president), had said when reassuring one young YWAMer that God would provide for him. Referring to the above Scripture, Loren asked, "Did you ever see a worried bird?"

Nearly nine years earlier, I had "retired" from my salaried position with our denomination and determined to spend the rest of our years traveling in the cause of world evangelism. We faced the same dilemma that young YWAMer was facing.

It's human nature to worry and fret if things don't go the way we think they should. But this is God's work, and He has chosen to have us be dependent on Him.

The birds were not worried when the food was gone. They weren't even concerned about how reliable Jewell and I were as sources of food. They simply trusted God, and we can do the same. He will never fail us.

T.C. Cunningham, an American, represents missions and missionaries internationally. He is also the father of YWAM's Founder and President, Loren Cunningham.

Thursday

If anyone has material possessions and sees his brother in need but has no pity on him, how can the love of God be in him? Dear children, let us not love with words or tongue but with actions and in truth. I John 3:17-18

First, there was no hot water for my shower. Then the staff joined our class for intercession. What was happening?

When all had assembled, one of our base leaders said, "You have all probably noticed there is no hot water this morning. There's no money to pay for the propane to heat the water. We have other unpaid bills, as well. Many of us have not paid our staff or student fees." One by one, various leaders encouraged us to look to God not only as our provider, but also as the One who might ask us to give, even in our time of need.

According to the instructions, anyone owing money to the base should stand with the other "debtors." *How humiliating,* I thought.

Dozens hesitantly stood to their feet. Each looked as embarrassed as my husband, who was standing beside me. I was surprised to see highly respected staff people among those standing.

After prayer together, I watched in amazement as scores of individuals moved from their places and handed others either money, checks, or pieces of paper with a written promise of money. Some simply tucked the papers into the pockets of those standing.

I watched and listened with a sense of awe. There were tears of relief and many warm embraces, even squeals of joy.

One by one, those standing sat down as God sent someone to meet their needs. Some of those standing went to others to give money, even before their own bills were covered. After about 20 minutes, no one was left standing.

Watching this demonstration of God's people loving one another was one of the most tender mornings of my life. We later learned that tens of thousands of dollars exchanged hands that day. Enough to pay fees, to order propane, and to pay other bills.

Beverly Caruso, an American, is a Bible teacher and author who leads YWAM Writer's Seminars. She lives in California, USA.

Friday

You are the light of the world. A city on a hill cannot be hidden.
                                                    Matthew 5:14

After 13 years of occupation by the Soviet Army and civil war, Afghanistan is a devastated nation, economically, emotionally and spiritually. This country has been closed to the Gospel for centuries, and most of its residents are Muslims.

Yet in the midst of the agony and suffering of the Afghan people, God is revealing Himself to the Afghans in many ways. Christian ministries are working in such varied ways as eye care and rehabilitation projects. Afghans who accept Christ face extreme persecution, yet many hold strong to the faith.

One young man was hired to serve as night watchman for a Christian ministry. Each morning, he watched as the workers, singly and in groups, prayed and sang to their God. The man was amazed at their consistency, their obvious devotion, and the joy in their praises.

Over several months, a yearning grew in his heart to learn more about the God these young people served. He questioned them and studied their answers. He also questioned his own Islamic beliefs. After continuing to watch the lives of the Christians and researching both religions, the young man made an open confession of faith in Jesus Christ.

Despite persecution, he became a radiant witness and influenced many others.

Steve Cochrane, an American, is Regional Director for YWAM in South Asia

Saturday

A time to tear and a time to mend, a time to be silent and a time to speak.

Ecclesiastes 3:7

"Never plan for an hour's work to be done in an hour." Have you heard that one before? How many times do we get frustrated because we can't accomplish a task in the time we have allotted for it? We over-schedule. We need to leave room for the unexpected—the interruptions that come along. We should learn to be flexible. True, we must establish priorities. We must find the Lord's perspective on our schedule, and then endeavor to stick to it. But that should always be balanced with being flexible and open. It's a tricky tightrope at times. But our schedule should never be a bondage; it should always be a tool.

There will always be the unexpected. Indeed, the unexpected is often part of God's plan. One pastor calls this the "theology of interrupting." We must keep a concrete awareness that even when there are many interruptions, the Lord gives grace to carry us through and to keep things in balance and in line with our priorities. He may even be bringing a blessing our way. And we wouldn't want to miss anything God has for us.

James 1:2 says (in J.B. Phillips' rendering): "When all kinds of trials and temptations crowd into your lives, my brothers, don't resent them as intruders, but welcome them as friends!" In maintaining this kind of flexibility, our schedule may have to be totally ignored. The two aspects of scheduling and flexibility must be kept in balance. The key link between the two is discernment and sensitivity to the voice of the Spirit to guide us in each situation.

Sally McClung, an American, has a ministry of hospitality and speaks internationally. She lives in California, USA.

From Where Will I Find the Time? by Sally McClung. Copyright © 1989 by Sally McClung. Published by Harvest House Publishers, Eugene, Oregon. Used by permission [from pages 71-72].

Sunday

Meditation

Do you not know? Have you not heard? The Lord is the everlasting God, the creator of the ends of the earth. He will not grow tired or weary, and his understanding no one can fathom. He gives strength to the weary and increases the power of the weak. Even youths grow tired and weary, and young men stumble and fall; but those who hope in the Lord will renew their strength. They will soar on wings like eagles; they will run and not grow weary, they will walk and not be faint.

Isaiah 40:28-31

Monday

For the Lord will be your confidence and will keep your foot from being snared.
Proverbs 3:26

Some time ago, I visited an old army friend whom I hadn't seen for ten years. We greeted one another warmly, and began to share stories of the past and the routes our lives had taken. He commented on a mutual friend who had received a commission and was rising rapidly in military rank. I quickly responded by explaining my administrative role in the organization, dropping comments about "lawyers" and "bankers" along the way.

As I drove away from his house that afternoon, I was smitten with guilt and disgust. I thought I had overcome the feeling that everyone seemed to have it so much more together than I did. But my intent that day was to impress my friend. God used this to reveal deep insecurities in my life.

Previously I had tried to deal with insecurity by reminding myself that the other person probably didn't have it together, either. What a totally false concept this is. I can only overcome my problem by recognizing God's call upon my life and by walking before Him with a whole and pure heart.

Insecurity is a lack of trust in God's ability to use my life. Yet those of us who struggle in this area are in good company. Great pillars of faith like Job, David, and Paul each found that the way to deal with these insecurities was by acknowledging God's ability to use them.

David Cowie, from New Zealand, serves as director of YWAM's mercy ship, m/v Pacific Ruby.

Tuesday

Therefore, as God's chosen people, holy and dearly loved, clothe yourselves with compassion, kindness, humility, gentleness and patience.

Colossians 3:12

Remember those mouth-watering aromas that came from Grandma's kitchen on Thanksgiving? For me those moments from the time we arrived at her house to the time we sat down to eat seemed like an eternity. But when I took that first bite, I knew it was worth every second of the wait.

Unlike my childhood visits to Grandma's house, I must admit I'm definitely less patient nowadays. One day, I put some leftovers in the microwave, and set the timer for three minutes. I found myself furiously tapping my foot. "Hurry up!" came spewing from my lips.

Then the Lord quickened my heart. What was I saying? Why couldn't I wait three minutes for my meal to heat up? By the time the microwave shut off, I was almost too ashamed to eat.

That little incident got me to thinking seriously about my walk with the Lord and my attitude in general. Had I grown that impatient in other areas of my life, including my relationship with Jesus? I started thinking of all the times He had been so patient with me. Had I even begun to reciprocate? Did I ever acknowledge His unending grace? My Savior had called my name for many years before I responded to His call. He waited patiently for me to invite Him into my heart.

And what about my prayer life? Had I given up on praying for my lost family and friends because my prayers weren't answered the *way* I thought they should be and in the *timing* that I thought best?

Those 180 seconds I spent waiting for my leftovers to warm in the microwave had changed my attitude.

Jeannè Piraino Sigler, an American, works in the editorial department at Last Days Ministries in Lindale, Texas, USA.

Wednesday

*"Do not be afraid of them, for I am with you and will rescue you," declares
the Lord.*
Jeremiah 1:8

Many of us respond just like Jeremiah did when God gives us
a hard task or one that will go unnoticed by man. Jeremiah was
a very young man when God appointed him as a prophet to the
nations. He panicked when he first heard God's plan for him.
But God reassured him of His deliverance and protection. "They
will fight against you but will not overcome you" (Jeremiah 1:19).

God promised Jeremiah that He would be alongside him and
would personally deliver him. This promise holds true to all of
God's sons and daughters whom He appoints to a specific task.
"I will be with you always, to the very end of the age," he said in
Matthew 28:20.

When the prophet first heard of God's plan, he was reluctant
to accept the responsibility. He answered, "Behold, I do not know
how to speak." It was only natural for Jeremiah to consider himself
too weak. It is also natural for God to choose a weak man to do
His task. It's often through the weak that the name of God is
glorified.

When God sends us, we are not to look at ourselves and feel
inadequate. He promised to protect us and help us to accomplish
what He intends.

God knows us personally and will never command us to do
something without His enabling us. All He requires is obedience
and trust.

Judy Olson, an American, lives in Austria.

Thursday

May your unfailing love be my comfort, according to your promise to your servant.
                                              Psalm 119:76

As the daughter of missionaries, I've missed some of the usual things American children do. But God has blessed me with many experiences which most children don't have. I've seen many countries of the world. I have friends all over the world and from most countries of the world.

When David and I were small, Mom took our sleeping bags everywhere we went for meetings. The bags were our "home away from home." While our parents were occupied with the meeting, we rolled out our bags and felt the security of home. We often went to sleep to the sounds of worship, preaching, or a Bible study.

Now, as an adult, I sometimes find it hard to leave family and friends to go to the mission field myself. God has been faithful to fill the gap. Because we frequently travel separately, our family seldom has planned vacations together. But before I attended a Bible school in South Africa, God arranged for us to come from our various locations for a short time together in Sweden.

Meeting for such times together is one way God compensates for the long stretches of time when we are apart from one another. It's an extra blessing God gives us to experience time with our family members. I see this as not only a personal blessing, but also as an expression of God's overall concern for family units.

Karen Cunningham, an American, teaches at Small World Christian Kindergarten in Hong Kong.

Friday

My children, with whom I am again in labor until Christ is formed in you....

Galatians 4:19 NASB

When we are single, we long for the intimacy of marriage—just to have somebody of "my own." We fantasize about moments of emotional and physical intimacy. Eventually, we may get married and face the reality of actually dividing our time, money, and space with another person. That's where we discover how much we really need Jesus.

And then come children. Tiny, poopy, little creatures who demand constant attention. Ah, but what love fills our hearts at the first sight of Junior. Our selfish focus on personal rights is swept away the moment those big baby eyes look into ours.

When a baby is born into a family, the parents virtually become his slaves. We clean him, feed him, warm him, protect him, and sometimes we do it all night long.

Our major concern is for the physical safety of our children during their early childhood. That is often the focus of our prayer life, but then they reach their teens. The day my oldest son entered junior high school, I knew that my prayer life would have to change. Now I can truly identify with Paul's statement in Galatians 4:19. God, our Father, uses the experience of parenting to help us to identify with Him.

John Dawson, a New Zealander, is YWAM's International Director of Urban Missions. From Taking Our Cities for God by John Dawson. Copyright © 1989 by John Dawson. Published by Creation House, Lake Mary, Florida. Used by permission [from pages 206-207].

Saturday

No one who has left home or wife or brothers or parents...for the...kingdom of God will fail to receive many times as much in this age and, in the age to come, eternal life.   Luke 18:29-30

We minister to street kids in Belo Horizonte, Brazil. Because each staff member has left home and family in different countries, it is common at Christmas time to think of our families and to desire to be with them.

On top of such thoughts, we think of the people who roam the streets hungry, lonely, tired, afraid, sad, angry, and hurt. They don't know about the Christ of Christmas.

Cicero is typical. He came to the city looking for work, and was robbed of all his personal papers during the first week. Without them, he could not get a job. He started living on the streets and drinking heavily.

A Brazilian couple from our team found him sick, hungry, and dirty, living under a viaduct. Burns covered one foot. When Eduardo and Sandra examined Cicero's foot, they found signs of gangrene. With loving care, they washed it and prayed over it in Jesus' name. For two weeks, they came every day, and the foot healed miraculously!

Not only was Cicero's foot healed, but his heart was also healed as they shared the message of the Gospel with him. He eagerly accepted Christ. Now he lives at a YWAM halfway house and is growing in the knowledge of the Lord. He now understands what Christmas is all about.

Jeannette Lukasse and her husband, Johan, both from the Netherlands, are the leaders of YWAM's urban ministry base in Belo Horizonte, Brazil.

Sunday

Meditation

Though the Lord is on high, he
looks upon the lowly, but the proud
he knows from afar. Though I walk
in the midst of trouble, you preserve my life;...with your right hand
you save me. The Lord will fulfill
his purpose for me; your love, O
Lord, endures forever—do not
abandon the works of your hands.

Psalm 138:6-8

Monday

Seek first his kingdom and his righteousness, and all these things will be given to you as well.   *Matthew 6:33*

In 1964, as a 17-year-old high school graduate, I joined a YWAM group from San Francisco known as The Roving Team. We went to small islands in the Caribbean Sea which are accessible only by boat. We learned much from God about His ways of working in men's lives.

When we arrived on the island of Andros, we wondered what would happen if we really practiced the concept of putting God's Kingdom first. Normally we spent time looking for housing and making contacts for our food and various living needs.

We decided that this time would be different. We wouldn't ask for anything; we wouldn't look for our needs. We would seek only His work, His righteousness. We wondered, *Will He take care of us?*

In small groups, we went in different directions to witness. When we gathered at the end of day at a prearranged place, we were a strange-looking group. One guy carried a big watermelon, another held loaves of bread. Someone told us that a lady who lived down the road had a big empty house. "She says we can stay there," he said.

All of our needs were met because we shared Jesus first.

Al Akimoff, an American, directs YWAM's Slavic Ministries.

Tuesday

Jesus Christ is the same yesterday and today and forever.   Hebrews 13:8

As I reached for a bunch of spring onions in the produce aisle of the supermarket, I saw a small child standing beside her mom, who was busily inspecting the packaged tomatoes.

Little by little, the toddler made her way past the fruits and vegetables toward a colorful display of blooming daffodils and other potted plants. Soon the child had drifted to the far end of the aisle.

Then she became frightened and started screaming for Mommy, who hadn't budged one inch in the twenty seconds it took her daughter to wander away. Immediately responding to the child's cry, the mother crouched down and stretched out her arms—the little girl ran straight into her place of refuge.

How many times are we drawn away by the greener grass on the other side of the fence? When we find ourselves far from the place of safety, we cry out, perhaps even questioning why we feel so alone and abandoned.

God promises that He is unchanging. When you feel far away from your heavenly Father, examine the situation and ask yourself the question, *Which one of us went away?*

Jeannè Piraino Sigler, an American, works in the editorial department at Last Days Ministries in Lindale, Texas, USA.

Wednesday

For the eyes of the Lord range throughout the earth to strengthen those whose hearts are fully committed to him. II Chronicles 16:9

During the intervention by the United States Army in Grenada in 1983, I was a volunteer in the revolutionary People's Militia.

At 4:00 a.m. on the second day of battle, we were ordered to flee for our lives. Grateful Grenadians were informing the American soldiers of our whereabouts.

I discarded my AK-47 and my boots in the brush, stole some clothes off a clothes line, and changed out of my fatigues. In two minutes, I looked like any other country woman. Looking for a place to hide, I started toward a small house, but just in time, I saw an American soldier perched on the roof. Had I been in my fatigues, I could have been killed.

I headed down the road and ended up at the home of an elderly woman I had never met. I started pouring out my frustration and my hatred for the "dirty Yankee Imperialists."

"I want to die!" I shouted. "There's nothing to live for now."

"Child," she said, "don't you know you must thank God for saving your life?"

Her words hit me hard. In our culture, we pay close attention to what elders say. In the coming months, I kept thinking of what she had said. It prompted me to start my search for God.

In 1987, I accepted Jesus as my Savior, and in 1988, I joined Youth With A Mission. During my training, the Lord reminded me of the events of that day in 1983 and showed me His purpose for my life. I realized how He had saved me from deception and confusion.

Today, my heart is completely changed. I now love my American brothers and sisters in Christ, and thank God for equipping me with the weapons of spiritual warfare, which are greater than the gun I once held. He is now preparing me to return to Grenada to establish a Christian school to train the coming generation "to know God and to make Him known."

Rose Henry, from Grenada, is in teacher training at YWAM's Christian Heritage School in Tyler, Texas, USA.

Thursday

He who dwells in the shelter of the Most High will abide in the shadow of the Almighty. I will say to the Lord, "My refuge and my fortress, my God, in whom I trust!"   Psalm 91:1-2 NASB

One day, I took a walk out on our back property to spend some time with the Lord. It was near the end of a beautiful day, and long shadows were starting to fall across the field. After walking for a while, I decided to go sit under a tree I saw on a hillside.

The sun was setting behind me as I leaned back against the trunk. Its shadow fell across me and spilled all the way down the hill. It was sort of a skinny tree, but I was almost totally enveloped in its shadow. In fact, when I scrunched my arms and legs in real tight, you couldn't see me at all. As I conformed my image to the image of the tree, my image couldn't be seen.

Almost immediately, the Lord brought a phrase to my mind, "abiding in the shadow of the Almighty." As I sat there, I started meditating on that portion of Scripture, and peace filled my heart. I thought about how we need to conform ourselves to the shape of any shadow we're trying to hide in—and how we usually need to be very close to the source of the shadow for that to happen.

We talk about "standing in someone's shadow" or "being over-shadowed." Neither connotation is very positive. But the ways of the Lord are opposite the world's ways—and as Christians, it's our goal to "stand in the shadow" of Jesus, hoping He's the One people notice.

As the fruit of the Spirit grows in our lives, we draw closer to Jesus and, as a result, start looking more like Him—making it easier to abide in His shadow. And when we do that, we are enveloped in Him. Being close to God is our safety, our shelter, our provision, our joy, our comfort, and our salvation.

Melody Green-Sievright, an American, directs Last Days Ministries in Lindale, Texas, USA.

Friday

Show the wonder of your great love, you who save by your right hand those who take refuge in you from their foes. Psalm 17:7

A small group of believers in the town of Timisoara, Romania met secretly. The Lord led them to pray against the spirits of fear and terror—these were controlling every aspect of Romanian society. They were impressed to go out in small groups late at night, taking prayer walks around their town. In front of various official buildings, the Christians prayed against the principalities and powers—in whispers, lest the secret police hear them.

They felt foolish, but they kept obeying God. Over the months, things actually got worse. Finally, on October 23, 1989, the word of the Lord came, saying that a fire would begin in their town and "blaze across Romania." What a difficult message to believe—especially for a little band of people whispering their prayers.

However, the spark began in Timisoara, just as God had said. It began with the house arrest on December 15, 1989, of a Reformed pastor named Lazlo Tokes. What usually followed such an arrest would be the disappearance of the minister, but this time was different. Word spread of Tokes' arrest, and instead of the usual cowed reaction, Christians streamed to the pastor's home, forming a human chain across the entrance. The police threatened them, but they began the first chant of the revolution: "Without fear, without fear! Liberty!"

The flame had been lit. The army turned around and fought the secret police with the people. The brutal reign of Ceausescu was over by Christmas of 1989. The newspapers of the country reported, "The band of fear and terror has been broken." Fear and terror—the same spirit powers God had directed a small group to pray against two years before.

Dean Sherman, an American, is an international Bible teacher, and lives in the USA.
From Spiritual Warfare for Every Christian by Dean Sherman. Copyright © 1990 by Dean Sherman. Published by YWAM Publishing, Seattle, Washington. Used by permission [page 97-98].

Saturday

And my God will meet all your needs according to his glorious riches in Christ Jesus. Philippians 4:19

I was born into a middle-class Brazilian home. Because my Christian parents paid for everything, I never had a chance to see personally God's provision in my own life.

In 1985, I went to the United States to further my studies in psychology. Two years later, I became interested in Youth With A Mission (YWAM). I prayed, "Lord, if this is Your desire and Your time for me to join YWAM, provide all the money that I will need. I don't want to depend on someone else, but just on You."

I would need $2,000 to attend a Discipleship Training School. My pastor advised me to send in my application and to pray, and he asked me to share my plans with the church one Sunday evening. Unfortunately, inclement weather kept many people home that night. Before the end of the service, the pastor called me to the front and asked me to share my testimony. He closed by taking an offering for me.

A month later, I received an acceptance letter from YWAM. Because I'm Brazilian, they offered me a scholarship for half of the tuition.

I immediately called my pastor to tell him the news. I was dumbfounded to learn that the offering that Sunday night had come to $2,300. This enabled me to pay the remaining $1,000 tuition and have $1,300 to cover living expenses, outreach, and tithe.

I've been able to see God's provision for 100 percent of my needs.

Sonja Melo, a Brazilian, works with street children in Belo Horizonte, Brazil

Sunday

Meditation

For to us a child is born, to us a son
is given, and the government will be
on his shoulders. And he will be
called Wonderful Counselor,
Mighty God, Everlasting Father,
Prince of Peace. Of the increase of
his government and peace there will
be no end. He will reign on David's
throne and over his kingdom, estab-
lishing and upholding it with justice
and righteousness from that time
on and forever.

Isaiah 9:6-7

Monday

But he who is greatest among you shall be your servant.

Matthew 23:11 NKJV

Though young myself, I had been assigned as leader of a team of 15 young people who would spend two weeks witnessing in Paris, France. Soon, Loren Cunningham, the founder of YWAM, arrived to visit. Since we were staying at an old, dilapidated theater, I expected Loren to stay at a nearby hotel. It was a shock when he asked me, "Denny, where do you want me to sleep?"

I stammered, embarrassed to have to explain our inadequate facilities, "You're the boss. Don't you sleep wherever you want?"

I'll never forget the patient, gentle look on Loren's face as he said, "No, Denny, you're the leader of this team. While I am here, I am under your leadership. Where do you want me to sleep?"

I was stunned, but there was no place of "honor" I could allocate to Loren. We single men had set up our quarters on the stage at the front of the theater, and had attempted to wall it off. The area was small, and each of us had defined our personal "space" by surrounding our sleeping bags with chairs and suitcases.

I was about to offer my carefully defended spot to Loren when I noticed him eyeing the grand piano. Surely he didn't want us to move it! There was nowhere for it to go. Instead, Loren bent down and examined the space under the piano. Without thinking, I blurted out, "You can sleep under the piano, if you like." Loren nodded, smiled graciously, and said, "That sounds just fine."

Even though that incident took place years ago, its impact was so great upon me that I still remember every detail. I was deeply impressed and humbled at the same time. Here was the founder of a successful ministry graciously submitting to my immature leadership.

Denny Gunderson, an American, serves as North American Director for YWAM, and lives in Seattle, Washington, USA.

From Through the Dust...Breaking Leadership Stereotypes by Denny Gunderson. Copyright © 1992 by Denny Gunderson. Published by YWAM Publishing, Seattle, Washington. Used by permission [from pages 113-114].

Tuesday

In a loud voice [Elizabeth] exclaimed, "Blessed are you among women, and blessed is the child you will bear!"　　　　　　　　　　　　　*Luke 1:42*

Elizabeth is a wonderful example of rejoicing in another's calling. She must have been in a state of awe herself over her own pregnancy in old age and the angel's announcement concerning the child. Now here was Mary, her young relative, with a greater calling—to be the mother of the Messiah Himself.

Elizabeth easily could have questioned the justice of Mary's calling, or have been jealous. She and her husband had served God faithfully for many years. Mary was little more than a child.

However, we find no record of doubts or jealousy on Elizabeth's part. She knew God's place and calling for her. With joy and awe, she accepted her place and humbly and wholeheartedly rejoiced in Mary's calling. She was thus free to participate in what Mary was going through, and to be an encouragement and support to her.

Do I joyfully accept God's calling for me? Am I willing to know fulfillment where He has placed me? If so, I am freed to support and encourage another in his God-given task.

Paul wisely cautioned us not to compare ourselves to others. Am I caught up with comparing my ministry to another's, or can I sincerely rejoice, as did Elizabeth, when I see another called by God to a ministry greater than mine?

Christine Alexander, from New Zealand, serves on YWAM staff in Amsterdam, Netherlands.

Wednesday

Take captive every thought to make it obedient to Christ.

II Corinthians 10:5

Many times I have not wanted to face up to reality. God would say something which was really the best for me, but I didn't listen to or accept His Word because I wasn't courageous enough to live in accordance with it.

Now, God is teaching me to live according to the reality of my life and accept the truth, even though it is sometimes difficult or painful. This is what God wants for each person.

When we don't face up to reality, we shut ourselves in with our own fantasies and ideas, which leads to frustration and destruction. It also keeps us from having the life that God intended for us.

God cannot help us if we exist in a fantasy world. He wants us to be strong and courageous. He asks that we trust in Him and in His ways. He asks that we be teachable. And He requires that we live in truth.

Margarita Piña, a Spaniard, works with children, drama, and accounting with YWAM Spain.

Thursday

These commandments that I give you today are to be upon your hearts. Impress them on your children. Talk about them when you sit at home and when you walk along the road, when you lie down and when you get up. Deuteronomy 6:6-7

We need to take time to develop traditions in our families. Traditions give security and continuity. Certain meals, special holidays, and various events become a part of our individual family heritage through the traditions we set. They strengthen our family bonds.

I learned how important this is one year at Christmas. I had been away at a conference, and returned just a few days before Christmas. Because of the limited time, I suggested that we omit some of our usual things, taking a few shortcuts to save time. My children almost left home! They couldn't imagine how I could possibly not decorate the whole house, put all our favorite and special ornaments out, hang up our stockings, and put our ragged-looking angel on top of the tree. These (and many other things) were part of who we were as a family, and how we expressed ourselves at that particular festive season. It gave the family security and a sense of continuity.

We need to share our family heritage with our children. Misha and Matthew love to hear things from when Mom and Dad were kids. We have a unique little book of drawings of escapades from Floyd's childhood that we love to share with guests in our home. Our children also like to hear stories from our early days in Youth With A Mission. Stories of how God "healed" a leaky air mattress, saved a criminal, and multiplied our mosquito repellent never grow old!

Sally McClung, an American, has a ministry of hospitality and speaks internationally. She lives in California, USA.
From Where Will I Find the Time? by Sally McClung. Copyright © 1989 by Sally McClung. Published by Harvest House Publishers, Eugene, Oregon. Used by permission [from pages 62-63].

Friday

For He satisfies the longing soul, and fills the hungry soul with goodness.
Psalm 107:9 NKJV

My husband and I moved frequently when we first joined Youth With A Mission. This was a challenge for us as newlyweds, trying to establish a sense of home and family. My first Christmas was a time of learning.

Traditionally, my mother and I made Christmas cookies and gave them to neighbors we visited during the holiday season. Now my mother was in West Africa, translating the Bible for local villages. Many of my single friends were making plans to visit their families.

With all the talk of going home for the holidays, I began to wonder, *Where is home for me?* I knew it was not my father's house where I grew up. It wasn't my college dorm where I'd lived for two years before getting married. My last connection with "home" was with my mother before she left for Africa.

I was praying about this and began to cry. But I felt God's presence around me. Then my husband came and put his arms around me.

I asked the Lord, "Where is home?"

"Your home is in My arms, and sometimes that means in your husband's arms, too."

That brought comfort and encouragement. Soon I felt so much better that I got up and made Christmas cookies. I realized that wherever I am, I'm home.

I no longer feel the pain when I think of "home," because the reality is that I only have to whisper His name: "Jesus."

Sandy Falor, an American, teaches at YWAM's Christian Heritage School in Tyler, Texas, USA.

Saturday

To Jesus,

Help me not to keep You in the manger
As a baby, warm and comfortable
Silent and somewhat helpless
Loved and cared for by Your parents
Honored by those who knew of Your birth.
But, rather, to let You grow up to be the One
Who was a Stranger among men
Who had no place to lay His head
Who knew pain and was acquainted with grief
Who spoke with boldness the Truth, and had
The Power of God at His command
Who rarely saw His family
And for all His kindness and compassion
Was rewarded with rejection and was forsaken
By even His closest friends
To die the death of the earth's worst
In someone else's stead.
Help me not to keep You in the manger of my heart
Where it's warm and cozy and, oh, so easy
But to let You grow up in me, so I will be willing
To walk dirty, noisy streets
To love unlovely strangers
To suffer pain and share sorrow
To speak boldly the Truth of You
To be rejected and forsaken
By those for whom I care
To die to myself whenever it's needful
To help someone else.
Help me, Lord, to let You grow up in me
That I may always live for the purpose
For which You lived...
To bring hungry, lonely, helpless people
To the loving Father
Of that Baby in the manger.

Sandy Devisscher, an American YWAMer for 16 years, lives in Texas, USA.

Sunday

Meditation

But the angel said to them, "Do not be afraid. I bring you good news of great joy that will be for all the people. Today in the town of David a Savior has been born to you; he is Christ the Lord." Suddenly a great company of the heavenly host appeared with the angel, praising God and saying, "Glory to God in the highest, and on earth peace to men on whom his favor rests."

Luke 2:10-11,13-14

Monday

And when you stand praying, if you hold anything against anyone, forgive him, so that your Father in heaven may forgive you your sins.

Mark 11:25

Forgiveness is not a feeling, and neither is it simply trying to forget the bad things done to us. It is an act of the will and heart. It is giving a person something they have not earned the right to have—pardon. Forgiveness acknowledges that we have been wronged, but it goes beyond that and extends mercy.

Sometimes, forgiveness is a process. If we have been deeply hurt, it takes time for the wound to heal. In this case, forgiveness acts as a continual cleansing of the wound so that it can heal properly. As we think about a person who has hurt us or has sinned against us, feelings of resentment and emotional pain well up. Then we must reaffirm our commitment to forgive them. It is not that the first act of forgiveness is invalid, but that an ongoing process may be necessary until we are completely healed.

I was deeply hurt once by a friend. I could not get over the anger and disappointment I felt every time I thought of him. Another friend advised me that I should tell the Lord I forgave the friend each time these feelings surfaced, and should say, "Lord, I choose to do this with Your love, and I will not give up until You put love in my heart for him. I receive that love by faith."

I prayed that prayer many times each day for months, but nothing seemed to change. Then one day as I prayed, something finally happened—I began to see my friend through new eyes. I saw his wounds and hurts; I saw how he had been hurt by his father, and how he was passing those hurts on to me. The Lord released compassion into my heart for him, something I thought would never happen. The Lord did more than I could ask or think!

Floyd McClung, an American, directs Leadership Development Programs for YWAM. He lives in California, USA.
From Learning to Love People You Don't Like by Floyd McClung. Copyright © 1989 by Floyd McClung. Published by YWAM Publishing, Seattle, Washington. Used by permission [from pages 55-56].

Tuesday

All this is from God, who reconciled us to himself through Christ and gave us the ministry of reconciliation.   *II Corinthians 5:18*

One of Loren Cunningham's early visions for Youth With A Mission was that of a bridge. A bridge is easy to get on and off. Many see the mission as a bridge in other ways. It bridges denominational, ethnic, cultural, and national barriers by working together to help spread the Gospel.

The apostle Paul said that we've been given the ministry of reconciliation. The dictionary definition of *reconciliation* is "to make friendly again."

When we pioneered YWAM in Singapore, I was instructed to concentrate on street evangelism. "Don't develop any other ministries," I was told, "just evangelize." I took that so literally that I didn't do what I had always done previously: take time to get to know pastors and other Christian leaders in the community, and hear their heart for this city.

The result was almost fatal to the ministry. Rumors spread among the Body of Christ in Singapore. I felt like leaving.

We prayed, and encouraged others to pray. Then I started contacting pastors and other Christian leaders. I learned about their goals. I answered their questions about me, about YWAM, and about our goals. We prayed together.

Our evangelism efforts continued, but we served the Christian community in many ways. Gradually the barriers dropped. News of the reconciliation spread through Singapore's Christian community. Trust and cooperation developed.

As a result, we had more invitations to minister than we had time to accept. We soon averaged 20 services a month in churches, youth groups, and Christian camps.

Evangelism is still the emphasis in Singapore. But Singaporeans now attend Discipleship Training School. Some are serving the Lord in various places around the world. Many are serving God in their local churches.

Bridges take time to build. There aren't any short cuts.

Dave Hall, an American, serves on base council in Kona, Hawaii, USA, and is General Manager of YWAM's radio station, KFSH-FM on The Big Island.

Wednesday

Indeed, my heritage is beautiful to me.   Psalm 16:6 NASB

In many nations where significant church growth is occurring today, much of the groundwork has already been done by earlier Christian workers who gave the people a heritage factor and rendered them receptive to the Gospel.

In America, 75 percent of the population claim to believe in God. Most give at least mental assent to the notion that Jesus was more than a man. So, having a heritage factor, we must go out, build on it, and see many won to the Lord. Studying average evangelical churches and training schools, I found that over 50 percent of those surveyed came from some type of "Christian" upbringing, be it nominally Catholic or Protestant.

I met John Pipolo one day while street witnessing, and my wife and I soon became good friends with him and his brother Anthony. They were in a sense true twentieth-century "God-fearers" from a strong Italian Catholic background. We began visiting them from time to time to share the Gospel, but we eventually lost contact with each other.

Other Christians, though, shared the love of Jesus with them through both personal testimony and literature. John and Anthony were encouraged to follow Jesus, and eventually they did— along with John's wife, mother, sister, and older brother. Today, the Pipolo family are among some of the most committed Christians I know. Their strong Catholic heritage provided a wonderful foundation on which to build.

Danny Lehmann, an American, directs the YWAM base in Honolulu, Hawaii, USA, and travels extensively in a teaching ministry.
From Bringin' 'Em Back Alive by Danny Lehmann. Copyright © 1987 by Danny Lehmann. Published by Whitaker House, Springdale, Pennsylvania. Used by permission [from pages 41-42].

Thursday

Behold, I stand at the door and knock; if any one hears My voice and opens the door, I will come in to him, and will dine with him, and he with Me.

While traveling down the busy highway, I wrestled with God over something He had asked me to do. My confused thoughts manufactured a special bargain for God, "Okay, Lord, if You really want me to do this, then give me a sign."

I was stunned when I noticed a billboard with a huge picture of Jesus about 300 yards up the highway. As I got closer, I realized that the billboard was not a mirage.

My heart froze as I saw the picture of Jesus knocking on a slammed door. The words of Revelation 3:20 scrolled along the bottom of the billboard cut deep into my pious heart.

Then I heard the Lord whisper powerfully to my spirit, "Son, the issue is not what I have asked you to do, but that you've pushed Me right out of your heart."

I quickly realized that this Scripture wasn't written to unbelievers, but to one of the seven churches John had addressed in the Revelation. They had pushed Jesus out and had gone on being religious. A "coup" had taken place! They were performing lip service, but their hearts were far from Him.

As I went on past the billboard, my tears flowed freely. I repented and invited the Master to rule my life again.

God is a gentleman knocking on the door of our hearts. He enters only at our invitation, and longs to sup with us. Let's invite Jesus to dwell in our hearts forever, and let's keep an open-door policy.

By the way, I haven't asked for a sign lately.

David Gustaveson, an American, leads YWAM's Global Opportunity Network, mobilizing local churches into missions. He lives in California, USA.

Friday

You are the light of the world.   *Matthew 5:14*

The four-wheel-drive truck crawled along the dirt road of West Africa's Sahel desert. My dad, Loren Cunningham, and I had looked forward to this time alone together. As we drove, he shared with me his vision for a torch run. "It will involve young people—teenagers. They'll run the length and breadth of each continent. It's an opportunity for your generation to give of yourselves physically—something tangible toward the Great Commission."

He continued, "We'll start at the Mount of Olives, then carry it to Tel Aviv. From there, the flame can be carried by airplane to other continents."

As we rode along, I visualized the event. One runner would start out, run a while, then pass the torch off to another runner. On and on we would run, to the edge of the continent. Along the way, other young people would tell the local people about Jesus and distribute Christian literature.

The heat of the dusty Sahel became oppressive. Dad grew quiet. After a while, I realized he was sick. I felt his brow—it was hot with fever.

We dragged on to the YWAM base in the mountains of Togo, where Dad was supposed to speak that night. When we arrived, Dad was barely able to talk, but he said, "Son, here are my notes. Tell them about the torch run."

"I'm only 16 years old! I can't speak."

"Sure you can. Just tell them what God wants to do; that they can be a part of it."

I was scared, but I couldn't let Dad down. While speaking that evening, God lit the flame in my heart. God had ignited the torch of missions in my heart that already burned so brightly in my dad's heart.

David L. Cunningham, an American, runs a film and television production company in California, USA.

Saturday

Before the mountains were born or you brought forth the earth and the world, from everlasting to everlasting you are God.

Psalm 90:2

When my 16-year-old daughter, Kristal, died of leukemia, I desperately needed to know that she was okay. I longed to see her just as I envisioned her: in glorious white robes, preferably standing beside Jesus. It didn't seem like too much to ask. I told God all about it, but I didn't see a thing. No visions, no impressions. Nothing.

My mother had died just seven weeks before Kristal, and Dad moved in to help during Kristal's last days. After her funeral, Dad, my son, Jeff, and I needed to get away. We packed up Dad's motor home and took off.

We toured the northwest corner of Washington State, hiking through the Olympic Peninsula's beautiful old-growth forest where 600-year-old fir trees live. Their enormity overwhelmed me as I walked 44 feet around the trunk of just one tree.

Next, we camped at the ocean. One windy afternoon, I sat on a log and watched for hours as perfectly timed waves crashed on the sand. As the sun set, I realized that I could sit there forever and never see the last wave. Only our Creator saw the first wave, and they'll keep rolling in long after we're gone.

Through nature, God gave me a revelation of His patience and faithfulness. I saw eternity through His eyes. The same God who tends giant trees for 600 years watches over me. The One who controls the waves, the entire universe, is in charge of me.

I had asked for a glimpse of my daughter. He gave me something far better—a long look at His character.

Shirley Walston, an American, is a freelance writer for YWAM, living in Washington State, USA.

Meet Our Editors

Our editing team has turned the stories of YWAMers into devotions for you. Meet the team.

Teri Anderson is a widow who resides in Marysville, Michigan, with her three children. She is actively involved in ministry with women in her home church. She occasionally speaks to women's groups about the faithfulness of God.

Frances Bradley is a freelance writer, mother of four grown children, and grandmother of eight. During her Discipleship Training School outreach in Asia she visited 17 of the international students she had previously taught in her home church in Texas. Frances serves on staff of YWAM's Writer's Seminars.

Joy Cooley has three grown children and three grandchildren. She earned a Master's degree in Communication in her mid-50s. Joy is working in YWAM's communications department in Kona, Hawaii, and is part of an author's team. Her current project is her own story.

Myrtlemay Pittman Crane is a freelance writer/editor and speaker who lives in Alderwood Manor, Washington.

Regina Masters-Dagen served on YWAM staff in Titusville, Pennsylvania, in the areas of journalism and mass media. She and her husband, Don, have a daughter, Ellysa.

Joanne Holden earned a degree in English/Creative Writing after involvement with YWAM in Ontario, Canada. She lives in Long Beach, California.

Nancy Kington holds a degree in journalism, is an editor for a private firm, and does freelance writing. She makes her home in Huntington Beach, California.

Marianne Miller holds a Masters degree from Regent University. She wrote *Barefoot to the White House* (about Mercy Ship's ambassador-at-large) with Carolyn Sundseth for Creation House Publishers. Marianne lives in Tyler, Texas.

Shirley Sells holds a journalism degree, has worked as associate editor for a magazine, and does freelance writing. She has edited books for YWAM Publishing, and lives in Saratoga, California.

Dianne Shober is a busy wife and mother. She worked with YWAM for six years in Kona, Hawaii, leading missions tours in

North America and directing West Coast operations for Night of Missions. She now directs a Writer's Conference in California.

Shirley Walston wrote for the University of the Nations-Kona campus newspaper, *On Line,* for four years, and has worked on staff with several YWAM Writer's Seminars. Shirley lives in Gig Harbor, Washington.

Pam Warren is an editor with YWAM Publishing, and has served on staff with YWAM Writer's Seminars. She has worked with YWAM since 1973, and lives in Lindale, Texas.

Beverly Caruso is the mother of three grown children and grand-mother of three. She has authored four books and leads YWAM Writer's Seminars. She speaks at retreats, conferences, churches, and YWAM schools. She is senior editor of *Around the World.*